THE APPALLING STRANGENESS OF THE MERCY OF GOD

The Appalling Strangeness of the Mercy of God

The Story of Ruth Pakaluk
Convert, Mother, and Pro-Life Activist

Edited with a Biographical Overview and Afterword
by
Michael Pakaluk

Foreword by the Most Reverend Daniel P. Reilly, D.D.

Introduction by Peter Kreeft

IGNATIUS PRESS   SAN FRANCISCO

Cover design by Riz Boncan Marsella

Photographs courtesy of Michael Pakaluk, Ruth's husband

©2011 by Ignatius Press, San Francisco
All rights reserved
ISBN 978-1-58617-451-4
Library of Congress Control Number 2010931415
Printed in the United States of America ∞

To Michael Sebastian

CONTENTS

FOREWORD

When a mother of six dies at forty-one, it is tragic. But it is not always a tragedy.

When someone has grown to embrace the Catholic faith, striving to live its tenets and to meet life's challenges with a hope, love, and joy that come from a deep commitment to Jesus Christ and an insuperable confidence in him, there is a fullness of life even if not marked by the fullness of years.

Such was the sense among Ruth Pakaluk's family and friends when Ruth died in 1998. To those who knew her, she continues to inspire. To those who didn't, this book offers that opportunity.

These pages, containing excerpts from Ruth's correspondence with family, friends, and others, give us a very personal and honest glimpse of the life and spiritual growth of a woman who in high school abandoned her belief in God but in her twenties became Catholic. It is a story of a Harvard grad who was a stay-at-home mom. It is an account of a wife and mother who saw meaning, purpose, and abundant opportunities for holiness in raising a family, struggling to pay bills, rushing to ballgames, singing in her parish choir, and teaching CCD.

Along the way she would bear seven children and bury one. She would debate abortion on college campuses, host her own television show, and become the president of a statewide pro-life organization. When her children were all in school, I hired her as the director of our diocese's Respect Life Office. Through it all, she battled breast cancer with a wit, grace, and joy of life that inspired longtime friends and casual acquaintances alike.

People would frequently comment on Ruth's selfless character, boundless optimism, and fervent faith. Ruth would respond, "Anyone can have this!"

Her zest for life and her zeal for the faith were gifts from God. They are gifts offered to us all that we might find strength, happiness, and peace not just in the absence of trials but, indeed, in their midst. So equipped by grace, our tragedies can become triumphs.

I pray these pages will remind you of the abundance of God's mercy and inspire you to be ever more open to those graces which strengthen us for our journeys and see us to our eternal end.

The Most Reverend Daniel P. Reilly, D.D.
Bishop Emeritus of Worcester

INTRODUCTION

Peter Kreeft

In this book you will meet a truly wonderful person. There are few things in life more precious than that. Even meeting a great fictional character enriches your life. But this one is real.

Since Ruth was a woman who loved God and loved life, this book of her letters and speeches is a book for everyone who loves God and who loves life. But it is especially helpful for mothers, especially stay-at-home mothers, homemakers, people with cancer, parents faced with leaving their children through death, and people who care about abortion.

How to describe it in a few words? All the following adjectives describe Ruth herself as well as her letters and her book.

Utterly honest, human, "homely", and humble. Simple. Direct. Full of the ordinary, but full of a light that shines on or through ordinary life, a light that most of us simply don't see twenty-four hours a day, seven days a week.

And always cheerful. Surrounded by many small children; infected by cancer; suffering in continual pain for seven years; facing uncertainties about death and then certainties (which is worse?); maligned and misunderstood for converting to Catholicism, for having "too many" children, for being consistently pro-life; working harder for the culture of life while in poor health than most people ever work when in perfect health—yet always cheerful. Like Mother Teresa. Like John Paul II. They show us that cheerfulness is neither a temporary feeling nor a genetic predisposition but a *choice*. A matter of free choice—of will, not emotion. This cheerfulness is not a teeth-gritting, "stiff upper lip" cheerfulness but one grounded in truth and in fact, in the certainty of the goodness and wisdom and power of God. (From these three non-negotiable premises logically follows the astonishing conclusion of Romans 8:28,[1] and the cheerfulness it generates.)

Full of faith, in all its senses: personal trust, personal fidelity, theological orthodoxy, and immediate acceptance of revealed data. Ruth had a brilliant mind, but I'm sure she would have loved the Southern Baptist preacher's famous definition of faith: "If God said it, I believe it and that settles it." Honesty often expresses itself in simplicity, even (especially!) in brilliant minds. (Read Saint Thomas Aquinas.) This simplicity was one of the secrets of her cheerfulness.

Full of hope, especially when things are most hopeless. (That's the whole hard heroism and preciousness of hope.)

Full of charity, of love. The real thing, not imitations. Full of the love of God, which is so immediately translated into love of neighbor that its heavenly origin becomes invisible, like air full of light.

Yet also hardheaded, rational, clear. (Why did I say "yet", as if there were some tension? Exactly the opposite: it is all of a piece.) Brilliant, even—in the sense that a light is brilliant, not in the sense that an overly clever scholar is "brilliant".

What was her secret? It's no secret. It's all here in print. Just meet her and see.

The reader must be warned not to bog down in the simple, homey, hobbitlike details of the first few letters. The letters start slow. It's right that they do. They are like the first fifty pages of *The Lord of the Rings*. Acceleration takes place, in due time, right up to the stunning conclusion, on p. 209.

I met Ruth five or six times, mainly at Boston College, where she gave the most persuasive, irresistible, and winsome pro-life talks I have ever heard. To explain my impression of her, I have to tell you a story that may sound strange, but it is right on target, on her wavelength.

---

[1] "We know that in everything God works for good with those who love him, who are called according to his purpose" (RSV, Second Catholic Edition).

A student asked a famous Zen Buddhist *roshi* (master) to teach him the secret of Zen. He agreed and promised the student that if he obeyed everything the master told him to do, he would attain *satori* ("Enlightenment"). The student came to live with the master in his monastery. Every day, the only command the master gave to the student was "Wash your dishes!" and the student dutifully obeyed. After a month, the student, impatient, asked the master when he would begin teaching him the secret of Zen. The master replied, "I have been teaching you every day, but you have not learned." "But master, all you have told me to do is to wash my dishes." "That is true, and if you had obeyed me, you would now be enlightened." "But I did obey you, master. I washed my dishes every day." "No, you did not. You never washed your dishes. You have never washed your dishes in your life." "But master, what did I do, then?" "You wobbled."

Ruth did not "wobble". She was totally "there" for everyone she talked to. When she spoke to an audience of one hundred, every one of them felt as if there were only two people in the room, not one hundred—because that's how *she* felt.

My first reaction, upon reading that people in Worcester had wished to consider opening her cause for sainthood, was surprise. Not because there was anything in Ruth that would contradict such a verdict, but because my concept of a saint, like that of most Catholics, I suppose, was a cartoon concept, full of strange and unusual accidentals like incredible penances, violent martyrdoms, and supernatural revelations. But the greatest of saints was the humblest, simplest, quietest, and most ordinary mother in Israel, although the Mother of God himself. And especially today, in the age of the laity and of the humanism of John Paul the Great and Vatican II, we need examples of "ordinary" saints—because all are called to be saints, and most of us are "ordinary".

I conclude with a "tease", a passage from the book that is typical of Ruth's mind and spirit. I have read and debated much about abortion, but I have never seen a clearer and stronger pro-life argument than Ruth's. In Michael's words, "the core of Ruth's argument about abortion and human rights may be summarized in this way: Human rights are rights that pertain to us simply in virtue of the fact that we are human, not for any reason above and beyond that; the fundamental human right is the right to life, and so, if that right is denied, then all human rights are in effect denied; the thing growing in the mother's womb is surely alive (otherwise it would not need to be killed by an abortion), and it is human; thus, to deny that the thing growing in the mother's womb has the right to life is to deny that anyone has any human rights whatsoever."

Michael goes on to say that this led Ruth "to reconceive the abortion controversy not as a difference of opinion as regards some philosophical thesis—'Is the fetus a person?', as people often say—but rather as a difference in two cultures: given that (as everyone really knows) the thing in the woman's womb is a living human, do we act on the principle that all human beings are fundamentally equal, or do we proceed as if we believe that it is permissible to kill some human beings to solve our problems? The first is the Culture of Life, the second the Culture of Death. The two cultures, she thought, were vying for the allegiance of the young people she was addressing."

I invite you to meet a warrior for life whose pen is truly mightier than death's sword.

BIOGRAPHICAL OVERVIEW

Michael Pakaluk

I have no difficulty in understanding what Plato was about. He loved Socrates deeply and recognized in his philosophical master an extraordinary man, a kind of natural phenomenon of ingenuity, power of personality, and truthful insight. Socrates *really* lived; he really knew how to live. Most of us in comparison just stumble through life as in a kind of twilight. So, when Socrates was snatched away in an untimely way—not at an early age, but suddenly, from an unjust accusation and a contrived trial that led, unexpectedly and horrifically, to Socrates' execution—Plato wanted somehow to capture Socrates and make him "alive" for others who would never encounter him. From this love, and skill inspired by love, came the Platonic "dialogue", a completely new literary form, which surely was originally intended to recapture what it was like to spend time with Socrates.

I similarly have witnessed an extraordinary human being, taken away from her friends in an untimely manner, by metastatic breast cancer, when she was forty-one years old: Ruth V. K. Pakaluk. When Ruth died, her friends believed that the best among them had been taken away. It seemed unjust that she should die and that we should continue to live, because the way she lived, and her love of life, seemed to make her so much more "worthy" of the gift of life. At the same time, she lived with such intensity, and accomplished so much, that we agreed with a friend who remarked in a newspaper article at the time that she "lived more in her forty-one years than most of us could hope to do in ninety-one years".

The True Greatness of a Christian

Unlike Socrates, Ruth did not start a new branch of intellectual inquiry and inspire schools of disciples. And yet it turns out that Ruth was in some ways like Socrates—she was a public figure, widely known in her home city (Worcester, Massachusetts), known especially for her skill in debating, and unpopular too for exhorting her fellow citizens to virtue and goodness. She wasn't put to death, but she certainly had enemies, and legal authority was in an important respect against her, where she was on the side of right, and the law was not.

She inspired the greatest admiration and devotion among her close friends. After her death, I felt in conscience that I should make a record of her life somehow. I began to collect her papers and memorabilia, together with recordings of actual "dialogues" or debates from radio and television. I enjoyed a big advantage over Plato in being able to bring a tape recorder to interviews I arranged with her friends. In these conversations, one friend compared her to Saint Teresa of Avila for the kind of effect she could make simply by entering a room; another likened her facile and quick reasoning, especially in delicate practical matters, to that of Saint Thomas More. Many said that she was a Joan of Arc in her own time and place, and many also said that she reminded them of John Paul II when it came to her solidity and reliability. Ruth was frequently compared to Mother Teresa, probably because the spiritual force of her personality made it easy to overlook her small stature (she was five foot three) and because she was a defender of unborn children in self-sacrificial action as much as in challenging words.

Now, here is a puzzle about this woman, Ruth V. K. Pakaluk: How is it that a housewife and homemaker could spontaneously be compared, by those who knew her best—and by sober and responsible people—to a great foundress, a lord chancellor, a warrior-saint, one of the greatest Popes of all time, and a renowned servant of the poor? Why did none of these comparisons seem like hyperboles—and they still do not—but, rather, the most apt way of expressing what one wants to say?

To resolve this puzzle, one might draw a distinction between the "greatness of the deed" and the "greatness of love". We account something as great, it seems, because it reveals something wonderful and marvelous. Now, some people, through providence and circumstances, are afforded the chance to perform actions that are extraordinary in extent, duration, or power. If they make use of this opportunity and are successful at what they attempt, we marvel at them because we take their actions to reveal the power of a strong human character or the glory that is bound up with heroic self-sacrifice. Such is the greatness of a victorious Olympic athlete or a hero in war. By its very nature, such greatness is rare, because it depends upon extraordinary opportunities. Moreover, when we see the greatness of the deed, we tend to attribute the greatness to the agent. That is why we celebrate and honor great people with statues and similar tributes. A housewife could not possibly be great in this way; it would be foolish to imagine that any ordinary person could be great through astounding achievements.

However, the "greatness of love" is something else. If an action springs not solely from a human virtue, such as self-mastery or courage, but primarily from charity, which is the love of God, then—because the love of God is also God's love—this action can be great because it reveals something about God in a striking and marvelous way. The love of God, we know, involves a gift of self for the good of another: "This is my commandment, that you love one another as I have loved you. Greater love has no man than this, that a man lay down his life for his friends" (Jn 15:12–13). But ordinary life consists of opportunities to show this love, especially in the relationships we have with one another, in families, as friends, and as fellow citizens. Thus, nothing hinders a homemaker from being great with the greatness of love. Whereas in the case of a hero or an athlete we trace the greatness of the deed to the greatness of the human person who achieves the deed, in the case of the greatness of love we trace its greatness back to God. We see that the Christian who exemplifies this greatness is simply allowing God to achieve something in and through her.

Pope Benedict XVI once explained the concept of heroic virtue for a Christian in this way:

Heroic virtue does not mean that the saint performs a type of "gymnastics" of holiness, something that normal people do not dare to do. It means rather that in the life of a person God's presence is revealed—something man could not do by himself and through himself. Perhaps in the final analysis we are rather dealing with a question of terminology, because the adjective "heroic" has been badly interpreted. Heroic virtue properly speaking does not mean that one has done great things by oneself, but rather that in one's life there appear realities which the person has not done himself, because he has been transparent and ready for the work of God.[1]

This sort of greatness can indeed be shown by a housewife and homemaker, and furthermore, it might be even more readily apparent under conditions of weakness, suffering, and death.

True Life Stories of Christian Heroes

Now, to capture what it was like to know Ruth and to be her friend—which is the goal of this book—I haven't, like Plato, devised a new literary form. Yet I have exercised a little editorial ingenuity through the selection of material for this book. My criterion for including material here is that it be something in which Ruth tells us about herself in her own words. The application of that principle results in an admittedly diverse collection: correspondence mainly, but also some talks given to friends, and a few public lectures besides (which tell us about Ruth insofar as they reveal the pro-life convictions and thought that animated her).

I mentioned that I began writing a biography of Ruth soon after her death. But that work, still in progress although almost completed, by the nature of the case has several infirmities that the present volume lacks. First, it is rather long, while this is satisfactorily short. Second, such a biography must be a memoir and therefore be about me as much as it is about Ruth, whereas this work can appropriately be primarily about her. Third, the biography gains its interest through the interpretation of experience and history, whereas the materials collected here speak for themselves and need little interpretation. Fourth, and perhaps most important, in any biography, no matter how well

[1] Joseph Cardinal Ratzinger [Benedict XVI], "Letting God Work", *L'Osservatore Romano*, October 6, 2002, special supplement (published on the occasion of the canonization of Josemaría Escrivá).

executed, the access that the reader gains to the subject is indirect, whereas here it is fairly unmediated and direct.

In favoring letters over a biography for what they tell us about Ruth, I have been much influenced by Blessed John Henry Newman's remarks on hagiography when, in his essay on Saint John Chrysostom, he explains that he loves the saints of the early Church because we know about them largely through their own letters. "What I want to trace and study", Newman writes, "is the real, hidden but human, life, or the *interior*, as it is called, of such glorious creations of God; and this I gain with difficulty from mere biographies." He explains that the biographer cannot remain a "mere witness or reporter" but must become a "commentator". Yet in contrast, "when a Saint is himself the speaker, he interprets his own action; and that is what I find done in such fulness in the case of those early luminaries of the Church to whom I am referring. I want to hear a Saint converse; I am not content to look at him as a statue; his words are the index of his hidden life." The "Ancient Saints" are so appealing because they "have left behind them just that kind of literature which more than any other represents the abundance of the heart, which more than any other approaches to conversation; I mean correspondence." [2]

In this collection I have excluded letters and passages that deal with business, passing matters, or personal matters that could have significance only to a few. By the same token I have purposefully not followed the rule of including only putatively "edifying" discussions about spiritual or religious topics, although there certainly are plenty of those. I want the letters to convey a portrait about Ruth, and Ruth, like any other sane layperson, did not talk solely about religious topics. Moreover, for a layperson, the details of ordinary life must provide the "matter" for which one's devotion provides the "form", and so it would be necessary, to understand Ruth's love of Christ, to be familiar with this "matter". Ordinary life is the foundation for Christian devotion for a layperson, and for Ruth in particular, how she lived her ordinary life as a housewife and homemaker was an indispensable preparation for

[2] John Henry Newman, *Historical Sketches*, vol. 2 (London: Longmans, Green, and Co., 1906), pp. 217, 220, 221.

the heroic way in which she endured suffering and accepted death.[3] Our Lord refers to the man who builds his house patiently on rock—only in that way can his house stand firm when the storms come. Tolstoy once remarked that we die how we live and that we can hardly expect to die a good death except through living a good life. Similarly, I wished, through giving instances of humble and simple letters, to avoid the common misimpression that heroism comes "out of the blue".

A final goal of mine was to avoid any kind of falsifying idealization. A collection of letters, which were not originally written for any set purpose and certainly were never intended for publication, can hardly err in that direction. Newman commented, "A Saint's writings are to me his real 'Life;' and what is called his 'Life' is not the outline of an individual, but either of the *auto-saint* or of a myth."[4] There is no myth concocted in these pages, nothing projected or imagined by a well-intentioned piety but perhaps not true to daily life or adequate for its trials. Admittedly, letters might seem to err in another way, by exposing seeming shortcomings or faults, from which someone might mistakenly conclude—from the mere fact that these letters are published and therefore seemingly offered as a model—that faults which were such as those would not be faults or that a reader might, in his own case, safely acquiesce in them. But of course this collection must be read with good judgment, just like anything else. And to attempt to remove anything that potentially could be misleading would turn this collection of letters into "spiritual lessons" and "spiritual reading", as Newman remarks, which is not their purpose.[5] They aim not in the first instance to edify but to display and reveal. Along similar lines, Newman warns sharply against what he calls "the endemic perennial fidget which possesses us about giving scandal": "facts are omitted" and "glosses are put upon memorable acts, because they are thought not edifying, whereas of all scandals such omissions, such glosses, are

[3] Saint Josemaría Escrivá writes, "Some biographers of saints have in the past been interested only in highlighting extraordinary things in the lives of God's servants, from even their earliest days in the cradle. They have, unintentionally perhaps, done a disservice to Christian truth." ("The Christian Vocation", in *Christ Is Passing By* [New York: Scepter Publications, 1974], no. 9).

[4] Newman, *Historical Sketches*, p. 227.

[5] Ibid., p. 229.

the greatest." [6] This seems a common judgment among saints: Saint Josemaría Escrivá says, "I have never liked biographies of saints which naively—but also with a lack of sound doctrine—present their deeds as if they had been confirmed in grace from birth. No. The true life stories of Christian heroes resemble our own experience: they fought and won; they fought and lost. And then, repentant, they returned to the fray." [7] The life of a Christian hero who is a housewife and home-maker actually doesn't *resemble* our own experience; it *is* our own experience, and is most typically simple, humble, and ordinary.

****

I Want to Live Like Them

Ruth V. K. Pakaluk was born Ruth Elizabeth Van Kooy on March 19, 1957, in East Orange, New Jersey. Her father, Hank Van Kooy, was the son of Dutch immigrants and worked first as an electrical engineer designing submarine simulators for the U.S. Navy and then as an instructor at a vocational high school. Her mother, Sheila (née Max-well), the daughter of Scottish immigrants, stayed at home to raise the children when they were very young but later worked as an executive secretary for a company that devised some of the original multiplexers for computer communication over phone lines. The family lived at first in Kearney, New Jersey, an immigrant town near Newark, but when Ruth was a young child they moved to Norwood, at that time a rural village nestled in the valley that runs along the western base of the Palisades, a line of cliffs north of New York City.

Ruth attended Northern Valley Regional High School in Old Tappan (NVOT), where she achieved straight A's; played the oboe, flute, vio-lin, and bass drum in various musical groups; was an accomplished vocalist, chosen for the All-State and All-Eastern choirs; played on the field hockey team; and produced, directed, and acted in numerous plays and musicals under the auspices of Northern Masque, a theater group founded and managed by students. She won the English depart-ment prize and other honors upon graduating in 1975. Ruth was keen

[6] Ibid., p. 231.
[7] Escrivá, "Interior Struggle", in *Christ Is Passing By*, no. 76.

21

on attending stewardess school afterward ("All you need do is smile, and you can see the world"), or maybe McGill University, where her boyfriend was going, but she applied to Harvard on the suggestion of a local Radcliffe alum. Like many others, she found that she could hardly turn Harvard down when accepted: "I would never have known whether I could compete with the best", she said.

Her first year's academic work was so brilliant that, besides winning several honors, she was invited to help teach a course on cosmology the following year. That is how we met—we began to date when I took that course as a sophomore and she was my teaching assistant.

Although by conventional signs Ruth's life up to the time we met would have been judged a complete success, interiorly she was, as she later described herself, completely miserable. There came something of a crisis point one evening in the first semester of her sophomore year. As she told the story, she was sitting in bed comfortably propped up by pillows, reading the week's assignment for Alan Heimert's course on American literature. The assigned reading was Governor Bradford's journal, with its account of how the Pilgrims survived their first, bitterly cold, winter in America. A serious illness had struck the settlers, and Bradford movingly describes how, with great heroism and sacrifice, those Pilgrims who had sufficient strength would devote themselves to caring for the sick and dying until they became sick themselves, at which point they were cared for in turn by those who had survived their maladies and had regained some of their strength. Ruth was profoundly affected by the heroic love of these religious and idealistic people, which she contrasted with her own hedonistic and, as she saw it, aimless life. She sat up in bed: "I want to live like them", she said to herself. "I don't even care whether what these people believed is true. I want to live like them." Her thought—that she didn't care whether what they believed was true or not—was voiced in defiance of those around her who scoffed at Christianity and were far from admiring the Pilgrims. The Pilgrims were living better lives than those who would claim that they were better off for not believing anything "false". In any case, since it is not possible to live heroically without also believing dogmatically something to be true, what Ruth implicitly resolved at that moment of crisis, even though she did not realize it, was to search for certain knowledge of the truth.

22

When Ruth and I met in our sophomore year, I too had recently experienced a moment of crisis—a narrow escape from death by drowning, and a miraculous rescue, in the previous summer—followed similarly by a conviction to search for the truth. So for us, falling in love looked inseparable from being faithful to a common yearning to investigate whether Christianity might possibly be true.

We both regarded ourselves as atheists, or near to it, when we met. As a teenager Ruth had rejected as incoherent and confused the religion she was familiar with from the Presbyterian church in Norwood that her parents attended. She had arrived at college an atheist with a social "religion" only, consisting of the very "progressive" social sympathies shared by her church community—for instance, she was enthusiastically "pro-choice". For my part, wide reading had caused me to go through so many revolutions of thought that by the time I entered college I had become a skeptic, and I simply thought it highly unlikely that any religion could be true. My own upbringing by nonreligious and nominally Catholic parents seemed irrelevant to me.

And yet here was this common experience of a crisis, and a common implicit intuition that we had to look into Christianity. We both thought that Christianity should be tested as if by experiment but that the experiment should consist in *how one lived one's life*: we hadn't read Pascal, who says the same thing, but we both believed that the best way to tell if Christianity were true would be to try to live as a Christian. One's entire person was the instrument for testing its truth. So we adopted in increments the sorts of practices we thought a Christian should follow. We began by reading the Bible regularly; then, after we had acquired that habit, we began praying; then we began examining our thoughts and actions each day. By the end of the year, we thought we should look to become part of a fellowship or church—because that's what Christians do, we thought. We did all of this on our own, not under anyone's guidance, and not even finding help through books—although there were plenty of signs and intimations that, even then, we would have interpreted as examples of our being led and guided. We knew no other Christians at Harvard. For all we knew, we were the only two; and also, for all we knew, that was no obstacle to Christianity's being true.

That summer, after classes were over, a friend who was an Evangelical Christian and had heard of our quest put into our hands *Mere Christianity* by C. S. Lewis. We read this greedily, followed by every other book by Lewis we could get our hands on. We started to say that we were Evangelical Christians ourselves because those were the *real* Christians, we thought, the ones who had a personal relationship with Christ and who rejected Christianity as a cultural artifact or mere routine. When we returned to school in the fall, we did not delay in joining the InterVarsity Christian Fellowship, which we learned was Evangelical. However, this placed us in a highly conflicted situation because the church that by happenstance we had joined the previous spring, when we thought it was imperative to join a church—First Church Congregational on the Cambridge Common—was as liberally Protestant as it is possible to become without lapsing into Unitarianism. Thus, we were pulled two ways: the InterVarsity fellowship pulled us toward historic Christianity, and First Church pulled us away from it.

This peculiar arrangement, which no one would have planned, and which we would never have gotten into if we had started attending the InterVarsity fellowship first, had the benefit of exposing us to pretty much the whole gamut of Protestantism, from fundamentalism on one extreme (on the fringes of the InterVarsity fellowship) to Marxian liberation theology on the other (actually not very far from the center at First Church). Yet we found that we were not entirely at peace anywhere in that range. Our friends at First Church did not believe, and did not seem able to believe, that Christ was God incarnate and that he was raised bodily from the dead. They tended to reduce Christianity to a political program; for them, radical professors of theology were the highest authorities, and these professors (mostly German, it seemed) had long ago given up on historic Christianity. Our friends in InterVarsity, in contrast, believed in miracles, and they accepted supernatural truths wholeheartedly, since they accepted the authority of the Bible. However, they seemed to identify Christian faith with emotional enthusiasm, and Christian discipleship with the maintaining of a certain kind of upbeat emotional mood. We weren't so capable of that, and we found that our faith could be viewed somewhat dubiously as a result. The InterVarsity fellowship, moreover, seemed to suggest a critique of itself: the fellowship fostered in us a desire to be connected with historic Christianity, and yet the very intensity and closeness of the fellowship seemed to derive from its insularity, from its being a group of students of roughly the same age, interests, and background. But if the fellowship were unconnected with Christianity across the world at present, we wondered, how could it be connected with Christianity across the ages?

A Friend's Conversion

In 1978, the summer after our junior year in college, and eighteen months after we started dating, Ruth and I were married. We knew within two weeks of dating that we wanted to get married, and we would have gotten married a year earlier if we hadn't thought it proper to give Ruth's brother the honor of getting married first (he was much older, had been engaged for a long time before Ruth and I met, and had already set a wedding date). Our decision was almost as unusual then as it would be now: only two other undergraduates at Harvard were married, but they weren't married to Harvard students or even to students at all; their spouses were older.

Although marriage is natural, and man and woman are meant to marry, it is still probably always a mystery when a couple wants to marry. But two considerations help to explain our decision partially. We wanted to spend all of our time together—to spend our lives together—and yet after becoming Christians, and therefore followers of the moral law taught by Christ, the only way open for us to do so was to become married. Our love of God's law, then, pushed us to marriage. Yet a love of family life did so as well: we were not happy at Harvard, and we both sensed from our own childhoods, which we looked back upon as happy, that human happiness can be achieved only through life in a family; we therefore wanted our relationship to constitute a family, and by getting married we could achieve that. (Not that we would have understood our decision in that way then; and although we certainly wanted to have children at some point in the future, we didn't clearly see then that a more concrete openness to children is essential for making a relationship a family.)

Christians now, and married—as if there could be anything less popular, in our senior year we set out on a path of investigation that led to our becoming Catholics. It started when a friend, Curt, in the InterVarsity small group that I was leading announced after one meeting that he was undergoing instruction to be received into the Catholic Church at Easter. Ruth and I smiled and congratulated him, but inwardly we were both horrified. Anti-Catholicism was strong in Ruth's Reformed heritage, despite any professed "liberalism" in other respects, and she had assimilated this. For my part, from the time I had discovered Evangelical Christianity, I firmly regarded the nominal Catholicism from my childhood as a snare and a trap—a false religion that blocked Christians from forming a personal relationship with Christ. When Curt made his shocking announcement, then, Ruth and I were worried that we had set a poor example somehow or hadn't been clear about the Good News. We wondered what impression Curt's conversion might make on the higher leadership of the fellowship, who would think that one of our flock going astray reflected poorly on our spiritual maturity. In our thoughts we likened Curt's new direction to that of the unfortunate Christians that Saint Paul tried to free from the snares of the Judaizers. So with great concern we each met with Curt, with the clear purpose of talking him out of it.

However, Curt was unmoved by our protestations and representations. He said that he didn't plan to lose his personal relationship with Christ when he became Catholic, or his love of Scripture, or any other good thing that we shared in the fellowship. He hoped only to gain clarity, stable teaching, and the "weightiness" of the Catholic faith. Then he surprised us by launching a counterattack and throwing some objections back against us. Curt's first argument involved drawing a contrast between the Orthodox Churches and the Protestant denominations: both had broken away from the Catholic Church, he pointed out, but the Orthodox Churches, which had done so over a thousand years ago, were intact, whereas the Protestant communities, which arose only about four hundred years ago at the Reformation, had fractured into *tens of thousands* of sects and denominations. What could explain such a difference, he asked, except that the Catholics and Orthodox Christians shared a proper understanding of governance in the Church, which Protestants lacked? Curt's second point was similar: he said that there had been so much drift in Protestantism over the centuries that if Martin Luther or John Calvin were to come back to life today, they would be horrified by Protestantism and would feel more at home in the Catholic Church. This showed that Catholicism was closer to the religion of the Reformers than contemporary Protestantism, and therefore closer to true Christianity.

Ruth and I could think of no way to respond to these arguments. Curt's first point made the deeper impression on me, because I felt keenly the relative isolation and parochialism of the InterVarsity fellowship. His second point perhaps made a stronger impression on Ruth, because she had recently been reading Calvin's *Institutes* for one of her classes. "I didn't say so then, but I knew full well he was right", Ruth said later. "Calvin wouldn't have hesitated to burn most Protestants today at the stake." Since we had nothing to say, we told Curt that we would investigate and find the answers to his objections, and yet interiorly we had the suspicion that Curt was right and his objections unanswerable.

Something else that Curt said made a deep impression on Ruth. From other discussions with Curt, we knew that his father was a Catholic who was divorced and had remarried outside the Church and that Curt was a child of this second marriage. So when Ruth spoke with Curt, she urged this difficulty upon him: if Curt were to become Catholic, he would be bound to accept the Catholic Church's view of his father's marriage; therefore, he would have to regard his father as living in sin, and, more than this, he would have to view himself as a bastard, the illegitimate offspring of an illegitimate relationship.

Curt didn't blink at this. He said he wasn't concerned about himself and whether he was an illegitimate child. But as regards his father, he said that it wasn't his business to correct his father; but if his father had concerns of conscience about his marriage, Curt said, he would direct him to a priest, who would be the best person to give his father guidance in such a matter.

As obvious and as sensible as such an answer may seem, to Ruth at that time, what Curt said seemed like blazing light breaking through the clouds. It suggested a new and liberating way of applying the Christian faith to one's personal life. From her Protestant background, Ruth was used to thinking that the individual believer, reading the Bible with the presumed assistance of the Holy Spirit, is the sole standard of

Christian faith and morals. From this it would follow that each Christian has the responsibility of being a kind of prophet; that is, if the Holy Spirit has illuminated his mind and helped him to see the wrongness of some human practice around him that perhaps had previously seemed obscure, then, in fidelity to this guidance, he would need to make this known to others and denounce that practice. Furthermore, since Christianity purports to be an all-embracing way of life, there is nothing, in principle, from which a Christian should hold back judgment. From this point of view, a Christian must try to settle everything in his own conscience and then declare his view publicly when he has settled it. For someone who takes this task seriously, it should seem an almost impossible burden. Ruth did take this task seriously, and that is why Curt's reply seemed liberating to her. "How refreshing to think that I don't need to decide everything," she thought to herself, "that I don't need to confront everyone. It's possible instead that, in a matter of conscience, one might with discretion rely on the judgment of someone one regards as having proper authority in some matter, such as a priest."

One might say that what Ruth had encountered in that conversation with Curt was the theological notion of *munus*, or "office". Curt in his answer to her challenge had drawn an implicit distinction between the fact that something is (or might be) wrong, and someone's having the authority to determine and pronounce that that is so (which would belong to an office). He was saying in effect that in some matters the priest, but not Curt himself, had such an office. But it would be a small step from accepting such an assertion to accepting that perhaps, as regards the Church as a whole, there are some who have a special office for determining doctrines of the faith and teaching them. Indeed, once one admits the good sense of the notion of office, what remains to be investigated is only whether, as a matter of fact, Christ established such an office in the Church, and if so, who occupies it.

This line of thought leads naturally to the recognition of a teaching authority in the Church, which belongs to the apostles and their successors. Thus it is understandable that for Ruth the next crucial step in her becoming Catholic was her reading of the so-called Apostolic Fathers. These early bishops—Clement of Rome, Polycarp, and Ignatius of Antioch—declare explicitly and repeatedly in their writings that when Christ was on earth he appointed the apostles as the authoritative teachers of the Church; furthermore, they say that Christ gave instructions that the apostles were in turn to appoint bishops, so that after the apostles' death these bishops would succeed the apostles in this office of teaching and governing, ensuring stability and continuity of government.

More than that, this government would be simply the extension of the government of Christ because—as these Apostolic Fathers stress repeatedly—just as Christ appointed the apostles, so the apostles appointed the bishops. Thus, Christ's authority is transmitted along this line of succession. Hence, it is not possible to reject the bishops without rejecting the apostles, or to accept the authority of the apostles without accepting the authority of their successors. Ruth and I certainly accepted the authority of the apostles because we accepted the authority of Scripture, and we knew furthermore that a condition for including a writing in Holy Scripture in the early Church was that the writing be either written by an apostle or written under the authority of an apostle. We saw, then, from the teaching of the Apostolic Fathers that we were being inconsistent in accepting the authority of Scripture but not the authority of bishops.

Encountering the Gospel of Life

Admittedly, it took a while for this argument to develop in our thoughts and present itself with full clarity and force. In the meantime, we were helped along by a growing respect and admiration for the Catholic Church as a moral teacher. It became clear to us that only the Catholic Church had stood firm on certain teachings historically affirmed by all Christians but which Protestant churches had abandoned in the face of strong forces of popular culture. It seemed that only a Church rooted firmly in something outside the world could have the power to stand firm when confronted by all of the forces of the world.

One such matter was abortion. When we came to see that abortion was clearly wrong, we also saw that only the Catholic Church clearly taught that it was wrong. We came to see that it was wrong in the way that, in principle, everyone might see that it is wrong—through a simple argument. As mentioned, Ruth arrived at Harvard a fervent believer in a woman's right to abortion. (Her friends told the story that, in a discussion in her high school English class, she became so passionate about it that she stamped down her foot and declared firmly, "If I ever get pregnant, I won't hesitate to have an abortion.") So it is not surprising that when the topic of abortion came up over lunch one day, not long after we began dating, Ruth took the "pro-choice" side of the argument. I took the other side, not because I had any settled views on the matter—although I suppose that in some vague and intuitive way I sensed that abortion was wrong—but for the sake of argument, and to see if I could defeat her. A good friend and fellow philosophy major, Doug, was at lunch with us, and he joined my cause. (Doug did have settled views, as he was from a fundamentalist background in Louisiana and was decidedly pro-life.) Doug and I argued in terms of who had the burden of proof because we often saw in our philosophy courses that disputes are more often settled by shifting the burden of proof than by refutation. The burden of proof, we said, was clearly on someone who maintained that there was a difference between killing a newborn baby and killing a fetus: Why is the former forbidden but the latter permissible? Presumably to discharge the burden of proof, one would have to appeal to some characteristic of the newborn baby that the fetus lacks. Also, if one accepts that one should not kill any human being, this characteristic, to which one appeals, would have to be one that could reasonably be counted as belonging to the "essence" or definition of a human being. Doug and I became increasingly enthusiastic as we argued, and came to see that this was an interesting and possibly sound line of thought.

Ruth replied that the relevant difference is that an infant is breathing but a fetus is not. "So then, once an adult is placed on a respirator, one may kill him?" we asked. Ruth admitted that that was absurd, so she said next that the fetus is *dependent* upon someone but the infant is not, and that's the relevant difference between them. "So then," we replied, "if a mother is alone on a desert island with her baby, she may kill the baby? The baby is dependent upon her." This was clearly not right, so Ruth explained that the fetus is *physically dependent* on the mother, through an organ (the placenta), but the infant is not. "So when Siamese twins share a single organ," we said, "it would be permissible to kill either one of them?"

Ruth was speechless; she couldn't find anything else to say in response. She didn't say on the spot that we were right. But much later, reflecting back on that discussion, she said that at that moment she thought to herself, "They're right. There is no difference between the two cases." The argument convinced me also. So from that point onward we both believed that abortion was wrong. Yet we saw that Protestant churches either did not oppose abortion, or they vacillated, whereas the Catholic Church was notorious for not bending in opposition to it.

Another such moral issue was contraception. Soon after Ruth and I became Christians, a friend of mine from high school, Rich Gill, also had something of a conversion experience. As a result, he began to practice his Catholic faith seriously, and he took a job as a research assistant to Father John Hardon, the renowned Jesuit theologian who was teaching at the university that Rich was attending, Saint John's in Jamaica, New York. Rich soon began plying us with books defending the Catholic faith, especially books by Father Hardon, including the famous "yellow catechism", which at that time was the only reliable and up-to-date conspectus of the Catholic faith.[8] When we asked a question about the Catholic Church that he couldn't answer, he would do research and consult Father Hardon about it and then get back to us with a thoughtful and typically convincing response.

When Ruth and I were getting married, for obvious reasons Rich frequently raised the topic of contraception. We were happy to discuss the matter, not simply because we always liked discussions about ethics and the Christian faith, but also because we wanted to follow Christ in every respect. Rich claimed that contraception was contrary to the will of Christ, and we couldn't be sure that he was wrong. So we wanted to discuss the matter until we acquired some kind of confidence. Moreover, we half suspected that Rich was right. To us it seemed that in every age the practice of Christianity involved some kind of test, some point of conflict between Christianity and the spirit of the age, and fidelity to Christ would hinge on faithfulness on this one point. We couldn't rule out that contraception was such a test in our own time.

[8] John A Hardon, S.J., *The Catholic Catechism: A Contemporary Catechism of the Teachings of the Catholic Church* (New York: Doubleday, 1975).

Rich's arguments had a great deal of plausibility. He pointed out that the use of contraception tended to go along with what he referred to as a "contraceptive mentality"—a generally selfish, individualistic, and consumerist outlook, which was clearly the opposite of the attitude that a Christian was supposed to have. Also, who could deny that widespread use of contraceptives had led to increased promiscuity and increased abortion? And how could consequences that were so bad follow from a practice that was morally indifferent or good? Again, Rich seemed right when he drew an analogy between contraception and binging and purging: to look for sex while acting to thwart its natural consequences indeed seemed similar to the practice of eating to the point of surfeit and then vomiting so that one could eat over again.

Finally, from Father Hardon's excellent *Christianity in the Twentieth Century*—one of those dozens of books that Rich passed on to us—we learned that, although rudimentary contraceptives were widely used in the Roman Empire, Christians rejected them from the start.[9] In fact, it wasn't until 1930, when the Anglican bishops declared themselves in favor of contraception at the Lambeth Conference, that any Christians of note had ever defended the use of contraceptives. The rest of the Protestant communities generally had gone along with these changes, although they did not have clear reasons why this was now permissible. So we concluded that the Catholic Church alone held firm to the historic teaching of Christianity in opposing contraception as well as abortion, and—since by this point we were married—we burned our bridges by disposing of the contraceptives we were using.

By this point, in our last semester of college, Ruth and I were just about resolved that we would become Catholic. We even began going to the early Mass at Saint Paul's Catholic Parish in Harvard Square before attending the Sunday service in our own congregation, in order to be sure that we got an adequate dose of historic Christianity before having to deal with the wildly heterodox viewpoints we would inevitably encounter at First Church.

Some of the other leaders in the InterVarsity fellowship were concerned about our Catholic sympathies, much as we had earlier been

[9] John A Hardon, S.J., *Christianity in the Twentieth Century* (New York: Doubleday, 1972).

concerned about Curt's. To forestall what seemed a pending conversion, the campus minister of InterVarsity arranged a lunch in Harvard Square where, it was proposed, Ruth and I would meet with an InterVarsity campus minister from another city who had the reputation of being very skilled in apologetics, especially in points of difference between Evangelical Protestants and Catholics. Also invited to the lunch would be a philosophy professor from a college in Boston who had recently converted to Catholicism from a Dutch Reformed background. The plan was that Ruth and I would observe the discussion and hear the InterVarsity campus minister confute the arguments of the professor, and this would then dissuade us from becoming Catholics. However, this lunch meeting had precisely the opposite effect, since the InterVarsity minister was refuted at every point by the telling arguments put forward by that philosophy professor—who introduced himself to us by saying that the double E's in his last name should be pronounced like the E's in the name Beethoven: although spelled K-R-E-E-F-T, his name was pronounced "Peter KRAYFT".

When the founder of Catholics United for the Faith, H. Lyman Stebbins, was considering converting to the Catholic faith from a Protestant background, he wrote to C.S. Lewis to ask what the main arguments would be against such a change. The letter he received in reply struck him as so weakly argued that he thought, *If that is all that can be said against Catholicism, then I should convert right away.* After that lunch, Ruth and I developed a similar conviction. It now seemed almost a pressing obligation to convert, at least out of a concern for Christian unity. At the Last Supper, Christ commanded his disciples to live in unity; the divisions in Christianity were therefore clearly contrary to the will of Christ. They could be justified, then, only so long as they were absolutely necessary. Hence, it seemed to us that if a Christian were not positively *obliged*, by compelling and serious arguments, to be outside the original fold of Christianity—which is the Catholic Church—then the clear implication of the commandment of Christ was that he ought to become a Catholic.

We needed temporarily to put off a final decision because we were about to move to Britain: I had won a Marshall Scholarship for study at the University of Edinburgh. However, the day after we arrived in Edinburgh, we went to the Dominican Chaplaincy in Georges Square to seek instruction. Ruth knocked on the door and was greeted by Father Marcus Lefebure, wearing the distinctive white-and-black habit of the Dominicans. This granddaughter of Scottish emigrants from Glasgow then began a conversation by declaring immediately, to the father's astonishment, "I want to become a Catholic. How can I join?"

Whoever Receives a Little Child in My Name Receives Me

Father Marcus at first planned to meet with Ruth on a weekly basis until Easter. But when it became clear to him that, through her study of Father Hardon's writings and the Church Fathers, she hardly needed to go through an extended catechesis, he moved the date for her reception into the Church to the midnight Mass on Christmas Eve 1980. For my part, I made a general confession and began the practice of the Catholic faith at the same time.

We lived in Edinburgh for two years. I wrote a thesis on the Scottish philosopher David Hume, who lived in that city and is also buried there. Ruth got a job in the mail order department of Jenners, a famous department store on Princes Street—at the time, the Edinburgh equivalent of Bloomingdale's. Her job lasted only through the Christmas season; after that, she didn't look for a job for the remaining time as was allowed by her visa, since we planned to travel through Europe during the six weeks of spring break.

It was a classic student trip, very low budget; we carried backpacks and slept in squalid pensions throughout Germany, Switzerland, and Italy; we took the ferry from Brindisi to Greece and a train back. But a big frustration for me during the trip was why Ruth was such a poor traveling companion, as she couldn't even stay awake when we were traveling through such beautiful scenery as the Bernese Oberland or Arcadia. I think it was from my repeated complaints in letters home that Ruth's mom drew the inference that her daughter was not merely tired. Indeed, soon after we returned to Britain, it was confirmed that Ruth was expecting—one of the first gifts of our conversion to the Catholic faith. At 3:33 on a Friday afternoon, November 27, 1981, at the Simpson Royal Maternity Pavilion in the medical center of the University of Edinburgh, we were blessed with a son, Michael.

The baby's arrival was like a conversion: everything changed, while most things remained the same. For example, Ruth continued to attend seminars at the Dominican Chaplaincy but now took the baby along. We found the Dominican Chaplaincy to be a remarkable center of Catholic discussion and thought. Father Aidan Nichols and Father Vivian Boland, now distinguished theologians and writers, were young priests then and taught seminars on Saint Thomas Aquinas' angelology and anthropology, on John Henry Newman, on the Fathers of the Church, and on famous papal encyclicals. Father Marcus was an editor of *Concilium*, the "liberal" theological journal founded in the wake of the Second Vatican Council, and he would frequently propose for debate ideas drawn from Hans Küng or Edward Schillebeeckx. These thinkers seemed to him provocative, fresh, and new. Ruth and I, however, had a different view. We argued vigorously against them, since we had encountered their ideas already in liberal Protestantism; to us the evident tendency of the teachings of Küng and Schillebeeckx was to induce the same confusion that we had just escaped from in converting to Catholicism.

The chaplaincy would also frequently host speakers who would give a presentation or lead a discussion after the Sunday evening student Mass. One week the speaker was a member of Parliament who had recently sponsored a bill to lower the time up to which abortions were allowed in Britain, from twenty-eight weeks to twenty-four weeks. He pointed out that medical technology had advanced so much following the passage of the national law legalizing abortion that now unborn babies in one wing of the hospital were being aborted at the same age at which, in another wing of the hospital, they were being saved and treated as premature infants. Any person of goodwill should be willing to support his bill, he argued, since no matter where one stood on abortion, surely no one would wish to allow abortion after the time of viability. But, more important, to lower the date as he was proposing, he said, would simply bring current abortion legislation back to the same scope as it had when abortion was originally legalized: if the date of viability had changed, then the law should change also.

Besides having very reasonable arguments, the MP himself was soft-spoken and kindly—he hardly seemed a threat to anyone. Yet the MP had become a notorious figure because of his abortion bill, and his public appearances elsewhere in the country had been met with demonstrations and protests. The same thing happened with his talk at the chaplaincy. During his presentation, a group of students in the audience who were dressed as punks stood up in concert and started chanting loudly. As no one could any longer hear the speaker, the group had to be escorted out. Outside the building other students were protesting. When their chanting friends were led out the door, these other students tried to disrupt the talk by repeatedly ringing the doorbell of the chaplaincy. A friar had to fetch a screwdriver and manually disconnect the doorbell.

Ruth and I were astonished to witness this discourtesy and hostility to free discussion. We couldn't understand why everyone wouldn't immediately agree with the MP's very reasonable proposal. But what most disturbed us was that on a university campus—supposedly dedicated to learning—those who disagreed with the speaker weren't interested in arguing with him but instead tried to drown out intelligent discussion. The students' behavior reminded me of a quotation from the philosopher Thomas Hobbes which was a favorite among the eighteenth-century thinkers I was studying: "As oft as reason is against a man, so oft will a man be against reason."

Ruth and I were so disturbed by this event that afterward we wrote both the major pro-life group and the major abortion rights group in Britain to ask for their best pamphlets and papers in favor of their points of view. We wanted to see whether what we had witnessed at the chaplaincy was representative of the abortion debate in the United Kingdom in general. We found that the pro-life pamphlets we received were packed with philosophical arguments and facts from biology. Significantly, the pro-life pamphlets took care to state and carefully rebut all of the arguments that might be advanced for the other point of view. But the materials sent by the abortion rights groups discussed only strategies for political action—*how* one should act in order to get this desired result but not *why* this desirable result was justifiable. They presented no facts and gave no arguments (except one frivolous argument, that we do not really suppose that a pregnant woman is carrying a human person because we don't require her to obtain more than one passport when she is traveling). Moreover, they either ignored or gave caricatures of the pro-life view, and they made no attempt to rebut it. It was easy to suspect that they realized that if they were to state the pro-life view accurately, it would make that view appear more plausible than their political goals could allow.

The birth of our son Michael caused Ruth to look at the abortion controversy in a new and more urgent light. She observed this change in herself, writing at that time, in connection with a miscarriage suffered by a friend, that she was no longer capable of being "philosophical about the deaths of other people's children" and that "what seemed sad and tragic before is now plain terrible to contemplate." Her opposition to abortion was now rooted in her own motherhood and was not simply the cool, intellectual conclusion of a philosophical argument.

After our two years in Edinburgh were finished, we returned to Harvard, where I began study in the Ph.D. program in philosophy. We lived in a small two-bedroom apartment on Oxford Street, in a building owned by a North Cambridge landlord for whom Ruth had worked as a bookkeeper and office clerk as an undergraduate. We were relieved that this landlord enthusiastically hired Ruth again when we returned, since we needed the income from that job to make ends meet. Ruth and I would trade off caring for the baby: I would come home from class and watch Michael, studying when he slept, and she would go off to the office to work.

President of Massachusetts' Citizens for Life

One afternoon in October in that first semester, when I was leaving the philosophy building after a day of classes, I noticed a poster on the bulletin board advertising a debate that evening at Harvard on the subject of abortion. The debaters were eminent: Jack Wilke, president of the National Right to Life Committee (NRLC), and Nanette Falkenberg, executive director of the National Abortion Rights Action League (NARAL). I took a copy of the poster and handed it to Ruth when she met me at home at the door. "This looks like something you might want to get interested in", I said. She decided that she would go. At the debate, Wilke gave a thorough slide presentation in which he illustrated fetal development, described methods of abortion, discussed current abortion law, and urged his audience to get involved. Falkenberg, in contrast, began her presentation by saying,

37

"Maybe the fetus is a person, and maybe not. What's important is who decides." She made no attempt to reply to Wilke and gave no attention to the question of the status of the fetus. Instead, like those materials we had received the year before from the abortion advocacy group in Britain, she discussed only what political action should be taken to ensure that abortion remained legal. Ruth was horrified by Falkenberg's complete lack of concern about the crucial question and judged her approach to be "utterly corrupt".

After the debate, Ruth approached Wilke and asked for information about getting involved. Wilke reluctantly gave Ruth only the phone number of the National Right to Life Committee because he thought that this intelligent and attractive woman, who seemed so concerned to get information from him, was likely to be a spy from one of the feminist groups at Harvard. The next day Ruth called that number and was referred to the state pro-life organization, Massachusetts Citizens for Life (MCFL). When she called MCFL, she was told that they had just received a call from a Harvard student in the School of Education, Paul Swope, who wanted to start a pro-life group at Harvard. Ruth was told that she should contact Paul and perhaps work with him to get something started.

So Ruth and Paul, after discussions, resolved to hold weekly meetings on campus where they would show a pro-life film borrowed from the MCFL office. Two other students who attended these first meetings also wanted to get more involved: Karin Morin, at the law school, and Carmen Giunta, in the chemistry graduate program. Together these students and Ruth founded Harvard-Radcliffe Human Rights Advocates, which eventually became an official Harvard student group, hosting regular film showings, presentations, and debates. Many residents of the city of Cambridge also attended these meetings, and within a year the number of these participating residents became so large (about three hundred) that Ruth founded a break-off group, which she called Cambridge Unborn Rights Advocates (CURA) and which became the Cambridge chapter of MCFL.

All the while I was studying full time and working part time, and Ruth was continuing her part-time work as a bookkeeper in our landlord's office. We were also blessed with a second son, Maximilian, born June 30, 1983.

Ruth's dynamism and talents were noticed by the president of MCFL, a Boston attorney named Fran Hogan. Fran recruited Ruth to the MCFL board of directors in 1985 and convinced Ruth to stand for the presidency of MCFL in 1987, a position Ruth held for successive two-year terms.

Ruth quickly proved her mettle as a member of the board by leading MCFL's effort to pass a state constitutional amendment on abortion. The goal of the amendment was to limit abortion rights in the state so that they extended no further than what the U.S. Supreme Court recognized. The amendment was designed to bring state funding of abortion to an end and also to serve as a check on the activist state supreme court. Although the amendment was voted down, the effort was regarded as fundamentally a success because the margin of defeat was small and because the public debate over the amendment gave many opportunities for the pro-life view to be broadcast.

When she became president of MCFL, Ruth worked with Paul Swope, who served as executive director of MCFL at the time, to modernize the office of MCFL, its fundraising capabilities, and its capacity to respond quickly with press releases to developing news. Membership in MCFL grew substantially during that time, and the communication between the state organization and local chapters was improved. Ruth founded a Massachusetts chapter of Teens for Life, and she helped to form an association called Concerned Central Massachusetts Churches, a coalition of Protestant churches wanting to get more involved in the pro-life movement. Furthermore, under Ruth's tenure the lobbying strength of MCFL was significantly increased, so much so that MCFL was able to ensure that several abortion rights initiatives were turned back in committee and never came up for a vote in the state legislature.

Although Ruth was a skillful administrator, she liked public speaking the best. Besides appearing many times on TV and radio to comment on current events as MCFL president, Ruth also debated widely on university campuses, including MIT, Wellesley College, Boston College, Columbia University, Harvard (at Harvard Law School), and

Northeastern University. In debate she was so effective that abortion rights activists often refused to go up against her.

Ruth's pro-life work was all in addition to our other responsibilities. In particular, our family was growing, as we were blessed with the birth of a third son, John Henry, born in April 1986—just before Ruth assumed the presidency of MCFL—and a daughter, Maria, born in October 1987.

Friendship with Christ

It was not uncommon for people to ask Ruth how she accomplished all that she did. How could she be raising several small children, working part time to help pay the bills, and on top of that taking on a purely voluntary position that would for most people be a full-time responsibility? She had no "help", did the cooking and the cleaning, took the dirty clothes to the local self-service laundry, and brought groceries home in a wheeled cart, or sometimes a child's wagon. Ruth would answer by referring to practices that, paradoxically, might seem only to diminish her available time—daily prayer, daily Mass, daily Rosary, daily Scripture reading, and other spiritual practices. These, she said, gave her clarity, energy, and a desire to use her time well in God's service.

Ruth and I were helped in living these practices through our becoming acquainted with Opus Dei. Opus Dei is a personal prelature[10] of the Catholic Church that was founded in 1928 by a Spanish priest named Josemaría Escrivá, who in 2002 was canonized by Pope John Paul II. The purpose of Opus Dei is precisely to provide Catholics with help in the spiritual life. Ruth and I had actually first heard of Escrivá in Scotland, because the fellow we had asked to be our son Michael's godfather, Peter Winstanley, who was a postgraduate student in biochemistry at the Edinburgh Medical School, had lived in an Opus Dei residence when he was an undergraduate studying in Manchester. When Peter saw how much we wanted to be faithful and orthodox Catholics, he said, "I know two books that you would really like", and he gave us a copy of Ludwig Ott's treatise on Catholic

[10] A jurisdictional structure of the Church similar to a diocese but without a territory, established for a specific pastoral mission. See the *Code of Canon Law*, canons 294–97.

dogma and also a book of spiritual considerations by Escrivá called *The Way*. Ruth and I loved *The Way* very much because its message seemed so fresh, youthful, and at the same time demanding. We had never encountered a presentation of a path like that for following Christ that seemed so well suited to students and young people. We would memorize points from *The Way*, and we also kept notebooks where we would write favorite points, followed by our own meditations and commentaries on those points. We did all this without knowing anything about Opus Dei itself. In my imagination I pictured Escrivá as a young professor, maybe thirty years old, maybe living in Spain somewhere, and I admired greatly the nobility of his love for Christ.

But our actual encounter with Opus Dei as an association took place in the following way. Soon after I began graduate studies at Harvard, there was a graduate student in physics named Jaroslav Olesiak, a member of Opus Dei, who saw that I was attending Mass most days and who therefore invited me to an evening of recollection at Elmbrook, the Opus Dei center in Cambridge. When eventually I was free to go and attended the recollection, I sought spiritual direction from the priest who was giving the recollection, Father Sal Ferigle, and over time became better acquainted with Opus Dei and its purpose. After meetings with Father Sal, I would explain enthusiastically to Ruth what I had learned. Ruth was very interested in my reports, mainly because, since the time we became Catholics, we had sensed the need for some kind of external assistance in our efforts to pray regularly and grow in the interior life. We wanted to go to daily Mass, for instance, because we wanted to pray every day, and it seemed to us that the Mass was the best form of prayer; yet our enthusiasm would wax and wane, so that we would succeed in getting to Mass for a few days in a row but rarely for a longer span than that. Opus Dei seemed exactly what we were looking for; it offered spiritual direction, instruction, and friends who were trying to live a life of discipleship with Christ with a similar intensity and so could provide real, friendly support. So Ruth began to see Father Sal for spiritual direction as well, and soon we both joined Opus Dei.

Members of Opus Dei make a commitment to follow a plan of life that includes the spiritual practices I mentioned (which are referred to as the norms of piety). The founder of Opus Dei used to say, "If you want something done, ask someone who is busy", and the same principle seems to apply to this plan of life—not only does it seem easier for someone who is already busy to do the plan of life, but also somehow the plan of life helps someone put his life into better order and accomplish more for God, no doubt fundamentally through the graces that he may thereby receive.

When we became members of Opus Dei, it seemed to us that our pilgrimage had in an important sense come to an end. Now we had not only found the true faith, Catholicism, but also discovered a way of being disciples in the manner of the early Christians—whom we had always wanted to imitate—that was also entirely suitable to our situation. We had the teaching of the Church and the sacraments, but we also needed "coaching", encouragement, practical assistance, direction in apostolate, and the fellowship of others—especially with those more experienced in the faith—and these were offered freely in Opus Dei. Our journey could also be viewed in terms of conversions, since a Christian life may be viewed as a succession of conversions. We converted first to theism, then to Christianity, then to Catholicism—that brought to an end our "religious" conversions—and yet something more was needed, something like a practice or habit of "personal" conversion. Opus Dei was not, and could not be, any kind of religious conversion, but it did provide us with help to see how, from that point on in our lives, we were called to constant personal conversion in the realities of ordinary life.

The responsibilities of family life, too, gave greater focus to our work. For me, the sight of our four children sleeping side by side on crib mattresses placed on the floor of our tiny second bedroom—which was the only way we could fit them in, like sardines, as we joked—certainly gave my doctoral work a certain urgency. I couldn't afford the luxury of dilly-dallying, and in workmanlike way I completed my dissertation on time and accepted an appointment at Clark University in Worcester beginning in the fall semester of 1988.

Brave New Family

We moved to Worcester in August, putting together a down payment for a house only by taking the most extraordinary measures. With the help of a sizable no-interest loan from Ruth's parents and by taking out the maximum student loan possible at the last moment (so that the loan, still in the grace period, wouldn't yet appear as current debt), we could just barely stretch an FHA mortgage to purchase what we knew from our research was the least expensive starter home in the city.

It was a modest cottage, located on a hill on the poorer east side of Worcester, on Shelby Street. Due to a recent housing boom, the area was in transition from being, in the previous generation, a neighborhood of Irish and Italian immigrants with stable families who owned their homes (largely triple-deckers), to a neighborhood where buildings were purchased by absentee landlords and rented out to Hispanic immigrants, many of whom were illegal aliens and typically had irregular or broken families. We lived very austerely there, as we had essentially borrowed the entire cost of the house, and my salary was modest. Moreover, we were discovering the reality that the U.S. economy was no longer designed for households supported by a single income. The reality was that even the least expensive starter house in the least attractive neighborhood of a relatively inexpensive city was not affordable for us, because now two incomes were usually chasing house prices. It was impossible for the family of the stay-at-home mom to compete. Yet our home was cheerful and in its own way blessed with abundance. For example, every day when school was over, Ruth would have something freshly baked waiting for the children and their friends; or on a hot summer's day she would pile everyone into the car, friends and all, and take them to Bell Pond or Rutland State Park to go swimming.

We had no hot running water (because the boiler arm was defective), our carpets were forty years old, we had almost no real furniture, the stove and refrigerator needed to be replaced, and our car was fifteen years old. But strangely, what seemed to many to be the real austerity was that we had only one car! As a consequence, either I would walk the three miles to and from work, or Ruth would bundle everyone up to drive me there or pick me up, so that Ruth could have the car. But this was a blessing as well as a burden, because Ruth and I were compelled to plan each day together and coordinate closely what we did.

It's impossible for a married couple not to communicate if they are both busy and their days revolve around a single shared car.

Our move to a poor neighborhood in Worcester was probably what solidified Ruth's drift toward political conservatism. Her first step was away from liberal politics, after her conversion in Edinburgh to seriousness about the pro-life cause, because she found herself unable to support any politician who defended the spurious right to abortion. After that she was a Reagan Democrat, someone who had never voted Republican before but was drawn to Ronald Reagan's optimism and expression of the American spirit.

But it was in Worcester that the failure and even injustice of "big government" social policies became clear to us. It was obvious that the two causes of the poverty of the people around us were broken families and a poor culture of education. But government programs did nothing to correct this while even providing incentives that only made things worse, promoting out-of-wedlock births and subsidizing deadbeat dads. It seemed unjust to us that families like ours, who made many sacrifices to live in such a way that children would be well taken care of by both parents, would have their money taken away through taxes, so that this money could be given to others who had abandoned their children. Also, we saw firsthand how inefficient these social programs were. Once out of certain desperation we signed up for one of the many social programs we qualified for through an income test. This was a program called WIC (Aid for Women, Infants, and Children), which was meant to give help in buying milk and other basic foods for nursing moms. However, to get her weekly check of twenty dollars offered through the program, Ruth had to travel with the children to an office in downtown Worcester and first have meetings with various social workers. Since two or three adults (besides Ruth) were occupied for at least a full hour in this process, we estimated that it cost taxpayers over a hundred dollars for that twenty-dollar check to be disbursed.

We faced our first real cross in life—and an opportunity for a deeper conversion—about a year after moving to Worcester. Our fifth child, Thomas Matthew, was born at Saint Vincent Hospital in Worcester on September 21, 1989. Seven weeks later, on November 13, when he did not cry as usual for his nighttime feeding, and Ruth awoke feeling that she needed to feed him, she went to his crib and found him dead, a victim of SIDS (Sudden Infant Death Syndrome). She brought him to me cruciform in her arms, saying, "He's dead!" I prayed to Mary, because we had dedicated Thomas to the Blessed Mother from even before his birth. The priest who came to our house in the middle of the night to anoint the body and say a Rosary with us, Father Joseph Coonan, thought aloud, "What does it mean that the baby of the most pro-life mother in the parish dies?" At least a thousand people attended the funeral, held in Saint Paul's Cathedral, because Ruth was president of MCFL at the time, and her infant child's death was viewed by many with complete shock and horror.

Many friends from Opus Dei attended the funeral and offered their prayers and solace. Opus Dei's solidity and the spiritual support it supplied us became especially clear during this time of suffering. Thomas Matthew's godmother was Jan Hardy, also a member of Opus Dei. Ruth and I had met Jan and her husband, Tom, at an open house at Elmbrook and soon became great friends. Tom sometimes worked as a high school math and chemistry teacher, and because he then had six children, he was sometimes obliged to seek more lucrative work, such as repairing cars at a gas station in Framingham that he bought in a business venture with a friend. At the reception following Thomas' funeral, the Hardys' eldest daughter, Catherine, who was thirteen at the time, made a comment that was repeated in Opus Dei circles and that for us seemed to sum up how we were looking at Thomas' death. "God must love the Pakaluks very much to have sent them this suffering", Catherine said. It was a difficult truth, which maybe a child could best see directly, yet it was a truth that we accepted in faith. As Scripture clearly teaches, God chastens with suffering those whom he loves. Also, he brings good out of evil, so that "in everything God works for good with those who love him" (Rom 8:28). Even so, when we heard Catherine's remark, we thought of the famous story of Saint Teresa of Avila, who complained loudly to God once when her cart was overturned and she fell into the mud. In response to the saint's complaints, God consoled her, "This is how I treat all my friends"— to which Saint Teresa smartly replied, "Which is why you have so few of them!"

45

Ruth and I had confidence that Thomas as a baptized infant was received immediately into the presence of God and enjoyed eternal happiness. (Yet when someone said something along these lines to Ruth and added that Thomas was not harmed and had not suffered anything, Ruth corrected her and said that Thomas had lost the real human goods of growing up as a boy and of enjoying all of the beauties and joys of the world that God had created.) A result of Thomas' death, therefore, was that Ruth's mind and heart were set on heaven in a very real and concrete way: she embraced this cross, letting its implications affect her whole heart and life, and so underwent another personal conversion. "Thomas is already doing a good job of keeping me on the straight and narrow", she wrote to her friend Katy Whisenant. "It's not contemplating Our Lord's wounds or the Virgin at the foot of the cross that moves me to do my norms.[11] It's the feeling of shame that my infant son is gazing at me and wondering why his mother is so silly that she thinks typing newsletters or folding laundry is more important than prayer."

Ruth prayed that her grief might be consoled by another child, and when Sarah Esther was conceived less than a month after Thomas died, and was born less than a year after his death, in the manner of many women of the Bible, she regarded this blessing as a concrete answer to her prayer. As Ruth later confided to Sarah: "You brought so much happiness and emotional healing to me after the sadness and emptiness of losing little Thomas. You were a great gift and blessing from God for your mother."

Thomas' death at the time seemed like the depth of suffering that our family would undergo. And yet in retrospect it looks to have been a kind of preparation, especially for Ruth, for a larger cup of suffering that she would be asked to drink. Not long after Thomas' death, Ruth developed breast cancer.

When Ruth was pregnant with Sarah, in the course of doing a routine breast exam, she found a lump in her right breast. She brought the lump to the attention of her doctor, who performed a needle aspiration and told Ruth that she shouldn't worry, that she didn't have

---

[11] That is, norms of piety. See also the explanation on p. 55 below.

cancer. Ruth was not the worrying type, so she put the lump out of mind. However, after Sarah was born and she was nursing Sarah, she found that she had difficulty nursing on her right side and that her breast was sore with an interior, not a surface, pain. She presumed this was merely a cyst and dealt with it by applying moist heat. Her doctor agreed with this treatment, saying that it was normal for cysts to develop and that she should just continue as she was doing. Even so, Ruth eventually had to stop nursing on the right side altogether because of the difficulty and pain.

In July of the following summer, after Sarah was weaned, and over a year after she had first noticed the lump, Ruth noticed that now the lump seemed to have grown and that its contours were even visible under the surface of the skin. She mentioned the lump once again to her doctor at a routine appointment. However, he oddly was not concerned and attributed it to a cyst. Ruth nonetheless was concerned and sought a mammogram, figuring in any case that, even if the lump were nothing, since she was thirty-five years old and happened not to be pregnant it would be a good time to have a basal mammogram taken.

Once the mammogram was taken, it was obvious that she had a serious cancer, and the consulting surgeon scheduled a mastectomy for the first moment that the operating room was available, on October 8, 1991. The lump was found to have grown to four centimeters, and two lymph nodes were involved.

Then began a regimen of chemotherapy, lasting five months, where Ruth received chemotherapy for two successive weeks, then had a week off. In the weeks in which she received chemotherapy, for the day of the treatment itself and for two or three days later, Ruth would be completely exhausted and sleep most of the time; the rest of the week she would feel nauseated and weak. Ruth's hair before that was famously beautiful among her friends—luxuriantly rich and brown, with golden and reddish highlights. She had not cut her hair from the time she was eight years old, so it fell down past her knees. The chemotherapy caused all of her hair to fall out, even her eyebrows and eyelashes. The treatment so weakened her immune system that at one point she needed to be hospitalized. A port was surgically inserted into a vein in her chest so that she could receive chemotherapy more efficiently.

Ruth's friends organized a schedule for coming around the house on a regular basis to help with cleaning and to watch the children on days when Ruth was completely incapacitated. Throughout all the months that Ruth received chemotherapy, every evening without fail one of her friends from Opus Dei, the parish, or a pro-life group brought a meal.

If breast cancer metastasizes, it is always fatal. When Ruth's chemotherapy was completed, there was no way of knowing whether the treatment had successfully destroyed every last cancer cell floating around in her body or whether a surviving cell or cells would eventually lodge somewhere else and grow. In light of this uncertainty, we thought it made best sense to hope and act as if the cancer would not return. It was in that spirit that we believed that the most life-affirming thing we could do would be to conceive a child, if God granted us this gift—as was still possible, because the particular form of chemotherapy she had received had not destroyed her fertility. We conceived within months of the end of chemotherapy and were blessed with another child, Anna Sophia (Sophie), born April 16, 1993.

There were two dangers associated with Ruth's having a child at that time. The first was that if some cancer cells had metastasized and were of a certain type, the hormones of pregnancy might have had the effect of accelerating their growth. The second was that if metastasis were discovered when Ruth was pregnant, then most forms of treatment would be ruled out because of potential harm to the unborn child. Ruth was aware of these risks and did not hesitate to wish for a baby anyway.

Ruth had stepped down as president of MCFL in the summer of 1991, just a few months before her cancer was detected and treated. When she stepped down she took the position of vice president in charge of pro-life education, which she preferred, as she believed her distinctive talents could best be put to use in public speaking. When chemotherapy was finished, she gradually took on an increasing number of speaking engagements, speaking at Harvard Divinity School, Mount Holyoke, MIT, and Assumption College, among other places. She also founded

48

and led monthly meetings of a local Worcester-based chapter of MCFL called Central Massachusetts Citizens for Life (CMCFL).

When the Supreme Court came down with the *Planned Parenthood v. Casey* decision in July 1992, Ruth decided in light of it that the pro-life movement needed to change its strategy.[12] Before *Casey*, the chief pro-life strategy had been to change public opinion sufficiently so that a pro-life president would be elected who, it was thought, would appoint justices who would overturn *Roe v. Wade*. In Ruth's view, the pro-life movement had succeeded at this. They had done their part, but their efforts were undermined in the end by Justice Anthony Kennedy, who by all reasonable expectation should have voted the other way in *Casey*, constituting a majority overturning *Roe*. Human beings are free, and much can hinge on our free choices; thus, although the pro-life movement did everything that it should have done, Kennedy failed to do the right thing correspondingly. But the result of this, Ruth believed, was that the opportunity had been lost, and *Roe* was now just about irreversibly entrenched as law. That is why after *Casey*, Ruth changed how she opened a debate and would invariably start by saying that she did not expect to see *Roe* overturned in her lifetime and that that was not what she was trying to accomplish.

After *Casey*, then, Ruth changed her efforts in the direction of influencing the culture, especially influencing individual hearts and minds through education. She thought it was essential to present the truth about abortion to young people when they were in high school or middle school, before they went to college and were exposed there to abortion rights propaganda or adopted a lifestyle that would make it very difficult to embrace wholeheartedly the pro-life view. To this end she developed under the auspices of MCFL a program that she called the Life Education Awareness Project, or LEAP. The basic idea of LEAP was to make it so that Ruth's success in giving pro-life presentations could be replicated by others. She crafted paradigms for pro-life talks, taking care to base these on three different topics that she believed would be especially appealing to high school teachers: "Abortion and the Culture of Human Rights", "Abortion and Women's

---

[12] The decision in which the Supreme Court considered overturning *Roe v. Wade* but, in a plurality decision, reaffirmed it instead.

Rights", and "Pro-Life Is Pro-Love". Then she cultivated a speaker's bureau of intelligent, reasonable, articulate, and attractive women whom she trained to give talks on each of these topics, using the paradigms as an outline and model. In this way, she thought, there would always be a LEAP speaker available to give a reliable presentation on whatever topic a teacher picked.

After chemotherapy Ruth also became involved in a local political race for the first time when her friend Mary Mullaney ran for school committee in 1993. Ruth had already worked with Mary two years earlier on a matter of public schooling. In January 1992, it became clear that the Worcester School Committee was on the verge of approving a new sex education curriculum, which was written by Planned Parenthood. One of the big attractions of this curriculum was that Planned Parenthood, relying on its extensive funding from state and federal grants, would provide the instructors, who would come into the public schools and teach the sex education classes free of charge. This looked like a bargain to the Worcester School Committee. But Ruth and Mary viewed the initiative as insidious: they were aware of Planned Parenthood's history as an early proponent of eugenics and of its more recent activism in favor of unhindered sexual activity and unrestricted abortion for minors. It would be a disaster, they thought, and a corruption of the schools, to invite Planned Parenthood in to give instructions on matters that were best left to parents to discuss in confidence with their own children. Even though Ruth was undergoing chemotherapy at the time, she formed with Mary the Committee for Responsible Sex Education (CRSE), which in a very short period of time mobilized hundreds of Worcester citizens to express their disapproval to the school committee. At the same time, Ruth and Mary crafted guidelines for alternative sex education programs. Their efforts were highly effective: on January 16, 1992, in a tense and highly publicized meeting, the Worcester School Committee by a narrow 4–3 vote rejected the Planned Parenthood curriculum and resolved to seek instead an alternative curriculum that conformed to the basic criteria set down by CRSE.

Ruth and Mary both drew two important lessons from this experience: first, concerned citizens could hardly complain if they themselves were unwilling to make the sacrifices needed to participate in local government; second, in a city the size of Worcester, it was possible for a relatively small cadre of committed activists to make real progress in changing the political structure and culture. That is why at the next opportunity, in 1993, Mary ran for school committee, and Ruth managed her campaign.

Mary had arrived in Worcester only seven years previously, just a year before Ruth. They were therefore both regarded as newcomers in a fairly closed political community. As a result, Mary's campaign was not taken seriously by the press. But Mary spent many hours going door to door and making appearances at local meetings, while Ruth coordinated a comprehensive effort to distribute leaflets to every household in the city as well as advertise Mary's candidacy by signing up other moms to hold signs every evening on street corners. On election night, Mary was the fourth-highest vote getter in a field of eight, unseating one incumbent and garnering more votes than two very popular incumbents. This victory was viewed with astonishment by local media and received much coverage subsequently.

A Turn toward Heaven

A few weeks after the successful campaign, in late November 1993, Ruth noticed a persistent soreness in her lower back. The pain had appeared earlier, but she had dismissed it as related to the exertion of the election. However, now it was clear that the pain was not going away but rather was only growing in intensity. X-rays followed by a CT scan and bone scan confirmed Ruth's fears and revealed tumors in the lower and upper vertebrae, in Ruth's right hip, and on a spot on her skull. Because no tumor was so advanced as to threaten the integrity of any bone, Ruth began a hormone therapy.

Metastatic breast cancer is invariably a fatal illness; no one recovers from it. But how dire was her condition? Ruth's oncologist preferred not to discuss percentages, since each case is different. But in general the oncologist said it was not atypical for someone in Ruth's condition to live perhaps three years. In any case, so long as the metastasis remained only in the bones, it might be managed, and Ruth's quality of life could be very good; only when the cancer jumped to a vital organ did it become imminently life threatening.

Ruth's response to this news was conversion and greater confidence in God. "I have total peace that God will bring good out of this experience, whatever the outcome", she said. Her thoughts, moreover, turned increasingly in the direction of heaven, which, as her friends noticed, she spoke of as a reality, not as something abstract or far off. One such friend later observed, "She was someone for whom heaven was real. This was clear to me from a talk I heard her give where, in talking about vacation and the sanctification of leisure time, she mentioned heaven. I could tell by how she spoke that she had spent time thinking about heaven and what it would be like. The thought of heaven seemed closer to her than it was to me. Heaven was a place she was really looking forward to." Likewise, her love for life was evident: "For a Catholic," she wrote to a friend in 1995, "it is truly a blessing to have almost certain knowledge regarding the imminence of death. I have enjoyed—no, savored—these past two years more than any others of my life. My youngest child, Sophie, is now two years old. She has been among the most enjoyed children in human history." [13] But perhaps most paradoxically, in the midst of this sickness and suffering, she acquired what seemed to others an astonishing and almost superhuman capacity to accomplish good works.

In late May 1994 she began to experience once again increasing pain in her lower back and now also pain in her right thigh. She had a series of bone scans and CT scans, and it was observed that the tumors had spread to the point where there was a tumor in her right hip joint so large that it was compromising the structural integrity of her hip. Her doctors decided that she should have a metal rod placed in her right thigh to prevent a fracture of the hip. The surgery, which took place in June, was followed by a course of radiation treatment and a different hormone treatment.

The doctors said that it could take months for her to regain the ability to walk around freely as before. But she used the crutches that she took home from the hospital for only one day, and an antique cane with gnarled wood that a friend had arranged to be shipped from

[13] Because Ruth's treatments after metastasis had destroyed her ovaries and induced early menopause, she added, "I have to admit the one thing I most frequently regret about my current situation is not having another baby."

England for use after the crutches also proved to be unnecessary, as Ruth quickly returned to normal activity. Later in the summer, within six weeks of the surgery, she climbed Mount Washington in New Hampshire.

It would require a small book to describe Ruth's life and all of her activities after metastasis. She continued running the Worcester chapter of MCFL and also regularly gave pro-life presentations on campuses such as Fordham University, Columbia University, Boston College, the University of Vermont, Suffolk Law School, Amherst College, and Boston University. She continued training LEAP speakers and giving LEAP presentations herself, both for CCD classes in parishes in the Worcester diocese and at local high schools, including Doherty High School, Saint John's High School, Lawrence Catholic High School, Boston College High School, and Newton South High School.

Her victory in politics as the manager of Mary Mullaney's campaign led her to become involved in the successful campaign of a pro-life candidate, Peter Blute, for the House of Representatives for the Massachusetts third district. She met frequently with Blute's campaign manager for strategy sessions and was Blute's campaign adviser for life-related issues.

She appeared on a weekly political talk show on local cable television, and she hosted her own monthly show called *Close to Home*, where she interviewed leaders in pro-family initiatives in the central Massachusetts area.

She continued leading a cooperators' circle through Opus Dei,[14] organized the women's days and evenings of recollection, and also was a leader in a weekly Rosary group of mothers in the Worcester area.

From the time that we first arrived in Worcester, Ruth sang in the professional-quality choir of our parish, Saint Paul's, the cathedral parish. In the years she was being treated for cancer, she became increasingly involved in other parish activities, especially after the appointment

---

[14] A cooperators' circle is a brief monthly meeting for spiritual formation, with Scripture reading, prayer, an examination of conscience, and talks given by a member of Opus Dei. The meeting is designed for "cooperators", that is, persons who are not members of Opus Dei but who wish to help its apostolic endeavors.

of Father Richard F. Reidy as rector. Reidy, a former lawyer and a "late vocation", was a sportsman and popular with the young adults and shared Ruth's vision of how an inner city parish such as Saint Paul's might be renewed. Father Reidy appointed Ruth as director of religious education, and together they revamped the CCD program, replacing the old books with the Faith and Life series of Ignatius Press.

To promote better learning, Ruth devised what she called the Quiz Game, which involved students' memorizing prayers and facts from the Bible or Church teaching and history to compete for weekly prizes. At the end of the year, there was a Quiz Game playoff with both individual and team competitions. With Father Reidy she introduced a change whereby CCD students were no longer dismissed to their parents when class ended on Sunday at ten o'clock, just before Mass. Instead, the students processed into the church and, kneeling before the Blessed Sacrament, said a prayer that they had memorized. Parents were told that it was part of the students' CCD education to stay after class for Mass and that it would be helpful if the parents attended Mass along with their children.

Ruth wrote a play for the Christmas pageant, which she organized and directed. With Mary Mullaney she organized weekly summer excursions for families in the parish, with trips to the beach or a water park or to historic sites. She supervised the preparation of the students for confirmation and also founded a youth group, conceived of as a means for young adults to continue to find fellowship at the parish after confirmation. During winter months the youth group went skiing on Friday nights at the local ski hill, Wachusett Mountain, and once a year they went on a more ambitious ski trip to New Hampshire. All of these activities were subsidized by the parish for any families that could not afford them.

Ruth also helped to organize adult education in the parish and taught two Lenten courses herself, one entitled "The Christian Family in the Modern World", on Pope John Paul II's apostolic exhortation *Familiaris Consortio*, and another called "Themes in the Gospel of Life", a consideration of Pope John Paul II's encyclical *Evangelium Vitae*. With Mark and Grace Cheffers, Father Reidy, and me, Ruth helped to organize an ambitious series called Cathedral Conferences, which were held twice a year and brought prominent speakers to the cathedral for day-long conferences considering some aspect of the faith—such as Tom Howard speaking on the Eucharist, Peter Kreeft discussing spiritual warfare, or Clayton Bower giving a multimedia presentation on the Shroud of Turin. Last but not least by any means, at Ruth's suggestion, Father Reidy instituted daily confession after the noon Mass, which proved to be very popular.

During this time, except for a few days when she might be incapacitated from her illness, Ruth ran the household, shopped, did the laundry, and cleaned. She did the usual share of chauffeuring children to music rehearsals and soccer games—and there was a lot of that, as often enough we needed to drive boys to soccer games held at the same time but on opposite sides of the city. In keeping with a resolution she had made after the metastasis was discovered, without fail Ruth attended her sons' Little League games at the local Joe DiMaggio field.

All of this time, she lived the norms of piety of Opus Dei, as she had since we first encountered Opus Dei in Cambridge; that is, she went to daily Mass, said a daily Rosary, read from one of the gospels and a spiritual book on a daily basis, and practiced mental prayer in the morning and afternoon. For morning prayer she would wake up before the children, at six o'clock or so, make a pot of coffee, and sit quietly in the living room for half an hour, with some spiritual book in hand. For afternoon prayer, she would stay in the cathedral after noon Mass and pray before the Blessed Sacrament.

Final Months

In January 1998 Ruth saw her oncologist because of dull pain under her right rib cage that would not go away. A CT scan revealed that the cancer had spread to her lungs and liver. Her cancer had entered a terminal stage, and her expected life-span was now a matter of months, not years. She began an aggressive course of chemotherapy.

Ruth had been appointed a few months earlier as director of pro-life activities for the Worcester diocese, and in that position, she had made it her goal to give a LEAP presentation in every Catholic high school and in as many parishes as possible. This involved two or three presentations a week over a period of months. As a result, for the twenty-fifth anniversary of *Roe v. Wade* in 1998, Worcester sent five buses to the March for Life in Washington, D.C., instead of the usual one or two. Ruth went to the March and walked its length, but immediately afterward she suddenly felt very weak and feverish, and she collapsed. Tom Hardy was marching with her and took her to the Suburban Hospital in Bethesda, Maryland. The aggressive chemotherapy had so weakened her immune system that bacterial pneumonia had overwhelmed her body. She stayed in a sterile environment in the hospital until her white blood cell count came up to safe levels.

Because of this event her doctors tried several other types of chemotherapy, but none seemed to work, and the cancer kept growing. However, a drug called 5-FU gave Ruth a temporary period of relatively good health.

By midsummer Ruth had difficulty breathing from the cancer in her lungs. A surgeon who did an exploratory operation on her right lung to see whether there was cancerous tissue that might be removed said there was nothing he could do, since the cancer had reduced the lung tissue to a kind of undifferentiated mush. The liver cancer was causing fluid to accumulate in her lower abdomen. Ruth resigned from her various responsibilities, and we spent most of the time available between medical treatments and going on little excursions together. Ruth began to explain to me some of her household routines, and friends planned with her a system for helping with the household for when she became incapacitated. We received visits from friends we hadn't seen for many years, some of whom traveled great distances to see Ruth.

By early September it seemed that 5-FU was losing its efficacy. Ruth had entered a lottery for an experimental drug called Herceptin, but when she eventually began taking it, the drug had no noticeable good effects—either the drug was simply not effective for her, or she had won the lottery too late. Ruth was now bedridden and had to be placed on oxygen. She became too weak to think of traveling to Boston for further Herceptin treatments. That was her last available treatment; when she decided to forgo it, we switched to hospice care.

On September 21, the birthday of Thomas Matthew, her condition seemed critical. Father Reidy gave her the sacrament of the anointing of the sick, and even though it was a Monday, many friends from the parish and Saint Paul's spontaneously gathered in the house and kept watch with us and prayed throughout the day. Ruth rallied, but in the evening she lapsed into unconsciousness and resumed labored breathing. I and a few close friends and family members took turns keeping watch by her side.

Her doctor said that someone with Ruth's strength might struggle in this condition of unconscious, agonal breathing (as they called it) for as long as two weeks. It seemed to me that on Wednesday I should teach my class at Brown University, where I was a visitor that semester. At dawn just before I left, I was alone with Ruth and praying over her, holding her hand, when I was amazed to see her open her eyes. They moved around in a directionless and uncontrolled manner, the way the eyes of a newborn baby move. But then for a moment they focused on me, and I could see in Ruth's eyes that she saw me and recognized me and that she saw that I saw her. Something was conveyed even through a glance in that moment—not a thought, but something like an act of affection and endearment, our last communication.

Later that day, Wednesday, September 23, I returned from teaching at about three thirty. As I came in the door, I saw that Ruth had been transferred from the couch where she had been lying to a hospital bed, which in the interim had been brought by the hospice nurses. Friends and relatives were standing around her, and they called out to me, "Michael, come here! Hurry! She's leaving!" It was one of those cases—priests are familiar with this—where someone who is unconscious and on the point of death holds out, perhaps continuing to suffer greatly, so as not to depart before a beloved spouse or friend arrives. I went to her bed and held her hand, and it was clear she had taken her last breath.

Then something strange happened. People started arriving from all over the city. In most cases, no one had called them. They just thought or "knew" they should show up. (This was a time before cell phones and immediate messages.) A woman even showed up from Boston. She awoke suddenly and sat up in bed after a dream about Ruth, told her husband she had to see her, and drove out to Worcester immediately. The group of us, maybe forty or fifty, prayed and kept a kind of vigil. Ruth's body was in the room; it seemed right not to have it taken away. Later in the evening I called the funeral home, and after the body was taken everyone left.

The funeral Mass was held on the following Saturday morning. The cathedral was packed with over a thousand people, even more so than at Thomas' funeral. Afterward we traveled by police escort to the cemetery, given the long lines of cars. It seemed that hundreds of friends came to the gravesite, including many children. Someone had handed out roses—the symbol of the pro-life movement—which the children held in silence during the service at the grave. But when the service was over and Ruth's coffin had been lowered into the ground, then spontaneously, not at anyone's urging, the children came up one by one and dropped their flowers on the coffin.

I stayed and prayed by the gravesite afterward. A handful of friends stayed by my side. I was oblivious of them, but Jan Hardy later told me that she was right next to me, along with her eldest daughter, Catherine. As I prayed over the grave, I pondered my years of fidelity to Ruth. I was moved and spoke aloud, "The vow says, 'Until death do us part.'" A kind of work or task had been faithfully accomplished.

****

The Records of a Love of Life

The letters collected below span twenty years. The first expresses Ruth's thoughts as a twenty-one-year-old student doing research at the Houghton Library at Harvard for her undergraduate thesis in history and literature; the last letters, almost exactly twenty years later, are to friends and express what Ruth understood to be her farewells. Two of her most faithful correspondents through the years are members of "the gang" from Northern Valley Regional High School: Larry Weller, her high school sweetheart, who studied at McGill University and became an engineer specializing in core sampling with the firm of Woodward-Clyde; and Tim Henly, a chemist whose political views, as is evident, were usually at odds with Ruth's but who loved a good and sharp debate as much as Ruth.

A fairly large number of letters are to her in-laws; since long-distance phone calls were still relatively expensive, Ruth had a habit of writing a letter once a week both to my parents and to hers. (Unfortunately, the letters to her own parents were lost.) There are also letters written for particular purposes, such as to give advice about cancer (written to a friend of a friend) or to explain how breast cancer could not provide a pretext for late-term abortion (written to Helen Alvaré, the spokesperson for the National Council of Catholic Bishops on pro-life issues). I include too a few less personal letters written to public figures or to teachers or the principal of the school her children were attending, when these give insight into how Ruth thought about some important matter.

Ruth never had an e-mail address or even a cell phone; only pagers were commonly in use when she died. In these days of social networking, instant messages, and Skype, it is unclear whether anyone will write lengthy letters that, like some of Ruth's, are carefully thought about for days before being penned. If so, then the collection that follows may end up being one of the last examples of the art of letter writing.

Ruth was a great reader with excellent literary judgment, and often in her correspondence she discusses the books she has been reading. *Vanity Fair, Lost in the Cosmos, The War against Population, The End of the Affair*, the short stories of Tolstoy—these are among the many works that receive mention. Likewise, music is a recurring theme—for example, Ruth had an ongoing and tongue-in-cheek dispute with Larry Weller about the worth of Wagner operas.

Many points of morality are touched upon—artificial contraception, abortion, suicide, in vitro fertilization, sexual morality—and also points of doctrine, such as baptism, John Paul II's theology of the body, and whether intellectual freedom is compatible with submission to the teaching authority of the Church. Toward the end of her life the great questions of what life is for and how one should approach death become increasingly important. This group of moral and doctrinal letters in particular may appropriately be said to constitute an "apostolate of letter-writing", which Saint Josemaría Escrivá advocated.[15]

The letters also show Ruth's journey over the years across the political spectrum, from views in college that matched the "progressive" wing of the Democratic party (she was an enthusiastic supporter of George McGovern in high school) to enthusiasm in her last years for William F. Buckley. She was for a time a political junkie and regarded herself as a political conservative. Certainly she was a social conservative first and foremost.

But without question the letters' main topics, as is fitting, involve ordinary life. It was actually having a child that converted her to the view that her highest calling was to be a homemaker—and from her descriptions of her first child it is evident that she was deeply in love with him and that therefore the central question of her daily life became how she might make life best for him.

Everything later in her life, I think, may be understood as flowing from this. For instance, when I was in graduate school, we devised a complicated arrangement (described in some of the letters below) that required her to take the baby to work at the landlord's office and then required me to pick up the baby in the midafternoon, to take him home and continue studying there—all so that one of us could always be with the baby and we would not need to put him in daycare. Later, when I was writing a dissertation and we could easily have relocated our household, Ruth turned down an offer to teach English at her former high school in New Jersey—a job that would have given her much satisfaction and paid a much-needed high salary—because, as she said, she didn't want to take away from her children the gift of being raised by a mother who stays at home.

Saint Josemaría has referred to the infant Jesus as a teacher who instructs us *ex cathedra* from a manger. One might similarly say that Michael, Ruth's first child, was her original instructor in the pro-life movement and, in essence, the first inspiration for all of the good that she subsequently accomplished.[16]

---

[15] Josemaría Escrivá, *The Way* (New York: Image, 2006), no. 976.
[16] Hence this book is dedicated to him.

This love of the family, which sprung also in part from love for her own childhood, was the reason, I think, that she was so simple in her affection for the little cottage on Shelby Street on Worcester's East Side, and the reason why she found nothing more delightful than watching her sons play Little League at the nearby Joe DiMaggio field. Of course, it was not that she romanticized family life in some distorted way or overlooked its real trials and difficulties. After all, she writes, "Mothers long for the same relief every day starting at about 4 P.M. My friend Katy and I call it the Arsenic Hour (it's either you or them, but someone's going to get it in the tea)", and she describes how sometimes she cranks up the volume of the music she is listening to in order to drown out the sounds of children quarreling in the background.

Besides letters, I have included talks on spiritual subjects and matters of interior life originally given by Ruth at Opus Dei cooperators' circles and recollections. These were written in a sufficiently polished form and could be published with only very light editing. Not surprisingly, Ruth wrote up in polished form only a few of her talks given in these contexts.

I include also two pro-life presentations. The first is a LEAP presentation entitled "Abortion and the Culture of Human Rights", given at Saint Peter-Marian High School in Worcester in November 1997. This talk is reprinted as a transcription of the actual event, so we may take it as representative of the pro-life presentations to which she devoted herself with increasing urgency as she realized she had little time to live. The second presentation I have included is one from almost a decade earlier, Ruth's opening statement in a debate at MIT in 1989. I include part of this earlier talk because it addresses the impact of abortion on women. It was standard for Ruth to deal with this topic in any pro-life presentation. She did not do so in the Saint Peter-Marian presentation because she was limited by class time—on the tape, one can hear the ringing of the class bell, bringing her talk to a close. The MIT debate statement, then, adds this additional and important dimension.

The core of Ruth's argument about abortion and human rights may be summarized in this way: Human rights are rights that pertain to us simply in virtue of the fact that we are human, not for any reason above and beyond that; the fundamental human right is the right to life, and so, if that right is denied, then all human rights are in effect denied; the thing growing in the mother's womb is surely alive (otherwise it would not need to be killed by an abortion), and it is human; thus, to deny that the thing growing in the mother's womb has the right to life is to deny that anyone has any human rights whatsoever.

Once, an interviewer of a student newspaper at a university where she was debating asked her, "So it's not a legal argument you are making but a humanistic argument?" Ruth replied, "It comes from this idea: either you think all human beings are equal, and you don't kill each other, or you don't. I have always seen abortion as an issue where you should not need to believe in God in order to be against it. If anyone wants to say human rights exist or that all human beings are equal, those statements are tautologous with 'Abortion is wrong.'"

A big turning point in Ruth's thinking about the abortion controversy occurred one day when she was looking for abortion-related books in the used book section in the basement of Harvard Book Store, and she came across *In Necessity and Sorrow: Life and Death in an Abortion Clinic*, by Magda Denes. The author is a firm advocate of tax-funded abortion on demand throughout all nine months of pregnancy. But she is a clinical psychologist, and therefore her intention is to gather facts about how abortion affects those involved with it. So in the book, she describes how she goes to an abortion facility and interviews doctors, nurses, counselors, the women having the abortions, and those who accompany these women. She even witnesses and describes an abortion. Paradoxically, this book by an abortion advocate was usually the first one Ruth would recommend to anyone who wanted to do further reading. What the book made clear to Ruth is that people directly involved with abortion are well aware that they are killing human persons—because that's how they themselves describe abortion. It's that very realization that causes them to be conflicted about abortion.

We perhaps resist recognizing this because it so shocking. But it was this recognition that led Ruth to reconceive the abortion controversy, not as a difference of opinion as regards some philosophical thesis— "Is the fetus a person?" as people often say—but rather as a difference in two cultures: given that (as everyone really knows) the thing in the woman's womb is a living human, do we act on the principle that all human beings are fundamentally equal, or do we proceed as if we believe that it is permissible to kill some human beings to solve our problems? The first is the Culture of Life, the second the Culture of Death. These two cultures, she thought, were vying for the allegiance of the young people she was addressing, and her concern was to teach them what they should know in order that they might choose life.

Finally, I include a brief afterword telling something of the continuing "roller coaster ride" (as Ruth used to refer to life) of Ruth's family after her death. There is much, much more to tell, but as they say, that's another story.

SELECTED LETTERS
by Ruth Pakaluk

Undergrad at Harvard

December 7, 1978—to Larry Weller

It's far more than about time I wrote to you. Fortunately, this year my excuse really is that I've been busy (though never so busy as you, just infinitely less organized) and not that I've been exceedingly lazy.

I have bitten off more than I can get into my mouth, much less chew, etc., this semester. However, it's all good stuff.

For instance, I could now build for you a full adder (the thing that does addition and subtraction in a computer). By January 14, I will (I'd better) know how to write a program (in machine language) which will cause the computer to translate numbers into musical pitches. What fun!

Next semester, Mike and I are thinking of taking a course at MIT— Introduction to Programming in FORTRAN (Harvard doesn't teach FORTRAN intro courses). I really should have majored in computer science. Strange to find that out at this late date.

Meanwhile, in my own field, I'm getting to do some interesting stuff. For instance, Harvard has this rare books library (named Houghton). In there, they have rare first editions, single copies of political pamphlets, etc. The place is really out of this world. First, there's a guard by the door. He does the following:

1. Check to make sure you have a legitimate reason to use the library.
2. Inform you that you need two IDs to register to use the library.
3. Take from you everything you're carrying (purse, bags, etc.), in exchange for which you get a numbered ticket.
4. Instruct you where to hang your coat.
5. See that you have nothing more dangerous than a pencil (no *pens* allowed!) and maybe a notebook with you.

Then he escorts you to the (locked, naturally) door to the Reading Room. He presses a little doorbell, and the librarian buzzes you in.

She then:

1. Obtains two IDs from you.
2. Registers you.
3. Asks you what book you want.
4. Tells you to wait (please).

And then she fetches you the book.

Quite an ordeal, but it makes one feel as though Important Research is being done. (By the way, the pamphlet I wanted was written by John Lilburne in 1649, protesting that Cromwell's government was as tyrannous and illegal as Charles I's. It seems that Houghton has the only extant copy of this pamphlet.)

Your description of hiking in the Adirondacks was marvelous. Mike's brother, Jim, has a beautiful Time LIFE book about the Adirondacks, and since I read it, I've been hankering to go there. It may take some time, though, as Mike and I have hiking trips scheduled for the next two years. This spring it's Tennessee (the highest mountain in the East is Clingmans Dome in Tennessee!);[1] then at the end of this summer, it's Wyoming; and hopefully next summer, we'll get to the Rockies. That's escalating pretty quickly, but I think we'll be able to do it.

Well, this is not much of a letter, but if I don't mail it today, you won't ever see it, most likely.

January 19, 1979—to Larry Weller

It's still exam period here, but I'm having a very tough time getting myself to work. Oh, it's shameful, I know, and I have no one to blame but myself. I'm convinced I'm going to get B's in all my classes, and B's don't seem worth working for. (Now that makes sense, doesn't it?)

[1] Actually, Mount Mitchell in North Carolina is highest, at 6,684 feet, but Clingmans Dome is a very close second.

I reread *Vanity Fair* for one course. I forget now whether you have read that or not. Anyway, it was sheer pleasure to read that book—every page of it. I can't tell you how glad I was to find that I still like books, even though I dislike studying them. I don't think I've ever read a book that managed to be so funny while cutting social norms and human selfishness to bits. Interestingly enough, I can't stand Becky Sharp, while I can't say enough good words about Mayor Dobbin. I thought that unusual because Becky is very like Scarlett O'Hara, and when I read *Gone with the Wind*, I quite liked Scarlett. Maybe I wouldn't like her anymore if I read it again.

Would you believe that the Harvard drama group is doing *Candide*, and I MISSED THE AUDITIONS!!?! I cannot tell you how miserable I was when I realized that I had missed what will likely be the only chance I will ever get in my life to be part of that final rousing chorus. It's just too, too awful.

I have to leave for work very shortly, so this letter is going to come to an abrupt halt. Enclosed is a copy of some of the wedding photos. We thought our friends might like to have a copy of some appropriate pictures. Hope you like these two.

February 12, 1979—to Larry Weller

I have two letters of yours to answer, so I suppose I'll be orderly. First, Abraham. I don't agree with you that Abraham was mistaken about sacrificing Isaac. There are men to whom the Lord speaks directly, and Abraham was one of those. He was called out of a rich, prosperous family of the city of Ur to travel as a nomad in the wilderness. He did not decide to do that by rationally contemplating what he should do to serve God—he got the call and went. Also, he was from a culture where human sacrifice was normal, so he would not have known that the Lord was going to reveal later on that human sacrifice is an abomination to Him.

One should also realize that Isaac was promised to Abraham years before he was born and that the birth occurred late in Sarah's life. Isaac was quite clearly a gift from God, not Abraham's by right.

I think the sacrifice incident is properly seen as a test of the strength of Abraham's faith. (It is good to keep in mind that the Lord promises never to test us beyond our strength, so the fact that this was Abraham's test shows how great was his faith.) God had promised to Abraham that he would be the father of a great nation. By asking Abraham to sacrifice his only son, God was testing to see whether Abraham would trust that God knew best what His promise meant. Also, the test showed whether Abraham loved God above all other things.

The final, most important thing to keep in mind is this—that God actually did what He asked Abraham to do. This incident strikes us as the most cruel, arbitrary command of a jealous God. Yet God Himself actually did what Abraham was not finally required to do—God actually let His Son be sacrificed for us. That is what makes the Abraham-Isaac story so amazing.

Which is not to say that all of us should stop thinking and obey "voices" which tell us to murder our sons. There are very few Abrahams, and anyone of sense can tell the difference between a man like Abraham and a Jim Jones.

I feel like you and I are on a seesaw. Last year, your letters did much to cheer me up and keep some semblance of spine in me when I was really in the dumps. Now I'm as happy as I can remember being in my life, and you sound so sad. I hope I can say something in this haphazard letter to cheer you up!

First, I simply must take issue with Frances' deprecations of Tolstoy's short stories.[2] Her interests are clearly American, and Tolstoy is literally of another world. But there is quite a consensus of critical opinion

---

[2] Frances Weller, Larry's oldest sister, was at the time a professor of American and Canadian literature at the University of Nebraska. Ruth's high school English teacher told the following story about Ruth and Frances. When he was writing Ruth's letter of recommendation for Harvard, he was asked to give Ruth's standing in relation to some comparison group (for example, she was in the top 5 percent of graduating students, or the top 10 percent of honors English students, etc.). He decided to figure out Ruth's standing in exact fashion. By his reckoning, he had taught six thousand students in his life. He wavered over whether Ruth or Frances Weller was the best. After reflecting on the matter for some time, he concluded that on their merits, the two were a tie. But for the purpose of recommendation he awarded the palm to Ruth. So he wrote in the letter that Ruth was in the top 0.017 percent of all the students he had ever taught.

regarding the worth of those stories. I really think they are as good as or better than any American stories. There is really no comparison between Tolstoy and Bret Harte when it comes to depth or profundity of thought. And the fact that Tolstoy's stories move you is precisely one of the reasons why they are great. His stories deal with issues that concern all human beings at the core. Bret Harte and Mark Twain and friends write well, wittily, etc., but they rarely plumb the depths or scale the heights of human emotion.

Oh! I could just stamp my foot and scream! How can you *of all people* talk about having a feeble mind?!? Now you just stop it!

You are most definitely correct in pinning the blame for this malaise on McGill (college in general). There comes a point in most people's lives when they have been in school too long. Studies lose all perspective—we lose the ability to judge the quality of our work, everything we read seems boring, and all our thoughts and works seem obvious, trivial, shabby. THIS IS A DECEPTION! You need only get out into the non-academic world for a little while, and you will quickly perceive that your brain works more quickly and soundly than other people's. (What is depressing—and here I commiserate with you in your dejection over that report which is going to be bound and kept for future reference—congratulations, by the way—certainly my mastery of punctuation has gone downhill since eighth grade—is the fact that our brains, which certainly seem to us to be feeble organs indeed, are among the best which the human species produces. It brings home the meaning of the psalm "What is man, Lord, that thou art mindful of him?")[3]

I finished the last two books of the *Narnia Chronicles*. They are without doubt the most enjoyable books I have read in ages.

Did I tell you I'm finally taking a Shakespeare course? It's amazing how easy it is to read Shakespeare, and how easy to understand. I can't imagine why I ever had trouble with it in high school, yet I know I did. Oh well, I guess I have learned something in four years, but I don't know what it is.

[3] Ps 8:4.

October 26, 1979—to Larry Weller

The church retreat was wonderful.[4] I was very glad to find that many, many people sincerely desired to talk about, so as to deepen, their spiritual lives. I often feel as though this church thinks political activism is equivalent to obeying God's will. It was deeply encouraging to realize that that is not the case. I wish the Norwood Presbyterian Church would turn its focus a little more toward our personal relationship with God and spend a little more time nurturing spiritual growth. Without that strength, a person can do nothing.

The strangest thing happened at work. I was reconciling the checkbook when I came across a check signed "Robert Farrington" (my boss' name is Richard Farrington).[5] The check was a temporary check—no name or address on it, just an account number. But the account number was *ours* (mine and Mike's). I called the bank, fairly disturbed. Evidently, they gave somebody temporary checks with our account number on them! So this character is going around writing checks out of our account! That struck me as a pretty big slip-up for a bank to make. Anyway, I assume the bank will have to make good on his checks if they can't trace him. Pretty odd.

Believe it or not, I think I saw a hawk yesterday. I was walking to work, looking up at the sky, and I saw this very large bird circling around and around overhead. It was soaring, not flapping, and its wings were bent like a hawk's. I don't know what on earth it was looking for in the middle of Cambridge.

Well, time to return to the thesis—I'm fixing it up so I can start typing the final draft on Monday. It gets handed in Thursday, but it won't be read until March! Isn't that silly. Oh well, by that time I won't much care about the grade.

May 23, 1980—to Larry Weller

Someday I would like to be able to write letters as nice as the ones I receive from you. But this is not the day, unfortunately.

[4] A retreat on Cape Cod held by First Church Congregational, Cambridge.
[5] Richard Farrington was the landlord who employed Ruth as a bookkeeper.

I'm at work, and even though there isn't really anything to do at the moment, I feel I shouldn't be writing letters, so I'll make this very brief.

Yes, Mike and I will be at the party at my parents' house on May 31. It's going to be an enormous open house, from what my mother says. I can't tell you how disappointed we'll be if you have to work that day.

I spent most of an evening listening to Wagner last week. I've been accepted at the graduate school in Edinburgh, but tuition is two thousand pounds a year, so probably I won't be able to go.

That is my news in a very small nutshell. Will see you next week!

Living Abroad: In Edinburgh

September 1980—to Mom and Dad Van Kooy

Well, we finally have an address! Apartment hunting here is very strange—it seems there were only four one-bedroom flats free in all of Edinburgh! I naturally find that hard to believe, but we looked everywhere: newspapers, real estate agents, contacts, and the housing office. In the end we took the apartment Mike heard about from the girl at Harvard.[6] Let me describe it.

It has what you'd call "atmosphere"—lots of it. The rooms are perfectly enormous: twenty by twenty-five by sixteen feet for the living room! That's right—the ceilings are SIXTEEN FEET high! The front door to the street measures five and a half feet in *width*. It's the biggest door I've ever seen. The windows are about ten by five—one pane is the size of Henry's bedroom window. The floors are wood, even in the kitchen. The walls are white or blue, and the furniture is late Victorian for the most part (and looking its age, though still serviceable).

Ours is a row house, one of about twenty, all grey stone blocks for three stories. Since our street is a circle, the row of houses curves—it's

---

[6] The apartment was at 4 Royal Circus in the Georgian "New Town" district of Edinburgh.

very picturesque. There's a garden in the center of the circle—beautifully kept, I must exclaim—and a street straight through the garden (which is fenced and tree-lined, so still extraordinarily quiet and secluded).

Our landlady is great. She teaches at a posh, private boys' school and is quite nice. She studies animal husbandry and suchlike.

No news on the job front. Haven't yet had time to begin looking. We're not desperate for money, though we do need to be careful. Already everything costs twice as much as it does in the States.... People are infinitely more frugal here—hot water is switched on only when needed; ditto with heat and electric.

October 18, 1980—to Mom and Dad Pakaluk

As to Mike's birthday, as usual I'm at a total loss. He's so anti-materialistic! I think a pocket watch would be lovely, and a vest so he could attach the chain. If I ask him outright, he'd probably say it was too frivolous, but when we read the letter together (yours), he didn't seem to object to the idea. I'll probably get tickets for us to go to a concert or take a weekend bus trip somewhere nice. He lost a tie clip in London, so that's also an idea. I think he truly appreciates getting money earmarked for hiking trips, and it is my opinion (not his) that he could use more nice shirts.... If Rich Gill could procure more books by Father Hardon, I know Mike would love those. We've got *Catholic Catechism*, *Theology of Prayer*, and *Christianity in the Twentieth Century*. That's about all I can think of.

I got a job! Did I already tell you? I'm getting so confused, what with the time lag. It's answering customers' letters for a very ritzy department store [Jenners]—something like the Scottish Saks Fifth Avenue. I get to use flowery language, and it's very interesting. Letter orders come from all over—U.S.A., New Zealand, South Africa, Italy. I get £54.40 a week, which is roughly $135, which is not high for here, but I'm quite satisfied. The job is only for the Christmas season, but my supervisor would like to keep me on longer if possible. We'll see.

We've started instruction for joining the Catholic Church. The chaplaincy at university is run by several Dominicans, and our advisor is

Father Marcus Lefebure. He's very intelligent, quite a scholar and philosopher, very nice, sensible, and we like him every much. I don't know when I'll be confirmed, but I hope it's soon.

Mike is hard at work on his studies. He's taking Greek, which meets Monday through Friday at 11 A.M., and a seminar on Scottish philosophy; and he works on his thesis: looks like it'll be on David Hume. He practices the horn about half an hour each day and keeps quite busy. We've fallen into the same old division of labor—he shops, I clean, we both cook. We have to do laundry at a Laundromat, and it's 60p ($1.50) for one wash!! I'm doing as much as possible by hand, as you might imagine.

December 3, 1980—to Mom and Dad Pakaluk

Thanks so much for the letter "just for me". It was really uplifting. You know, I'm not always the most demonstrative person, and I don't often say the things nearest my heart, but your letter made me feel so happy that I realized I ought occasionally to say these things.

You and I both know that Mike has his funny little quirks and that he can be difficult on occasions (just like Dad and my father and all husbands in general); however, what I don't say often enough is that Mike is in my opinion just about the ideal husband. Aside from the fact that I think he's cute, interesting, and fun to be with, and that I love him, he also has the qualities that make for a good husband and (someday—not too long away, I hope) a good father. He is 100% trustworthy, always trying to be considerate and loving, and he handles me with a certain firmness which in my better moments I freely admit I need.

Now, in a fundamental sense, it is Mike's commitment to Christ and the grace of Our Lord which enable him to be so loving. But the grace of God always works with a raw material that can be more or less easy to manage. And, to an enormous, almost frightening, degree, parents are responsible for the state of the raw material that God's grace must act upon. In Mike, you and Dad instilled a very fine mix of kindness, love, discipline, honesty, all kinds of good qualities, for which I am most sincerely grateful.

To top it all off, you have overwhelmed me with motherly love and affection in a way that I'm afraid very few daughters-in-law ever experience. From the first moment I met you, I have felt the warmth of your most remarkably loving personality. I would have loved you for Mike's sake alone and am so glad to be able to love you even more for your own sake.

Life is going along so well for us—I am often amazed at the quantity and quality of our blessing. Harder times may very well come—this is always in God's almighty hands—but I do not worry. How few people receive in a lifetime all the joys I've had in just two years!

Thanksgiving dinner was a lovely affair. We invited Jean Melious (last year's Marshall Scholar); her boyfriend (who is Scottish); Pat Conrad (another of this year's Marshalls); Calum, a Scots friend we met at a Christian fellowship meeting; his roommate, David; and a fellow, Eric, from the Catholic students center. Mike gave a brief history of Thanksgiving before dinner which included a reading from one of the Pilgrims' diaries regarding the hardships of the first winter. It was very good.

The menu was as follows: turkey, onion-apple stuffing, mushroom-walnut stuffing, turnips, Brussels sprouts baked with chestnuts, baked potatoes, and cranberry sauce. For dessert I made apple pie (I couldn't find pumpkin at all), date-nut bread, and honey raisin bread. The company was great—none of them knew each other, but they all got along just fine.

January 31, 1981—to Mom and Dad Pakaluk

Well, yesterday was my last day of work. I'm not thrilled by the prospect of unemployment, but I'm sure I'll adjust. Mike thinks I ought to learn to type—something I've been fighting for years. But I think he's right; at least I'll try for the next few weeks.

Believe it or not, I kind of miss winter. The winter here is nothing like a proper winter. It's never really gotten cold—it hasn't been below freezing for more than a day. The grass stays green! It really does. There's no snow. Strange to say, I really like the way in New England everything goes stark and bare during winter—no green, just bare black trees, blue sky, white snow, and the occasional evergreen. Then, when spring comes, that first patch of soft mud and those first few blades of yellow-green grass look *so* beautiful! I remember as a kid thinking how exciting it was when the temperature rose above freezing for the first time, and you could smell the earth again. I don't suppose there will be anything like that here.

I took Teresa as my confirmation name, for Teresa of Avila. I've been reading her biography and enjoying it a lot. She was a very fascinating woman and a great saint. She also wrote a lot of mystic books which I hope to read, but I thought it would be better to start with a biography—to get a feel for when and how she lived.

February 2, 1981—to Mom and Dad Pakaluk [mailed with letter above]

I'm mailing this tomorrow no matter what happens! Today was my first day of unemployment. I think I need to get a job so I can take it easy! I walked all over the town doing errands—to the bank, to the library, to the post office, back to the library, to the vegetable store, to a friend's house, then grocery shopping, home to make dinner—oh, I forgot the visit to the JOB CENTER (where they list available jobs)—not very encouraging. Oh—I also bought opera tickets—next Thursday, we're going to see *The Barber of Seville*. The friend I went to visit is a lady we met on Christmas Eve who plays piano. She offered to play duets with us. I've been able to play with her twice and am going again on Thursday. It's great fun. My oboe playing should improve.

Postage went up here by about 50%! It's just revolting how expensive things are, and inflation is even worse than in America. Also, the taxes are unbelievably high. I know people get free university and free medical help, but I don't think it's worth all the taxes they pay. The longer I stay here, the less socialist I think I'll get. I used to be in favor of government social programs, but now I'm more skeptical. I don't think it's good in the long run for government to take over so much responsibility for people. I think it makes most people lazier, softer, and irresponsible. *Especially* students. Do you know, here the government gives students their room and board money?! Tuition is free, and at the beginning of each term, every student gets a check from the government. I think that's crazy. Students ought to work for their education, at least a little anyhow. If it's just handed over, I think people fail to appreciate the real value of an education.

As you know, I don't pay much attention to the news (that's why I'm eagerly awaiting our *Time* magazine). Anyway, what I do hear makes me uneasy. [U.S. president Ronald] Reagan is saying some very harsh things about Russia. [British prime minister] Mrs. [Margaret] Thatcher is saying some very scary things about the need for NATO [North Atlantic Treaty Organization] to back the U.S. I don't like to seem paranoid, but things like that make me nervous.

April 8, 1981—to Mom and Dad Pakaluk

Mike and I are somewhere off the coast of Yugoslavia or Greece right now on the ferry which runs nightly from Brindisi to Patras. It's almost an eighteen-hour trip over what must be the calmest body of water in the world. There's not a wave, barely even a ripple, to be seen.

I can't remember where I ended the last letter—I hope you'll forgive me if I repeat some things. We got to Rome early on Friday morning. By about 11:00 we had found a good room at a *pensione* for about twelve dollars per night. We spent the afternoon trailing all over Rome to see the great sights—the Colosseum, the Forum, the monument to Victor Emmanuel, various churches, the Pantheon, etc. We were quite hungry, so we stopped for dinner on the way back to our hotel. Mike ordered some wine, and we each had a pizza (they're served one per person here). What with our fatigue and the wine, by the time we returned to our room, we were exhausted and slept about twelve hours.

On Saturday we went to see Saint Peter's Basilica in the Vatican. It's perfectly enormous—about the size of two aircraft hangars. By afternoon we felt we had seen enough statues, paintings, and buildings for a while, so we went to the city park and then the city zoo. This turned out to be one of our most relaxing and enjoyable days so far.

On Sunday we took a day trip to Assisi, which is a beautiful old city set in the mountains that run down the interior of Italy. Despite the hordes of tourists, we had a lovely day walking around the ancient town, exploring the ruined castle, and seeing the great basilica that was erected in honor of Saint Francis. Saint Francis' tomb is under the church and is a favorite place for Italians to visit since he's Italy's patron saint.

On Monday we headed to the Vatican Museum. It has got to be the most crowded museum in the world. There were hundreds of tour groups, class trips, and you name it. Some of the smaller rooms were so jammed you literally couldn't see what was in the display case. The collection is a strange assortment: Egyptian mummies, Greek and Roman statues, lots of religious paintings, scientific instruments from the 1600s and earlier, lots of old maps, etc. We also saw the Sistine Chapel, which is of course very beautiful but difficult to appreciate as one must stare straight up at the ceiling.

We took it easy for the rest of Monday afternoon, then had a big dinner and then caught the night train to Brindisi. Taking an Italian sleeper is quite an experience. In Britain you sleep two to a compartment. In Italy, it's six. Mike and I and four other men all slept in the same compartment. We arrived in Brindisi at about 8:30 and spent the morning doing errands—getting tickets for the ferry, getting our passports stamped, changing lire for drachmas, etc. Brindisi itself is a rather dull town. But millions of tourists must go through the town en route to Greece each summer.

When we got to Greece, we wanted just to stay put for a while. I don't know how people can go on extended journeys for months on end—we find it very tiring. You never know where you'll find your next meal, bed, or shower (showers being the most elusive of the three). We've met people who will be travelling all summer long—about three months. I couldn't put up with that.

Lots of the people we meet also do a lot of shopping while touring. That seems to be one of the big pastimes of tourists. Since we're carrying backpacks, we're not at all eager to buy lots of stuff, but I did get two nice things—a pair of sunglasses (the sun here is so strong, I found myself squinting all the time) and a very small white leather evening bag with a gold and rose floral pattern etched into it. I didn't have any kind of nice evening bag in Edinburgh, so when we went to the Jenners dance, I brought nothing rather than lug around a big, ugly pocketbook. But I prefer to always keep at least my contact lens case handy, so I thought this would be a good idea. Mike, as usual, has bought nothing.

May 7, 1981—to Larry Weller

Our life has taken a decidedly lovely turn, as you already know, thanks to my mother's enthusiasm for grandmotherhood. Our baby is due sometime toward the end of November or beginning of December. This is a very exciting venture. I find that, in spite of having three younger siblings and in spite of years of baby-sitting experience, I actually know very little about the care of babies. There's going to be whole worlds of things to learn.

The news of Louise's sad misfortune came just after I had confirmation of my pregnancy.[7] I spoke to my doctor about it, and he said, as you mentioned, that up to 20% of all pregnancies end in miscarriage during the first three months. He said most doctors believe this figure represents the bulk of non-viable fetuses which for some reason started off wrong—with metabolic abnormalities, etc. So in some way it's a blessing to lose the child so early on rather than carry it to term and deliver a stillborn. But it's cold comfort, and I'm very sorry for Louise. I hope all goes swimmingly next time.

May 8, 1981

I, too, seem unable to complete a letter at one sitting. One of my friends asked me the other day how I was liking the life of a "lady of leisure". Well, there's precious little leisure to it! I think what happens is I do everything slower, so I'm just as busy as ever but I have less to show for it. But in honesty, I must admit that I'm able to do some things for which I previously had no time. For instance, I nearly always attend Mass daily. I don't know why more Catholics don't do that— the only other people there (except at the university chapel, where a fair number of students do show) are old ladies. Catholics believe that receiving communion is the best way to be strengthened in faith and virtue and grow closer to God. Virtually every Catholic church celebrates

---

[7] Louise is Larry Weller's second-oldest sister.

daily Masses in the early morning, at midday, and in the early evening. So you'd think more people would show up. I suppose most
people are just too busy.

I have to leave in seven minutes, so I have to decide whether to close
here or carry on to yet another page. I've chosen the latter, much to
your dismay—another two sides of *this hideous scrawl.* Hope your eyes
are up to it.

It's 10 P.M. and the sky is still light. Summer in Edinburgh is going to
be very lovely—just like *A Little Night Music*—perpetual twilight. I
can remember my grandmother trying to explain what the "gloam-
ing" was, and I just couldn't understand how the sky could stay light
after the sun had set. I'm still not sure I understand—does it have
something to do with the sun not sinking very far below the horizon?

Did I tell you that I finally got into a choir? It's about time. As it is,
I'm rather annoyed at the conductor's rehearsal technique—no warm-
up, we sing straight through without adequate nit-picking, and his
counting is *very* sloppy. A conductor must really be bad at rhythm if *I*,
who am not the world's best counter, have cause to complain. But
we're doing the Bach B Minor Mass, a piece I've long wanted to
perform, so I will put up and shut up. The members of the chorus are
incredibly friendly, which, of course, goes a long way to sweeten one's
impression of the group. And, for once, I'm in a choir that has plenty
of basses *and* tenors. That's a pleasant switch.

We were very pleased to learn that Scotland is a geological sister to
the Appalachians. Perhaps that helps to explain why we feel so at home
here. After traveling (albeit rapidly) through Germany, Switzerland,
Italy, Greece, and France, we still feel that Scotland is the most beautiful country and Edinburgh the most beautiful city that we've ever
seen.

Michael saw a vocal score to the Saint Matthew Passion on sale for
twenty pence today, and *he didn't buy it.* The silly creature got confused as to which score I owned—the Saint Matthew Passion or the
Brahms Requiem. Anyway, he's been given clear instructions to march
back on Monday and, if by some miracle the score is still there, purchase it posthaste.

I'm sitting here sipping soda water, one of the vilest concoctions known to me. The reason is, unlike most pregnant ladies who suffer morning sickness, I seem to suffer evening sickness. I've also taken to having dizzy spells, which are a frightful nuisance. But if it weren't for these symptoms, I'd have trouble believing that there really is another human life getting under way inside of me. It's all so incredible.

Your comment about it being easier for penniless students to travel than for hardworking full-time employees like you struck me as quite true. I don't know how it is, but on about six thousand dollars per year, we seem perfectly able to get by and enjoy all the comforts of life. That's less than what you paid in taxes. But of course, this won't last. As our family grows, we'll start needing things like a home, insurance, etc. But while it lasts, the student life is a great bargain.

I read a very sensible essay about the value of work in *Time* magazine. I agree with you that many young people have lost an appreciation for hard work, which is a great shame for the country as well as for themselves. I shall always be grateful for the values instilled into my family by my grandmother and parents. It's really not so much dull work that is soul-destroying as it is not valuing one's work for what it is.

May 13, 1981—to Mom and Dad Pakaluk

I'm doing OK, though I'm bothered by indigestion and feelings of nausea. Lately, I've had fainting spells, which are both annoying and embarrassing. Yesterday I was just standing talking to a friend in a store when suddenly the room started going black and my ears started ringing. I made it to the ladies' room before falling over, but only just. I had to just lie on the floor for about fifteen minutes—then I was OK, finished my shopping, and walked home.

I bought my first maternity dress today, and what a bargain! I was walking home from Mass when I saw a rummage sale. I decided to go have a look, as I've got my eye out for a pinafore apron. I asked one of the ladies if they had an apron, and she went off to see. One of the other volunteers, in true-blue salesman form, asked me what size I was. When I told her, she pulled out this very pretty, very simple dress by the maker Laura Ashley. Now, I've been eyeing the window of the local Laura Ashley shop for months. The dresses are beautiful, well-made, but rather expensive (about twenty-five pounds). So I was mildly interested. I asked the price and was shocked to hear "One and a half pounds." That's about $3.35. The dress is blue with a high waist and a very, very full skirt (enough for triplets, I'd guess). So I bought it. The trim (white lace) needs to be replaced, but that seems to be the only fault. Not bad.

June 12, 1981—to Mom and Dad Pakaluk

It's very hard to believe that it's 12 June—we still use the electric heater, and I always wear a sweater and light jacket outdoors. It just doesn't get very hot or very cold here. I suppose I'll be very glad of that toward August and September when I'm looking very expectant.

The nausea and dizziness have passed, though I still have a little indigestion (so did my mom), and I sleep a few hours more than before. I dislike intensely the bulge in my stomach, but there's no way out of it now. I like the idea of having a baby: I'm just not wild about the effects on my figure. Oh well—I suppose I'll get used to it.

We've been reading *Time* cover to cover every week. So far I get an overall favorable impression of Reagan. Some of the problems in foreign policy that face the U.S. right now seem impossibly complicated. I'm especially interested in his African policy. I'm very opposed to the South African regime, though I think the problem of how to express that disapproval politically is very complex. They are a strong ally in a hostile corner of the world. If only they would reform their system of government!

Similarly, the Polish crisis is fraught with difficulties. Much as one applauds the unions, if that country doesn't get its economy back in shape and its productivity up, there's going to be a huge crisis, since Poland owes Western banks and governments billions of dollars.

Do you recall that I write letters for a blind lady? Well, she took me and a friend of hers out to lunch the other day. It was a real swanky hotel restaurant of the good old British school. First, we had drinks in the parlor by an open fire, then a three-course lunch in the dining room (I had crab salad, roast potato, carrots, and spring cabbage followed by a very lovely bread pudding), then coffee back in the parlor. Drinks and coffee were extra (I don't know how much), but the flat charge for lunch was £4.75—something like $9.50—just for lunch! I don't know how people can afford to eat out like that. Needless to say, I was very overfed that day.

I went to a store called Mothercare to look at maternity things and baby equipment. The maternity clothes look big enough to clothe a Toyota. I'm not thrilled about walking around looking like a circus tent.

We're thinking of the name Esther if Baby is a girl. Nana's name was Esther, and I'm very fond of Biblical names. Also, I have always enjoyed being the only Ruth around, and I think it's nice to choose a somewhat uncommon name. Boys' names are more of a problem. So far, we've come up with William, Joseph, Robert, and Thomas. Any suggestions?

June 26, 1981—to Mom and Dad Pakaluk

I just don't know about these vitamins. Both you and my mother took them while pregnant, but the doctor here never mentioned them. I've never taken vitamins consistently in my life; I've just never felt a need for them. We eat a bit more meat now, so I'm probably getting the required B-12 vitamin. But I just don't know how to gage whether they're needed or not.

I haven't yet decided what I'll do for a coat—Mike thinks I'll fit into his navy blue raincoat, but I don't know. I'm looking for one in that style that was popular recently—beltless and very full. Haven't yet seen one, but will keep looking.

I've been baby-sitting to earn a bit of extra money. So far I've had four jobs, one to start 6 June and to last for ten days, 9 A.M.–3 P.M. It's nice to have the extra money and also nice to get in a little practice changing diapers. Yesterday I had a five-month-old girl, very cute and well behaved. I just hope ours is as cooperative.

Mike feels his Greek exams went well. He studied very, very hard for them, so I can't imagine that he'll do worse than an A. Since his exam, he continues to work on Greek every day. He's also putting in two hours per day reading Aquinas and also working on his thesis. We have a very pleasant lifestyle: I do all the housework, and he studies most of the day. Since there's not too much to keeping a one-bedroom flat in order, I get to read a fair amount as well. We're together nearly the whole day (unlike nearly all other married couples, who only spend a few hours together each day), yet both of us get our work done.

July 9, 1981—to Mom and Dad Pakaluk

Well, I'm playing the part of a "hiking widow" for the first time. Mike, Robin,[8] and I went to the west coast last Saturday (4 July): I returned on Tuesday, and Mike and Robin are on Skye (I think) tonight. Mike is *supposed* to phone me at some point so as to reassure me they're still OK, but I don't expect the call just yet.

My part of the hike was loads of fun. Robin arrived early Friday morning after an all-night bus trip from London. We had a nice day of visiting and packing, then a very nice "farewell" dinner of roast chicken and baked potatoes, with chocolate cake for dessert. We caught the 4:30 A.M. train to Glasgow, then the 6:30 A.M. train to Rannoch Station, where we got off. Rannoch Station comprises one hotel, three houses, and one train station stuck literally in the middle of an eerie, desolate, moorish wasteland. We hiked thirteen miles (all level walking, in deference to my delicate condition) to where the moor meets Glencoe. Glencoe is a very narrow pass between two remarkable mountain ridges. We pitched tent and had a nice dinner of noodles, meatballs, and tomato sauce.

By Sunday morning, it was raining. (What else.) We hung around in the tent, hoping the rain would break, but it didn't. Finally, by around 3 P.M., it let up enough for us to climb a small hill nearby. We no sooner reached the top of the hill when—you guessed it—it started to rain again. We descended along a magnificent, fast-flowing stream with marvelous waterfalls and water chutes. By the time we reached the by now very boggy moor, the sun was shining once more, and we saw two of the most gorgeous rainbows imaginable. We slogged through

[8] Robin Russin, a friend from Harvard studying English literature at Oxford on a Rhodes Scholarship.

the wet moor back to our tent and had just time enough to eat a very hearty meal of cornmeal mush and ham before it started to—that's right—rain again.

Monday morning again arrived raining. We decided that rather than walk through Glencoe (the tops of whose mountains were hid in clouds), we'd catch the bus which ran through Glencoe to Fort William, which lies at the base of Ben Nevis, Scotland's highest mountain. That proved to be a good idea. We arrived in Fort William around 2 P.M., had a delicious, hot fish-and-chips lunch, then headed off into Glen Nevis (a glen is a narrow valley, in case you were wondering). We pitched camp, then hiked along a beautiful river and up to a spectacular water-fall. Unfortunately, it never cleared enough for us to see the top of Ben Nevis.

On Tuesday morning we hiked back into town, where I caught a train back to Edinburgh. Mike and Robin's train to Skye was to depart an hour later. Their plans were still rather flexible.

Yesterday (Wednesday) I began my most recent baby-sitting job. I look after three girls, ages fourteen, twelve, and ten, from 9 A.M. to 2:30 P.M. Their mother works part-time as a botanist in one of the university labs. I'll be doing this for two weeks, until they go away on vacation. They're very pleasant girls: yesterday, we went for a walk in the hills behind their home. Today (it rained) we played cards and watched TV. Tomorrow I think we're going to bake fudge, and next week we plan to go swimming, go ice-skating, and (weather permitting) go for a picnic. It's a very nice way to earn a little extra money.

Today (after work), I went to the doctor. Everything seems to be going just fine. The baby moves around quite a lot now. The only things wrong with me are unrelated to the baby—I have a wart on my right pinkie and a corn on the bottom (the bottom!) of my right little toe.

September 13, 1981—to Mom and Dad Pakaluk

It's encouraging to see that most people approved of Reagan's action. I feel that occasionally one might be justified in breaking the law to serve a higher good (as, for instance, when it was illegal to help escaped slaves along their way to Canada); however, one should always be prepared to suffer the consequences of such an act. If the air controllers felt their case warranted a strike, they should first have counted the cost and prepared for the chance that they'd be fired.

I just realized today that Baby's due on Thanksgiving. I think I'll just go ahead with preparing an elaborate feast and invite friends, hoping Baby decides to be cooperative and doesn't choose to arrive in the middle of dinner. What chaos!—Can you imagine a half dozen frantic guests running about trying to be helpful? Still, it would be horribly dull to do without a proper celebration only to find that Baby decides to be a week late.

Summer is quite definitely over. It gets dark around 8:00, and the sun doesn't rise 'til about 6:30. The air is delightfully nippy and fresh. We both think this kind of weather is far nicer than the summer. Summer's just not distinctive or extreme enough, whereas spring and fall are beautiful, long, and fairly mild. Last winter (we're told) was exceptionally mild, so perhaps we're in for a more exciting time this year.

Mike's worked hard this week: each day we get up at 7 A.M., go to 7:30 Mass, return and eat breakfast, and Mike gets to work by 9 A.M. He takes a break for lunch around 12:30 lasting about forty-five minutes, then works again 'til dinner at about 6 P.M. He's usually back at the books by 7:30 and reads 'til 10:30. Meanwhile, I keep the household going and do my own reading in spare time. Sunday is truly a day of rest—we usually just goof around all day, writing some letters, joking around, reading novels or magazines, etc.

Last night we had dinner at a friend's. He specializes in Indian curries, a type of food [Mike and I] both really enjoy. He had some truly hot sauces, which I'm surprised to find I like very much—in small doses. He invited another couple over, Canadians who've been married nine years and have two children. It was fun listening to their experiences with their kids. The fellow, Dale, urged Mike to be present for the birth. Mike figures he'll come along, though I wonder. If I weren't having the baby, I'm sure I wouldn't want to watch. I'm far too squeamish for that sort of thing.

87

You asked about typically Scottish recipes. There's very few I can think of. The Scottish foods we most like aren't the kinds you make at home: they're black pudding (a blood sausage) and haggis, both of which one gets at a butcher. Most American cookbooks have scones and short-bread. There is one dessert I could tell you how to make which is very popular here. It's called trifle. Basically, you get some sponge cake (either home-baked or bought), break it into small chunks, and spread these with raspberry jam. Lay these in the bottom of a bowl. Next, douse the cake with a fair amount of cream sherry. Then do a layer of fruit—canned peaches and pears are especially favored, but you can use any mix you like. Pour enough juice over it to really soak the sponge cake. Next, pour a layer of thick custard over the fruit and chill thoroughly the whole mix. Before serving, spread a thick layer of whipped cream over the top. This has rapidly become one of Mike's favorite desserts.

Another Scottish favorite is called sultana cake. It's just a rich raisin fruit cake topped with about a half inch marzipan and a half inch white icing. At Christmastime they often make much richer fruit cakes, again topped with marzipan and white icing (just confectioner's sugar with a little milk, melted butter, and vanilla).

What were the "input" answers to the question on the ERA [Equal Rights Amendment] like? I didn't realize it was only three votes short of ratification by states. I halfheartedly hope it doesn't pass. I don't know very much about it, but I find the feminist movement so odious that I'd prefer to see anything they sponsor fail, except for equal pay for equal work, which seems adequately guaranteed already.

September 20, 1981—to Mom and Dad Pakaluk

We've had nice letters from Jack and from Rich Gill.[9] Rich has decided to join an order of priests called the Legionaries of Christ, so he's Brother Rich now. They have a long novitiate! He probably won't be ordained for nine years. We're very glad—the Church needs more priests as dedicated and loyal as Rich. Our only regret is now he can't be godfather to our baby.

[9] Jack was an Evangelical Christian friend who was instrumental in Michael's conversion from atheism to Christianity.

Who says you can't teach an old dog new tricks? For the first time, Mike has given me a list of desired birthday gifts. I figure I'll get to this early so we can coordinate who's getting him what, when, and how. He'd like (1) a metronome, (2) a lightweight storm suit (those pullover waterproof pants and tops that hikers and bikers use), (3) gaiters, (4) boots (I think he means hiking boots, which he'd really have to pick out), and books. The books are a real problem. New books here cost a fortune. Further, many of the books Mike wants aren't available in modern editions. I keep an eye out in secondhand book stores, but the ones he wants are scarce. I'll list a few for you just on the off chance that you find a way to obtain some of them: John Henry Newman, *Development of Doctrine, University Sermons*; Boethius, *On the Consolation of Philosophy*; Saint Augustine, *On the Trinity*; and any writings by the following authors: Duns Scotus, Albert the Great (also called Albertus Magnus), Avicenna, Averroes, William of Ockham. These are almost entirely theological writers from the Middle Ages or before, so you can imagine how unlikely one is to come across their books in your average bookshop. In addition, Mike needs new bedroom slippers. You might want to pass this list on to my mom, especially since I just remembered that my father knows several good used bookstores in New York City. Perhaps he might be able to round up a few of these elusive books. Let me know what you want to do about the birthday, as I won't purchase anything but books 'til I hear from you. There's only a one in a million chance we'd duplicate book purchases, so I'm not worried on that score.

I saw my GP for the last time on Thursday. From now on, I go to the hospital clinic for my checkups. That way, the doctor who's to deliver the baby gets to know me, and I get to know the place and the midwives. My GP takes over again after Baby arrives. As of Thursday, I seemed to be in perfect health: good iron level, normal weight and blood pressure, no swollen feet or varicose veins, etc. It's only ten weeks 'til Baby is due! I keep calculating things like: "I only have to wash my hair ten more times contending with this enormous belly"; "I only have to do ten more grocery expeditions lugging around these eighteen extra pounds"; "Only ten more Saturdays of housecleaning in peace without an infant crying every half hour or so", etc.

A friend has lent me a camel-colored cape which is the ideal winter garment for a pregnant lady. I look like a recruit to the Salvation

Army, but it's warm and it fits easily 'round my blossoming middle. It's quite chilly here now. Autumn has arrived in spirit, if not in fact according to the calendar. I find I prefer these nippy, breezy days to the hazy, warmish ones of summer. One thing I regret, though: soon there'll be no vegetables but potatoes, turnips, carrots, onions, cabbage, and Brussels sprouts.

September 29, 1981—to Mom and Dad Pakaluk

Well, September's just about over. That went fast. Hope the next two months speed by, as I'm getting very impatient, as you can well imagine.

Last week a friend of mine from high school, Larry Weller, most unexpectedly popped into town. He had been working for four weeks in the jungles of Liberia (on the west coast of Africa) doing geological survey work. Somehow, he managed to return via London and take two weeks' vacation to boot, so he popped up here for a couple of days before heading back to the States. We had a most pleasant visit. On Wednesday, we packed sandwiches and went for a short hike in the Pentland Hills. It started raining fairly hard, but fortunately we had arranged the hike so as to end up near to where the other Marshall Scholar, Pat Conrad, lives. So we warmed up in the kitchen of her residence, visited the lab where she works, then went out for a pub supper.

I've been playing my oboe the past couple of days. Actually, Mike and I have been playing Bach's two-part inventions for piano as if they were duets for oboe and horn. Sounds odd, but it's fun. I don't know if pregnant ladies should play the oboe. Sometimes I doubt it, as it leaves me quite red in the face, huffing and puffing for several minutes afterward.

October 12, 1981—to Mom and Dad Pakaluk

We're planning to have Thanksgiving dinner here, but Pat Conrad is going to be the actual person in charge (just in case Mike and I have to make a speedy exit). We figured it was better to risk my having to leave my own party than risk having the baby born out at Bush Campus, a twenty-minute car ride from the hospital.

I continue to feel great, still not too big. This is my thirty-fourth week; six to go. I see my doctor again on Thursday. On Wednesday, I attend my first labor class—this is where they teach breathing techniques, etc. That should be interesting.

Mike joined the Mountaineering Club again this year. He also talked Brian and Pat into joining. The three of them may very well head off with the club to Glencoe this weekend. I'd love to go along, but I'm just not up to much walking now. Aside from the fact that I can't walk too fast, my feet have spread out so that they don't fit into my hiking boots very well.

Mike's first Greek class meets today at 2 P.M. I'll probably do a bit of shopping today—it's time I packed my case for the hospital, and there's a few things I don't yet have. Not that it's very likely the baby will arrive early, but it's better to be prepared.

October 17, 1981—to Mom and Dad Pakaluk

I had tea at a friend's home this afternoon. She found more baby clothes for me to borrow. Also, she has lent me a baby's bath—one less item I have to buy. I'm beginning to feel that if I just wait long enough, everything we need will appear from out of nowhere. Only six weeks left!

I've got another recipe if you're interested. This is one Nana used to make often. I tried it for the first time last week, and it came out really well. It's called apple dumpling and it's a type of steamed pudding, a favorite kind of dessert here.

Mix thoroughly:

1 cup flour
$\frac{1}{2}$ cup brown sugar
1 teaspoon baking powder
$\frac{1}{2}$ teaspoon salt
1 teaspoon (or more) cinnamon

Cut in with a pastry cutter: $\frac{1}{4}$ cup margarine. Mix in: one egg. Add enough milk to moisten all ingredients, but not enough to make the mixture liquidy. Add one apple, chopped in bits, and some raisins. Put the gloppy mix into a greased, heat-proof (or plastic) bowl with steep sides. Cover the bowl with a clean cotton cloth, tied around the bowl with a string. Set the bowl in a large pot of boiling water so that the water comes halfway up the bowl. Cover and steam about two and a half hours. Serve hot with hard sauce (confectioner's sugar with a little milk and melted butter mixed in).

October 23, 1981—to Mom and Dad Pakaluk

Another week gone by! Mike had a great time in Glencoe last weekend. Saturday was beautiful—a one-in-a-million day for Glencoe. Once on the ridge, they could see all that part of Scotland stretched out beneath them. There was some snow on the mountains, but not enough to be a hindrance. On Sunday it rained quite hard, so they were happy to come home.

I bought just about all the baby things that we still needed: diapers, plastic pants, baby soap, pins, powder, diaper disinfectant, a carry sling, you name it! I think all that's still needed are diaper pail, blankets, and a pram or carry-cot.[10] A lady from church has said she can find a friend with a pram I can borrow, so I'm not going to buy anything like that until I hear from her. She's expecting her fourth baby in January and has offered to let me borrow her pram 'til January if nothing turns up by 26 November. So we seem to be all prepared.

We've started eating fish on Fridays (Rich Gill told us that that requirement hasn't ever been revoked—it's just if you really don't want to eat fish, you're supposed to perform an alternative penance). Anyway, tonight we're having smoked herring for the first time. Mike's very fond of herring—I hope I am, too! (Actually, I had "kippers" once, and they weren't so bad.)

November 15, 1981—to Mom and Dad Pakaluk

Well, only one and a half weeks left. Can't wait! We had a very funny experience last night. Two weeks or so before birth, the baby is supposed to "engage", as they say here, which means he drops lower

---

[10] A pram is a baby stroller; a carry-cot is a portable baby bed.

down into the pelvic cradle. This takes a lot of pressure off the mother's lower rib cage. Anyway, I was getting very impatient for this to happen, since my ribs have been really sore. So last night, I complained to Mike, saying I wished the baby would drop. He tapped the top of my bulge and said, "Now you get down there, you hear?" I said, "Yes, do what your daddy tells you." Lo and behold, twenty minutes later, I felt my whole abdomen sag, and the baby shifted down about two inches. I'm much more comfortable now.

Today we had a new American philosophy post-grad and his wife over for lunch. They're both from the South, though since their parents were military employees, they moved around a lot. They like Edinburgh pretty well, but we enjoyed sharing gripes about the way everything closes at lunchtime and the awful way Scotch drivers treat pedestrians. I made lasagna, something Mike always appreciates. After lunch we went to the National Art Gallery to see a special exhibit of paintings by Poussin. It was quite good.

Where Two or Three Are Gathered Together: A New Life

December 13, 1981—to Mom and Dad Pakaluk

First, let me tell you about Mikey: he's a beautiful baby and (so far) as good as an angel. I always tell Michael that he reminds me of the archangel Michael (the one who according to tradition does battle with the devil and casts him out of heaven), so it's only right that an archangel's son should look and act like a little cherub. So far we can't decide whom he looks like: the nurses in the hospital said Mikey looked just like me; I don't see it, nor does Michael, nor did my parents. My mom thinks Mikey has Michael's mouth: I agree, Michael doesn't. I think Mikey looks like a miniature of Michael, but no one else agrees, so it seems my eyes are blinded by love. But they both wake up in the same way—they raise their eyebrows as if trying to open their eyes, but the eyelids stay shut and all they do is wrinkle their foreheads.

My parents' visit was lots of fun, though a bit lopsided. Usually when we have visitors, I like to get everything organized and keep things running smoothly. As it turned out, I hardly lifted a finger during their entire visit. My mom did all the cooking and cleaning up, Dad did most of the shopping, and I just got practice doing things like changing Mikey, giving him a bath, etc. I know that's the way my mom wanted it, but I felt a little badly about it.

Mom, thanks so much for the Christening outfit. Little Mikey looked beautiful. The shawl especially is gorgeous. He was Christened on Wednesday, 9 December. We were so pleased to have a new little Christian in the family! He cried a bit, but that's probably because it was quite cold in the chapel. He really dislikes the cold.

We wanted to bring Mikey to Mass tonight, but because it's so cold, we decided to leave him with a next-door neighbor. (She's been a great help to me. Her youngest is two, so she lent me a lot of infant's clothing.) Not only is it a half-hour walk through the cold to the chapel, the chapel itself is so cold that by the time we got home, Mikey would be freezing. Everyone is eager to see him, so I *do* hope it warms up a bit.

So far, Mikey is a very sleepy baby. The health visitor at the baby clinic where I take him to (in some ways this welfare state is a bit overbearing) thinks he ought to be gaining weight faster, so I have to rouse him every two and a half hours for a feed, except at night, when he usually goes four hours.[11] It's very hard to wake him, and he usually drops off to sleep again after only ten minutes or so. In this respect he does resemble his mom; if I'm too comfortable, I often drop off as well. I take him in again tomorrow to be weighed: he must be gaining weight since his cheeks are much fuller now and his hands are looking quite chubby.

December 22, 1981—to Tim Henly

By now you'll have heard, it's a boy, so what more can I say? After that, everything pales to insignificance. So steel yourself for an insignificant letter.

[11] In Britain, a health visitor is a nurse trained to help mothers with their newborn babies.

On the Long Trail in Vermont with Ruth, Michael's brother, Jim, and his wife, Debbie

July 1981: Robin Russin on a hike with Ruth and Michael on the Isle of Skye in Scotland

June 1980: Ruth and Michael at their Harvard College graduation

December 1981: Ruth with newborn "Mikey" and her parents on the tower in St. Andrews, Scotland

June 1984: Hiking near the Mull of Kintyre, Scotland, carrying Michael, and Max is in the backpack

Summer 1987: Ruth with baby John Henry

Summer 1989: Ruth expecting Thomas and holding Maria
(with John Henry, Max, and Michael) at Clark University

September 1989: The baptism of Thomas Matthew at St. Paul's Cathedral in Worcester. Brian Frykenberg and Jan Hardy are the godparents

Early 1991: Ruth holding baby Sarah, and Michael holding Maria, at the reception following the first Mass of newly-ordained Fr. Rich Gill in his hometown, at St. Ignatius Loyola Church, Hicksville, New York

June 1991: The family in vacation in the White Mountains of New Hampshire, the summer before Ruth was first diagnosed (Sarah, Michael, Max, John Henry, and Maria)

1994: A family visit to Cardinal Law's residence, after Ruth had stepped down as President of MCFL. The children are John Henry, Sarah, Maria, Michael, Max, and Sophie. Katy Whisenant, far left, was visiting from England.

June 1994: Hiking in the Colorado Rockies when Michael was an Aspen Institute Fellow

July 1998: With Michael on the doorstep of 17 Beechmont Street two months before her death

Mikey (as the poor infant has already been nicknamed) is beautiful and very easy to care for. Much less trouble than a puppy, though he generates more laundry. He was most cooperative in choosing to wait 'til after our Thanksgiving dinner before making an appearance. Once he decided it was time to be born, he was pretty quick about it; I was in labor for about five hours, as opposed to ten hours average for a first baby.

Two letters ago, you asked me if I liked jazz. (That was the letter that got locked in our secretary. Mike managed to pry open the back panel and retrieve the key.) Yes—I do like jazz. Very much. I listen to it whenever I can; since we have no tape player or stereo, that means I listen to it whenever it's on the radio. I don't know many names or titles, but I definitely like it more than any other type of popular music. We listen to classical music almost exclusively. Jazz is my second-favorite type of music, followed closely by authentic folk music—any folk; it can be Hungarian shepherds, African hunters, Gaelic fishermen, or American hillbillies as far as I'm concerned.

Strange to say, I've become almost appreciative of modern classical music. I still don't like the stuff that is nothing but blips and glitches, but I'm now able to distinguish "good" modern atonal music from the really awful stuff. Some of it I actually like. Mahler remains my least favorite composer (too whooshy), followed by Wagner, though I'm trying to learn to like Wagner since Larry thinks so highly of him. (Of course, Mike likes both Mahler and Wagner—they wrote great horn parts.)

I'll keep my response to your last point on contraceptives (mercifully) short. Yes, man is supposed to use his mind to solve problems and alleviate misery; however, some solutions, though they might be clever and effective, are ruled out because they are immoral. So, for instance, genocide isn't an acceptable solution to the problem of overpopulation. The use of artificial contraceptives is seen as being an immoral solution because it thwarts the primary, God-given purpose of sex, and it takes away the couple's openness to receive children from God as He, not they, see fit. Couples can still use their minds to use natural birth control (and believe me, there's plenty of scope for using the mind there). 'Nuff said for now—it's holiday time.

January 25, 1982—to Mom and Dad Pakaluk

Sorry to let a week elapse without writing: we've had a tough time resuming our normal schedule. To catch up on sleep, we've been lying in every morning 'til about 11 A.M., which hardly leaves enough hours in the day to get the daily chores done. Today we finally got up at an almost decent hour—8:30. Our goal is to rise every day at 7:00 or 7:30.

Last night Mikey slept from 1:30 'til *we* woke him at 8:30. I was afraid he was sick, but he doesn't seem to have a fever. Still, I'm going to watch him carefully today. He was weighed last on the nineteenth—eleven pounds exactly. He has started to "stand" more—when he's being burped on the shoulder, he straightens his legs and partly supports his weight. He seems to enjoy that a lot.

Last Saturday (23 January) we went to a Burns supper at the chaplaincy. The Scots are positively dotty about this poet, Robert Burns. Not only do they flock to gawk at every site where he's known to have sat, slept, or wrote (it seems Burns slept more than even George Washington did), they also celebrate his birth annually with this strange ceremony. Once the dinner guests have assembled, a piper escorts to the head table someone who carries a haggis on a platter. The guest of honor then "addresses" the haggis; that is, he reads an ode to the haggis which was written by Burns. At the appropriate moment in the poem, the haggis is stabbed open with a dirk.[12] Then we all partake of haggis, mashed potatoes, and turnips. At the end of the feast (?), someone toasts the queen, another toasts the lassies, another the ladies, and finally someone gives the "immortal memory" address, which recounts the glorious life of the poet. Needless to say, it was fun. Mikey was very well behaved. He wore his white shirt and tie for the occasion and looked quite the Little Man.

This term is getting going full steam now. Mike and I (hence Mikey as well) plan to take part in three seminars: one is about major Papal encyclicals of the twentieth century (Mike is presenting the session on *Humanae Vitae*—the one in which Pope Paul banned contraceptives); the second is on Aquinas' view of the angels; the third is a comparison of the modern

---

[12] A dirk is a decorative dagger usually carried by a man wearing a dress kilt.

theologian [Edward] Schillebeeckx to J. H. [John Henry] Newman. We'll be busy!

March 4, 1982—to Larry Weller

I'm glad my last letter did something to assuage your fears regarding the extent of my "computerization". Perhaps you would do well to view Mike's and my zeal for philosophical hairsplitting as Tristram Shandy viewed his uncle's passion for war games. (Have you ever read that novel by L. Sterne?[13] It begins well, but trips itself up in digressions by the middle and ends in confusion.)

Now for the tough paragraph. While I'm writing this, little Mikey is sleeping peacefully nearby. He no longer looks like the wizened old man you saw in my parents' photos; his little hands are dimpled at the base of each finger, his legs are getting longer and stronger, and his darling face is round as a pumpkin—the picture of healthy, adorable babyness. Why am I so lucky? Why is Louise not?[14] I say a little prayer every day for her and Joe, that things will go better next time. A friend of mine told me that once I was a mother, I'd never be able to be philosophical about the deaths of other people's children (not that anyone is just philosophical and cold, but she was right—what seemed sad and tragic before is now plain terrible to contemplate).

Thank you for clarifying your religious sentiments a bit. People are different, though I don't know just how different. For instance, as soon as I came (or rather, returned) to the conviction that a God exists, it seemed obvious that the only rational thing to do was to find out more about Him and what He wanted, since by definition God is infinitely more worthwhile and important than anything else. It's now hard for me to remember or imagine how a person can have a belief in God and yet not think that it's imperative that he strive to put God at the center of his consciousness. Doing that may sound terribly exhausting to you, but consider this—the Church has always taught

[13] *Tristram Shandy* (1759–1767), by Laurence Sterne.

[14] This letter refers to the death of the infant son of Louise and her husband, Joe. The baby was born prematurely and lived only nine days. (This had followed Louise's first miscarriage, referred to above in the letter of May 7, 1981. Louise suffered one further miscarriage, then thankfully was blessed with two healthy sons.)

that God made man in such a way that we cannot help desiring happiness, yet we can only be happy (truly happy, as opposed to momentarily amused or distracted) by being united with Him. So then, constantly turning one's attention Godward would be the most natural thing for a man to do.

Of course, the beautiful high-minded stuff like *Parsifal*, etc., is beautiful insofar as it reflects in its small way some of the infinite Beauty, Goodness, Truth that is God. I only wish I weren't so dull that I can't fully appreciate the resemblances to or reflections of God that must be in Wagner's music. But I'm getting there. Heard *Siegfried Idyll* for about the *tenth* time on the radio yesterday. It is extremely beautiful.

Did I tell you Mike gave me a flute?! I've been playing oboe and flute at least three times per week lately. It's great.

April 5, 1982—to Larry Weller

Your duck stationery is lovely. Did you know ducks are just about our favorite animals? They're always so amusing. We saw scads of ducks at Cambridge—they act as though the university greens and gardens were designed for them rather than for the students and professors. Since most of the students had departed for the spring holidays, the ducks had the place to themselves.

I've just returned from playing flute sonatas with a pianist friend. It is indeed a wonderful thing to have a flute. I don't think I'll bring it hiking—it's too apt to end up in a stream or at the bottom of a ravine.

Mike is off talking to as many philosophy profs as he can dig up (Easter break has a way of dispersing all university personnel) to get their views on Princeton versus Harvard. We just don't know yet where we'll go. For many reasons, we both hope Princeton wins, but professional considerations have to outweigh personal.

I never should have used the phrase "by definition". It's very weak and not at all persuasive. You were quite right to object to that phrase. But I would like to answer your other objections as best I can.

First, what do you mean by "my God"? I think what you mean to say is "as I understand God". If there's a God, He's everybody's God and

He's the same (essentially) to everyone. I don't say everyone under-stands God in precisely the same way, just as not everyone understands the *Mona Lisa* in the same way. But there's only one *Mona Lisa*, just as there's only one God.

You seem to want to make a distinction between the love of God and the love of man. I don't make that distinction the way you seem to think I do. The two are inseparable: one cannot love God and neglect the needs of his fellow men—God has forbidden that. What's equally true but more important—one cannot love mankind and serve the needs of others if one doesn't love God and get to know what He is like. If you wanted to be a great singer, you would study with and emulate a great singer. Similarly, if you want to do good to others, you must study with and emulate the One who is the source and pattern of goodness. Obeying the Ten Commandments isn't enough, nor is obeying the dic-tates of conscience—our own powers of reason often lead us astray. But by being with God, trying to become a more perfect likeness of His Son, a person becomes more able to do good in this sad, suffering world. I hope this makes my position clearer to you.

Mikey's not walking yet, so he's really not very exhausting at all. He's sound asleep on my lap at the moment—he spends one out of four hours sleeping during the day, then sleeps about ten hours at night.

April 22, 1982—to Tim Henly

Mike delivered his thesis to the typist today. This is going to be a controversial thesis, to say the least. He argues that none of Hume's criticisms of the Argument [for the existence of God] from Design actually go through, that it is possible to put forward a variant of the Argument from Design using Hume's own philosophy, and that Hume's philosophical framework is internally inconsistent. Since Hume is cur-rently in vogue among philosophers, Mike's thesis won't go down too easily.

Our newest interesting news is that we're returning to Cambridge this fall. Both Princeton and Harvard accepted Mike, but the faculty at Harvard is really better for what he wants to study. Much as we'd prefer to live in verdant Princeton, academically and professionally it's better for Mike to study at Harvard.

For Easter, we spent a week with a Catholic family we've gotten to know quite well. They have a rambling old house in the Highlands that used to be a hunting lodge. The weather was sunny and mild, so we did a fair bit of hiking in nearby Glencoe. The baby behaved beautifully and seemed to enjoy his first mountain climb. He got the benefit of the view without any of the effort.

To resume the birth control discussion . . . Yes, I do mean by "natural means" things like the rhythm method. There are several variations of that, all of which are based on avoiding intercourse on fertile days. This method is condoned, even, to a degree, encouraged, by the Magisterium, precisely because it does not violate the principle which precludes artificial contraception, viz., that one ought to *do* nothing to *frustrate* the generative possibility of the sex act. There is no sin in having intercourse on naturally infertile days (if there were, Catholic couples would be obliged to abstain on those days, which would be odd, to say the least). There is no sin in avoiding sex on probably fertile days (if there were, Catholic couples would be obliged to have sex on those days, which is no less odd). There *is* sin if a couple avoids having children for selfish motives, but that is a different sin from the one committed by frustrating the generative power of the sex act. One may also have good, even praiseworthy, reasons for wanting to avoid conception, but that would not change the fact that artificial contraception is wrong. It's important to understand that by "natural" the Church does not mean something which has to be spontaneous, easy, uncomplicated, etc. It means that one must not do any specific thing to render what would have been a fertile act infertile. If intercourse occurs on an infertile day, then it's an infertile act because of the way the human body operates, not because the participants did something to render it infertile. I'll leave it at that for now.

May 2, 1982—to Larry Weller

I'm glad you've enjoyed our last few letters—I'm looking forward to continuing the discussion in person, since I find it so difficult to put my ideas into sensible written form. I'll probably give it a try anyway before this letter's done, but first, some news.

We've travelled very nearly the length and breadth of Britain recently. On 14 May, we set off to visit a friend on Raasay, an isle off the coast of the Isle of Skye. You may have gathered, it's pretty remote. Mikey and I travelled by public bus; Mike travelled on a bus chartered by the university Mountaineering Club. The club members were hiking on Skye, but Mike caught the ferry and joined us on Raasay. Raasay has a nice little volcanic plug mountain named Dun Caan, which is easily climbed from one side. The opposite side is a vertical cliff face with a drop of about five hundred feet, so the view is exciting. The path of ascent commences on a spit of land in between two lochs. The sides of the loch opposite the mountain rise as a nearly vertical wall of rock, so as we walked down the path, we played echo games.

(Mikey is attacking a bunch of bananas. I put him in his high chair, then looked around the kitchen for suitable objects to put on the tray to amuse him. It usually takes him about ten seconds flat to knock all his toys onto the floor, but the bunch of bananas weigh a little bit too much for him to push them over the edge. It's almost time to give him his daily bowl of cereal—that's fun. He enjoys it so much that he tries to grab the spoon himself. All he manages to do is knock it over and cover himself with oatmeal, but that's enough to amuse him.)

That diversion almost made me lose track of the rest of my narrative. On Monday, we had a very nice day hiking in the Red Cuillins of Skye. The famous Cuillins are the Black Cuillins, but they're a bit dangerous if you're carrying a baby on your back. Dangerous even without a baby, as we were sorry to learn on Tuesday. One of the girls in the club fell to her death when a rock gave way beneath her. It came as a shock, as no one has been killed in the club for seventeen years, and she wasn't on a particularly difficult stretch.

After returning from Raasay, we travelled to London for the Marshall luncheon in honor of the departing scholars. We know quite a few of the Marshalls now, so we had a very enjoyable time. The luncheon was held at the assembly hall of the Worshipful Order of Glaziers, which is near Southwark Cathedral. The luncheon room was literally on the Thames—the water practically lapped up against the windows. It was most amusing to watch the barges and tour boats bustle by.

We were glad to hear that the Pope's visit to Britain is still on. There will be demonstrations of anti-Catholicism, especially now since the Argentinians are viewed by some throwback Calvinists here as a typically amoral Catholic regime. Nevertheless, the overall boost to Catholic morale and to sincere ecumenism will be very valuable. There will be an outdoor Mass in Glasgow on 1 June that I'll attend with Mikey. Mike is able to go to a private lecture given by the Pope to an audience of students that takes place on the same day as the Mass. Security measures will be so tight that we doubt he'll be able to join us for the Mass. (People will be admitted to the grounds as parish groups travelling together.) There's a real chance that violence might erupt, but I think one has to trust that the people in charge of security are competent.

Mikey is getting a bit unmanageable. It's time for a nap.

May 30, 1982—to Mom and Dad Pakaluk

Mikey just awoke from his late morning nap. His typical schedule these days goes like this: Wakes around 3:30 A.M. for a snack; back to sleep until about 6:30. Wakes again for a snack; back to sleep 'til about 9 A.M. Up, changed, and dressed, then eats again about 10 A.M. Usually plays for about an hour, gets some cereal, then sleeps 'til about 1 or 2 P.M. Up and active for a while, eats again between 3 and 4 P.M. We go to Mass at 5:15, meet Daddy there, and come home. We all eat dinner; Mikey has a bath and goes to bed around 8 P.M. He wakes around 11 P.M. when we go to bed, eats, and goes back to sleep until around 3:30 A.M. He doesn't always eat at every typical feeding time, but it's unpredictable which one he'll skip. We usually do our errands and visiting during his active periods, though often we're out most of the day and Mikey has to sleep wherever we happen to be.

... The Pope has arrived at last. His reception has been very enthusiastic. Anti-Catholic Protestant fanatics led by Ian Paisley from Northern Ireland staged a protest in London, predicting that thousands would turn out. Only eight hundred did, of which about forty were arrested for "actions tending to the disturbance of the peace". We're looking forward to his visit to Edinburgh and to the outdoor Mass in Glasgow on 1 June.

July 15, 1982—to Tim Henly

Two weeks from today we'll be flying to JFK. These two years have passed very quickly indeed. Neither of us is 100% thrilled about leaving Scotland, for in many ways our lifestyle and temperaments are better suited to this slightly behind-the-times country.

Henry was here for a three-week visit which ended on Sunday the eleventh. In three short weeks we showed him practically every corner of Scotland and also a fair bit of London. It will take a while for the scope of his tour to sink in. Right now I imagine he's still trying to catch up on sleep.

In an effort to be very organized, I packed up our household effects before Henry arrived. The effort was 90% successful, but a few things have gotten lost in the shuffle—like your last letter, for instance. I'm very sorry because I wanted to answer the points you raised but unfortunately can't remember them accurately enough. So lucky you!—a reprieve 'til next letter.

How odd to think that by the time you first see Mikey he'll no longer be an infant but will be well into the toddler stage. Not that you'll have missed much; newly born human beings are pretty scraggly looking. He's far cuter now.

I'm glad I'll be returning to the U.S. as Reagan's [first] term is heading to the end. I didn't vote for the man, but I did give him the benefit of the doubt once he was elected. I have sympathy with the budget-balancing, government-trimming side of his campaign rhetoric. Too bad that turned out to be the losing side. Now I wouldn't vote for him on any account. I have rarely been so utterly disgusted by a politician. I just hope against hope that Ted Kennedy isn't his opponent, as I have little liking for him and less trust in his integrity.

I can't seem to let a letter end without saying something about the Church. I seem to remember one of your points was about surrendering one's own will and intellect to the arbitrary dictates of an authoritative

Magisterium. That simply isn't how it is at all. It's more analogous to the case of a freshman in chemistry who accepts the teaching of his prof because the student accepts that the professor knows more about chemistry. Quite honestly, I'm confident that if you read seriously some of the Church's teachings you'd see that it offers a picture of the world and human nature that hangs together in a most intellectually satisfying way.

In Cambridge for Michael's Graduate Studies

October 1, 1982—to Tim Henly

Since I can't remember whether I owe you a letter or vice versa, I assume that the former is the case.

Well, we're back in the U.S. I wrote the month ahead of the date in my heading [October 1, 1982]; did you notice? That has almost become automatic. I find writing "£" in front of figures signifying money has become less automatic, and I've stopped asking people for "the way to the loo". My repatriation is practically complete.

I read *The World according to Garp*. While I was reading it, I kept saying I didn't know why people had made such a fuss about it. Now that I've been done with it for about a month, I've decided it's a pretty good novel after all. Certain passages and phrases and themes keep re-appearing in my mind. Several scenes replay as if I'd seen them in a movie, though I've not seen the movie, nor do I intend to see the movie. This forces me to conclude that the language of the book is vivid and memorable. That's just about what makes a book good, isn't it? Have you read anything recent (not "recently"; I know you've read recently)?

Cambridge is nice. I like it better the second time 'round. We've had practically no opportunities to see old friends yet. Mike's academic schedule is quite full, and I'm working twenty hours a week as well as bringing up Mikey, so I don't have a lot of time on my hands either.

Up 'til now our spare time has been devoted to unpacking, but now that's nearly entirely finished and we can start letting people know we're actually here again.

October 4, 1982

Well, the weekend has gone by. I spent all of Saturday alternating between two activities: putting our photos in the appropriate photo albums and putting our pots and pans back into the appropriate cupboard. Mikey loves to haul the contents of my kitchen cabinets out onto the floor. He then climbs into the cabinets and sits there looking silly.

On Sunday we went to the Harvard Arboretum. It was quite an experience. We sat down on a nice grassy slope next to a lily pond and started eating lunch. We spent the next one and a half hours trying to eat while fending off every unleashed dog in the park. People come to this park with their dogs and lose all sense of civic responsibility. They snap off the leashes, let Fido have a few hours of freedom, and turn a blind eye to all the helpless picnickers Fido decides to harass. After lunch we decided to leave the beaten paths and wander through the trees. After about five minutes of this rather poor replica of a "wilderness experience", we heard the roar of several engines and out popped three motorcyclists from the midst of a hemlock stand. We beat a fast retreat. I don't think we'll be going to the arboretum again. The next day Karen told me the park is a noted rapists' hangout.

Mike and I are learning Latin. The exercises are a scream. Get this: "Officium virum bonum semper vocat" (trans.: "Duty always calls the good man). The book is chock-full of similar noble, exhortative sentiments. "Pecunia et gloria virum animi superabunt": "Money and glory will not overcome the man of spirit." The language is also lots of fun, like doing a puzzle.

I forget to mention what work I'm doing twenty hours a week. I'm working for the same fellow I worked for as an undergrad. He's a landlord (also *our* landlord now), and I do most of his bookkeeping, bill paying, filing, and general office work. He lets me bring Mikey to work (Mike picks him up about 3:30, so I work with the baby 1:30–3:30 and alone 'til 5:30). It's fun work, very convenient, and adequately lucrative. What more could one want?

October 15, 1982—to Larry Weller

Well, Milwaukee did it! And they did it in the first quarter century of my life to boot. I may very well see them do this three times before I die. Of course, they haven't won the World Series yet, but I'm pretty much satisfied with the American League. Isn't it wonderful?

We've settled into a very nice lifestyle here. Mike goes off to work around 8 A.M. Mikey and I do the household chores in the morning. Mike sometimes returns for lunch, then studies at home in the afternoon. Mikey and I go to work about 1:30. Mike takes Mikey home at 3:30 (when he naps), and I come home around 5:30. Mike has one evening seminar; other than that, we're at home for the evening. Mikey goes to bed about 9 P.M., and then Mike and I do Latin together. On Sundays we go for a trip or have friends over. Not very eventful, but pleasant.

I'm just beginning to find time to read again, and I've chosen a monstrous, comprehensive book on U.S. history. I may only read through the Civil War, then take a break. Even that is likely to take several weeks, though. Then I must read some novels. I've got so many on my list of books I should read, I don't know where to start. I think it'll be Graham Greene—it's high time I read more living authors.

Our church runs the archdiocesan choir school, so every Sunday and weekday morning Mass is sung by the boys' choir. It is really something else to hear. They are very good. The church is extremely beautiful and has lively acoustics. Collegium used to do all its Renaissance-type concerts in this church.[15]

I know what I meant to ask. I'd like to know who are the major Canadian authors. Frances is probably the world's foremost expert on that. Could you relay some authors' names to me? I'm interested in

[15] The Harvard-Radcliffe Collegium Musicum is the choir in which Ruth sang as an undergraduate.

reading more non-British English lit. I've started reading some Scottish, some Irish, but Canadian is a big blank for me. Thanks.

February 13, 1983—to Larry Weller

You'd almost think I'd forgotten how to write. Sorry for the long silence.

Did you watch *Das Rheingold* from Bayreuth? We went to a friend's (Curt Dombek, from Saint Louis; I'm sure you've met him) to see it. I thought it was AWFUL. The music is beginning to appeal to me, but the direction was idiotic. Why, I repeat, WHY put gold bricks in plastic bags? And toss them around as though they were Styrofoam? Real gold would have weighed about three tons. Poor Freia would have been squashed flat as a pancake under that amount of gold. And why was Donner wearing a waxed toupee? The gods seemed to do little more than join hands and stumble about. And Rhinemaidens?!? I don't know quite what those creatures were, but they sure weren't maidens.

Nevertheless, Curt has invited us to see the rest of the series, and I certainly do want to take him up on the invitation. I can't help wishing my introduction to performed Wagnerian opera were going to be a little less traumatic, though.

Thank you so much for the list of Canadian authors. That plan of mine has taken a backseat for a while. I was suddenly struck by a Balzac craze and reread *Le Père Goriot*, and read *Les Chouans*, *Eugénie Grandet*, and *The Black Sheep*, all in the span of two weeks. That exhausted my private collection, so I'll have to go to the library for a few more. I was lucky enough to see the final episode of *Nicholas Nickleby* (oh, it *was* lovely), and now I'm all keen to read more Dickens.

Mikey's growing fast. He walks very well now and says a few words. He understands far more than he can say. We ask him to point at things, like the light, the window, etc., and he gets them all right, but all he seems to say is "Aaah."

107

Mike had five days free between his last exam and the start of the spring term, so we went to visit our artist friend, Robin, in Providence, Rhode Island.[16] It's rather a dreary city, completely under the thumb of the Mafia. Robin's girlfriend has an uncle who's a hotshot in the Mob, so Robin's apartment is taboo to crooks. He doesn't even have to lock his door. He lives smack in the middle of Little Italy, so the food shopping is gorgeous. On Sunday we drove south to Newport. The coast is very rugged and beautiful, and Newport is chockablock full of turn-of-the-century mansions, each more ostentatious than the last. Quite a contrast to drab Providence.

Michael's working hard on his various courses and papers. One item of special interest is a paper he hopes to prepare for the '84 meeting of the Hume Society, which will be in Reykjavík, Iceland. I don't know if we'll be able to manage it, but we'd sure love to do some hiking in Iceland. The terrain is supposed to be similar to northern Scotland.

May 3, 1983—to Mom and Dad Pakaluk

A million apologies for my lapse in writing. We've done a few special things this week, and it completely threw off my routine. Sunday is the day we normally catch up on correspondence, but last Sunday we met a girl at church whom we haven't heard from since we left Cambridge. We invited her home for lunch (I had made pierogi on Saturday, which explains why no letters got written on Saturday—what a time-consuming effort!). At 3 P.M. she was performing with the university choir in a concert of the Bach B Minor Mass. The concert was *free*, even though the chorus is top-notch and the soloists and orchestra were professionals. Mike volunteered to stay home so I could go to the concert. It was fabulous. But the consequence was, no letters.

On Monday morning I went into the Registry of Motor vehicles in Boston to get a Massachusetts driver's license. What an ordeal! I don't know why government offices seem always to be dingy and crowded and the workers always seem sullen, but this was no exception to that general rule. However, after about one and a half hours, I managed to

---

[16] After Oxford, Robin began studies at the Rhode Island School of Design.

get my license. (It took one and a half hours to fill in two forms, write two checks, wait in three lines, and get my photo taken.)

On Wednesday, we went to a reception for the new Marshall Scholars in the northeastern area at the British Consulate. We met lots of very interesting people and had a pleasant time chitchatting, but it's not the sort of thing we could stomach very often. Karen baby-sat for us, but Mikey was rather a terror and refused to go to bed. He's been a bit strange about bedtime lately—he gets so mad at being left in his crib that he jumps right out. He's done it enough times to demonstrate that he's not going to hurt himself seriously, but it's still a bit unnerving to hear him thud out of the crib.

Tonight we are going to the symphony. As soon as Mikey wakes from his nap, I'm going to take him for a very long walk so as to ensure that he falls asleep for the baby-sitter. I hope it works.

May 9, 1983—to Tim Henly

We heard the BSO [Boston Symphony Orchestra] perform Bruckner's Eighth Symphony. It was sublime. Strange how Bruckner and Mahler always get lumped together—I don't think they're really all that similar. Mahler is beyond a doubt whooshy and aimless—one lyric line fizzles into another. But Bruckner is just plain grand: the eighth has a pretty easily followed structure, and there's an air of surety about it. The brass playing was extraordinary, as was the string playing. The woodwinds had little of interest to do, but at least that meant I was spared listening to lots of clarinet solos. My aversion to clarinets gets stronger as the years pass.

My leisure-reading list looks quite impressive lately: I read Bede's (the Venerable) *History of the English Church and People*. That got me all fired up about early English culture, so I dusted off my Norton anthology and read in quick succession Caedmon's "Hymn", *The Dream of the Rood*, and *Beowulf*. Surprise of surprises, *Beowulf* really is superb literature. I read it in prose translation, of course—Anglo-Saxon is utterly unlike both modern English and modern German. Still, it's pretty good stuff.

I'd like to try out an argument on you concerning abortion. The classic stance of pro-abortionists is to say, since no one can prove the fetus is a human being, then the only fair thing to do is to leave it up to an individual woman to decide for herself. If she thinks the fetus is just a mass of tissue, then no one should prohibit her right to an abortion just because that person believes the fetus is a human being.

I'd like to suggest that the above argument is seriously flawed, for, if no one can prove the fetus is a human being, it is equally the case that no one can prove the fetus is *not* a human being. Since it is therefore the case that the fetus may be a human being (and I should hope we agree that the definition of "human being" is more than merely conventional), the only civilized and moral position to take is that abortion should be outlawed until we have knowledge that we are not slaughtering millions of innocent persons.

If you find that reasoning sound, may I ask you to write a note to your two senators urging them to support the Hatch-Eagleton amendment? The amendment reads, "The right to an abortion is not secured by this Constitution." Its effects would be (1) to take the force out of the *Roe v. Wade* decision, (2) to take the power to decide the abortion issue out of the hands of the courts, and (3) to place that power back into the hands of the legislature, where it was before *Roe v. Wade*. I could go on at much greater length trying to persuade you to do this, but I think the above-stated argument starts from the weakest assumption about the status of the fetus and therefore it is the least refutable argument. Of course, the argument also rests on the assumption that no woman's right to convenience can ever take precedence over the right to life of another human being. Even extreme emotional and financial hardship cannot justify killing another person (consider the mother whose three-year-old gets hit by a car and is paralyzed and retarded as a result—can the mother take the child's life?).

Baby no. 2 is due at the end of June. So far the weather has been mild and pleasant. I just hope we don't get a ferocious heatwave in mid-June. I've been feeling really great so far, but I think I'll wilt away completely if I have to carry thirty-odd extra pounds in ninety-degree weather.

Mike's got three exams and two papers over the course of the next two and a half weeks. Things will be really busy for a while, then June should be pretty calm—the calm before the storm. New babies have a way of disrupting households for a while. Still, we are very lucky he or she didn't choose to be born smack in the middle of exam period.

June 9, 1983—to Mom and Dad Pakaluk

Mike was at a luncheon for graduate students yesterday. He was seated next to James Baker, the fellow who provided Mike's scholarship. It turns out that Baker is a devout Catholic who left graduate school [at Harvard in philosophy] before completing his thesis because he and his wife had four children by then. He helped start a small computer firm and sold out for four million dollars when the company went public. He retired at age forty-eight, and he and his wife now have seven kids. As you can imagine, Mike had a good time talking with him.

September 17, 1983—to Tim Henly

This can hardly come as a surprise by now—our second son, Maximilian, was born on June 30. He's already two and a half months old. I marvel at how quickly the time is going by. He's quite an acceptable little chap, though a bit more work than his older brother was. Poor Max has what is called "colic"—a catchall word that basically means he suffers from gas (wind, as they say in Britain).

Michael just bought $120 worth of wood, braces, and cinder blocks. We now have used every available square inch of wall space for book-shelves. These now have to last another five years, but at the rate Mike acquires books we may have to sublet another room just for the overflow. Fortunately, he digs up most of his treasures in secondhand bookstores.

October 22, 1983—to Larry Weller

We are watching the extravaganza from the Met. Unfortunately, I can't attend to the singing with 100% effort because Mikey is awake and wants to look at picture albums, but what I do hear is very beautiful. Perhaps I'll be a knowledgeable opera fan by the time you are appearing on the stage.

I've started reading *A Man Called Intrepid*. It's spellbinding. I'm rather ignorant about the events leading up to World War II, and it comes as quite a shock to learn how much was known and foreseen by knowledgeable people concerning Hitler's intentions. That they were powerless to convince politicians and the public at large seems incredible. It also amazes me how clever and perceptive some people are. By many standards, I know I am considered intelligent, but I don't hold a candle to these characters. So, so much depended upon the wits and courage of these people. It makes me a little sad that in the life I have chosen I can be of so little direct service to what I think can still be accurately called the Free World.

Something rather ironic has come to pass: I've decided that I can no longer attend worship services in the Presbyterian church.[17] On Tuesday we received the October issue of the National Right to Life newsletter, in which appeared an article on the Presbyterian Church's most recent policy statement on abortion. They essentially have endorsed the status quo in the U.S.: abortion on demand into the third trimester. They even claim that it may be "an act of faith" before God to decide to abort rather than give birth to a child. This position is so utterly opposed to the gospel of Christ, to His example of boundless love for all of humanity, that I cannot give even the appearance of accepting a church that condones killing the most innocent and the most vulnerable members of the human race.

I can't be brief once I get onto the topic of abortion, but the upshot of this is, last Sunday was the last Sunday we shall spend at Norwood Presbyterian. Not that I'll miss the preaching, but I'm sorry for the breach it will cause between me and my parents and their friends.

The weather has been so wonderful. It's supposed to be rather dull to talk about the weather, but when it's so glorious at least a passing

---

[17] As a gesture of ecumenism and Christian solidarity, Ruth and I would attend services with her family at the Presbyterian Church of Norwood when we visited—after, of course, going to Mass at the local Catholic Church.

comment seems in order. There has been just the right degree of breeziness—not enough to be too cold or to blow grit in your eyes, but just a constantly shifting, playful little wind that keeps you from ignoring the splendid autumn world around you. I only wish we were in a place like Northern Valley so we could be outdoors enjoying it more.

October 2, 1984—to Tim Henly

Six and a half months have elapsed since I received your last letter. I think that's an all-time record. I shall make an effort to amend my ways.

The suicide of your colleague must be very troubling. Before mental disease was at all understood, suicide was considered one of the gravest of mortal sins. It is the ultimate rejection of God's gift of life. It also indicates a rejection of His forgiveness and compassion, a rejection of hope. Now, some people who commit suicide are truly rejecting God, rejecting the life He has given them; they may want to punish people in their lives, or they may be totally callous toward the family members and friends whom they will injure by their action. But it seems to me that the majority of people who commit suicide are victims of disease—be it mental or physical. The Church teaches that for a sin to be mortal, three things are required: (1) it must be a weighty matter, (2) the person must understand that the act is a serious sin, and (3) the person must freely choose to perform the sin. While the first condition holds for all suicides, the second and third conditions rarely hold. Now that depression and other afflictions are better understood, the Church, I believe, has rarely (if ever) withheld funeral Masses from suicide victims. I may be wrong, but this has been my impression.

No, Tim, I no longer support [George] McGovern. I'm on the verge of becoming a registered Republican. The Democratic party's wholehearted endorsement of abortion is what prompted my shift, but as I think through other issues, I find I am coming closer to the free-enterprise, minimize-government mentality of the current administration. I have serious reservations regarding that approach in areas like pollution. I have serious reservations about arms buildup. But I know that abortion kills a member of the human race. That is not a religious belief; it is simple biological fact. I know that the human being in the womb can feel pain certainly by the mid-second trimester, and probably much earlier. I know that there are at least forty thousand late second-trimester abortions (and some even *third* trimester) performed in these United States. I know that as well or better than any German citizen knew that Jews were being gassed in concentration camps. There is no justifiable reason to kill an innocent, non-threatening human being. As far as I can tell, all this adds up to one thing: I am obliged to do everything in my power to defend the rights of members of the human family who are being legally put to death. That means I cannot possibly vote for any political candidate who tolerates, let alone applauds, the status quo.

As for Ms. [Geraldine] Ferraro, she once stated on the floor of Congress that she believes a fetus is a baby. She also argued on the floor of Congress that it's cheaper for the government to pay for abortions than to pay child support. Even a pro-choicer should have reservations about a politician who says he or she believes abortion kills babies but wants to fund it anyway. At best, she's a hypocrite. At worst, she condones murder.

You're in pro-life country, I believe. You should try to see the film *The Silent Scream*. It shows an ultrasound of a ten-week abortion. The "fetus" twists and turns and squirms for five minutes trying to escape from the suction device before finally being dismembered. It's a strong dose of abortion reality.

On that cheery note, I give my very best regards.

February 10, 1985—to Tim Henly

We've been having a perfect winter—thirty-eight days straight with the temperature well below freezing (except for the occasional afternoon thaw). I really like consistency in the weather, at least within the framework of the seasons. Now I feel we have had a true winter, and spring will be most welcome. What I despise is a winter when the temperature fluctuates from minus ten to fifty every third day or so. The next worst thing is to have a two-day spring with temperatures in the sixties, then be afflicted with ninety-degree heat until mid-September.

The point is totally moot now, but I did vote for Reagan. I even urged others to do likewise and coordinated the distribution of roughly three thousand pamphlets aimed at persuading people to follow suit. My single reason for doing this (or, rather, the paramount reason for my doing this) is the abortion issue. It is to me quite obvious that abortion kills human beings. I used to ask myself, had I lived under Hitler, would I have spoken out in defense of the slaughter of innocent human beings? I still don't know what I would do if the price of speaking out were my own death, but it is inconceivable to me that I could sit idly by while our society condones the killing of innocent infants. I don't like leafleting, I don't like picketing, I don't like political activism; but I don't have the freedom to choose to remain silent.

As for the threat of nuclear war, it seems to me (and now I'll really sound grim) that if we don't stop the wanton slaughter of pre-born life, then nuclear holocaust will be the only fitting end for our society. The mentality that accepts killing on the scale on which abortion goes on in the U.S. is the same mentality that conceives of nuclear retaliation as acceptable. In both cases, reverence for human life is absent.

It also seems to me that what will cause nuclear holocaust is not so much the presence of the weapons as (1) extreme heightening of tension with the USSR, (2) a freak accident or terrorist strike, or (3) some upstart third-world country that is sick of its grinding poverty. Item no. 2 is totally out of my control. Item no. 1 is virtually out of my control. I honestly believe Reagan's relations with the USSR have been and will be as stable or more stable than [Walter] Mondale's would have been. Regarding item no. 3, my answer is to contribute to organizations like Bread for the World, Catholic Relief Services, and Oxfam and write letters urging fairer treatment of these countries by our own. It seemed to me somewhat hysterical to argue that a vote for Reagan was like a vote in favor of nuclear destruction; whereas a vote for Mondale was, as he himself said, a vote to oppose pro-life legislation.

In my letter [of October 2, 1984] that went astray, I said something about suicide. The Catholic Church teaches that there can be no sin if the person acting is not free. Psychological compulsion is better understood in our day. A person who took his or her own life while in a state where his or her will was no longer free would not commit any sin. It seems clear that many mental illnesses, like depression, deprive the victim of psychological freedom.

But it also seems to me that some suicides are prompted by a genuine desire to wound the people closest to one and to "make them sorry they didn't treat me better". This attitude is common in children when they are very angry, but they don't act on it. Some adults, it seems to me, are acting out this kind of peevishness on a grand scale when they take their own lives. Eternal punishment for such wanton disregard of God's gift of life and for the feelings of family and friends seems to me quite conceivable. Hell is not a punishment arbitrarily imposed—it is a state of rejection *of* God (not *by* God) that an individual makes of his own accord. I find it hard to understand how people can freely choose to reject the source of all joy and goodness, but that people do choose to do this seems fairly clear.

My sister is studying in Paris this year. Today, I learned that my parents are contemplating a jaunt to *Gay Paris* in June. Mike and I are contemplating a trip to Lawrence, Kansas (to see his brother). I think my sibs have better taste in educational milieu. But let's not get onto the subject of locales for universities—not one of your favorite topics, I'm sure.

August 25, 1985—to Tim Henly

It sounds as though your European jaunt was a total success. I hope you did manage to see Spain, etc. Since NATO footed the bill for airfare, it seems only right you should spread your American dollars around.

We bought a car from my aunt. A 1973 AMC Matador with sixty-five thousand miles. So far, it runs beautifully. We needed a BIG car to accommodate our growing entourage. Baby no. 3 is due March 21. I am in the throes of first-trimester nausea and indigestion. The funny thing is, I have three friends who are all also expecting babies in March. I feel we are doing our civic duty by providing future payees into Social Security.

Your parents are supposed to be at my mom's Labor Day picnic. I'm looking forward to seeing them. My parents' other friends seem to get a bit flakier as years go by—"Mother God" and other feminist trendy clichés. Somehow I can't picture your parents getting hung up on God's gender (silly notion).

You can take it as written that I apologize for the lack of letters.

July 13, 1986—to Tim Henly

Remember me? The girl who used to write letters?

This takes a world record for late birth announcement. John Henry was born March 12. He's like my other two—fat and cheerful. In one respect, he's quite different: he's bald. What little fuzz he does have looks (oh hope of hopes!) reddish. I really want a redhead, and I'd love to think he's the one. But truthfully, there's so little hair that I really can't be too confident.

I'm up to my eyebrows working for a referendum campaign. In Massachusetts, we pay for elective abortions out of state tax revenues, one of only twelve states that do so. The only reason we do is because our state supreme court struck down the state law limiting abortion payments to those done to save the mother's life. Anyway, we have a ballot question that will restore the right to regulate abortion funding to the state legislature.

I never thought I'd be so involved in politics, but here I am visiting candidates, addressing meetings, and organizing wards and precincts.

August 29, 1987—to Tim Henly

I almost don't believe it myself—I'm actually writing a letter.

Mike has written the first two (of three total) chapters of his dissertation. I am now confident that we will be leaving Cambridge next June. Since our fourth (due October 4) will be crawling by then, it will be high time to clear out of here. The three boys are all sleeping in one small bedroom, beds very strategically placed. My recurring nightmare is that Mike will get an offer he can't (well, we'll see if he can't) refuse from one of the prestigious but stingy institutions in this area. Rent for a two-bedroom apartment is now about a thousand dollars a month.

I actually shared, to some extent, the sentiments you expressed in a previous letter regarding Reagan's lack of delivery on pro-life legislation. But the guy really has done a tremendous amount to set in motion the machinery for a reversal of *Roe v. Wade*. That goal now seems almost inevitable within the next few years. Without Reagan, we would be waiting another decade at least for the reversal of that decision. Until it goes, it's virtually impossible to make progress in any substantial measure because what can be legislated is so very, very limited. (Public funding, basically—the current court has struck down legislation aimed at protecting babies that survive the abortion attempt, of which there are probably at least four hundred per year. If you can't even protect live-born "fetuses"—well, I think it's clear that the men currently on the bench just want to enable women to kill off inconvenient offspring, no matter what principles of law or logic have to be sacrificed.)

I'm now president of our state pro-life organization. It's rather exciting. I have to hire staff, deal with the press frequently, make decisions about computer systems, do market research, etc. Thank heavens I don't have a nine-to-five job, as most previous presidents have had. Towing three boys around with me is hard enough, but they're much more flexible than a boss.

You've probably figured out that we got a computer. Mike typed the first draft of the first twenty pages of the dissertation and saw the light. It is a marvelous machine. I haven't had time to do much more than word processing and mailing lists, but I look forward to high-tech whiz-kid-type applications (like maybe a budget, if we ever have enough money to warrant a budget).

March 3, 1988—to Tim Henly

This is a first in the history of my correspondence: I just finished reading your letter and I'm sitting down to respond. Perhaps I'll get this into tomorrow's mail (and then the world will come to an end).

MIKE HAS A JOB!! He got three offers: one at a very (VERY) small Catholic college in the mountains northwest of L.A. (called Thomas Aquinas College, a great-books program taught entirely in seminars). Mike loved it, but we turned it down for three reasons: (1) no time to write and publish, (2) difficult to move from there to a more conventional place if it turns out we don't like it, and (3) too far away from home base (my family is still very centered around Northern Valley).

The second offer was from Catholic University in Washington, D.C. Mike really wanted to accept this one, but in the end, essentially, family considerations prevailed: the cost of living is too high and the pay was rather low.

Offer no. 3 was from Clark University in Worcester, Massachusetts. They really wanted Mike and gave him a reduced teaching load, higher than normal pay, sabbatical after three years and again after another seven; cost of living is low; houses cost $125,000; it's New England; I love the wooded hills (sounds like a song); and it's where we will be. I am thrilled. So it's over. AMEN.

For once, we share a political opinion (several, in fact). I don't care whether [Pat] Robertson's pro-life or not, I don't think I could vote for him. My choice ought to be obvious to you: it's Jack Kemp. I have moved about seven-eighths of the way along the political spectrum to what would strike most people as an ultra-right-wing position. I support Contra aid, think the INF Treaty [Intermediate-Range Nuclear Forces Treaty] is of questionable value, consider lower taxes a sane approach to stimulating growth, oppose any form of protectionism, and am convinced that somehow or other, welfare has got to be reformed so that it works to strengthen traditional family structures. So, Jack Kemp is my logical choice. Too bad he appears to have no chance, but maybe in '92.

Between [Bob] Dole and [George H.] Bush, I guess I slightly prefer Dole, though my mind is not firmly made up. Lucky for me, I get to cast my conscience vote for Kemp on March 8, and the Republican Party will settle the rest.

As for [Michael] Dukakis, I haven't got much good to say. Politically knowledgeable people here say his "Massachusetts miracle" was all set in motion by his predecessor, conservative governor Ed King, who revived an essentially moribund state economy inherited from—who else?—former governor Dukakis. I have read estimates that Massachusetts will again have a huge deficit in about three years. It's not my field of expertise, so I don't really know how to evaluate it, except this is what I hear from people who are not even interested in the abortion issue. On that issue, he's probably the worst of the Democrats.

I am very surprised to hear you contemplating a return to academia. I think it's the best possible lifestyle, provided you like academic research and teaching. The life of an academic's wife is really the absolute best, because you have the long vacations and flexible schedule, as well as sabbaticals and guest professorships at interesting places (I can't wait).

I'll continue as president of the state pro-life group, seeing as we're staying in Massachusetts. I've been going to high schools for the past couple of weeks giving my pitch. It's a lot of fun. I still like high-school-aged kids better than any other age. Perhaps I'll end up a teacher after my flock leaves the nest (in a couple of decades or so).

Baby no. 4 (Maria) is entering the excruciatingly cute stage of gurgling, smiling, and convulsing her entire little body whenever something amuses her (momentous things like a light goes on or someone looks her in the eye and smiles). 'Tis a gift to be simple . . .

Hope all is going well with you. I read a great book recently—*Lost in the Cosmos* by Walker Percy (or Percy Walker; I never can get that man's name straight). It's a book every Californian should read.

April 3, 1988—to Larry Weller

We will be moving to Worcester in July if all goes well. Big "if". We haven't begun to look for apartments. With four kids, we'll be treated like gypsies.

Mike recently attended a lecture by one of the scientists who studied the Shroud of Turin. I've never forgotten your objection that Christ couldn't have died so fast. The shroud indicates he was flogged 120 times. The Roman style of crucifixion caused death by asphyxiation, unlike later copies (like [those used to execute] the Japanese martyrs), who[se creators] based their ideas of it on inaccurate medieval paintings.

I never stop hoping that someday you'll believe all the stuff of Christianity and see that life really is *just* as exciting and meaningful as a Wagner opera.

Making a Home in Worcester

August 23, 1988—to Larry Weller

I am reduced to hand-writing as our computer is being repaired. I promise to try to remember how to write legibly.

Thank you a thousand times for filling me in on Tim's wedding. I am terribly sorry I wasn't there, but I don't think I'd have seen my tenth anniversary if I had up and left Michael to move and unpack and tend the boys on his own, especially since the deadline for handing in his thesis was August 15.

Yes—August 15. And HE DID IT. What a remarkable fellow. We drove a (PACKED) Ryder truck to Worcester at 11 A.M. (I followed in the Matador), parked near our soon-to-be home, and drove to the lawyer's office for the closing. At 12:40 we picked up our keys and (after a celebratory lunch) began unloading the truck (with friends) at 2 P.M. I think that's some kind of record for close timing.

Mike helped unpack for the remainder of the week, and then the following Monday (August 8), he went back to Cambridge to the library to complete the final revisions to the thesis. It was completed and dropped off at the copier's about 2:30 A.M. Friday, August 11. *Deo gratias.*

Naturally, we're still unpacking. Friends tell me that's what we'll be doing for at least the next five years. I hope to abbreviate the interval by discarding at least half of what's still in boxes. It's disgusting how things accumulate.

(I pause to relate what I just saw out the window: Mikey hurtling down the hill at about 30 miles per hour on a toy truck. The boys like this place.)

You must promise not to tell Steve P. that we live in the Belmont Hill area of Worcester, not a neighborhood renowned for its exclusivity.[18] Our English-speaking neighbors are friendly, all lifetime residents, and they set a standard for lawn care that we will find hard to meet. The Spanish-speaking neighbors are friendly, all newcomers, loud, and— sad to say—not possessed of the same drive to keep their yards and lawns attractive. This is a dramatic example of how even small cultural differences can have a big and obvious impact on a neighborhood.

It's time to feed the hungry, a corporal work of mercy (that's Catholic talk for good deeds) that I can perform without stirring past my own kitchen. With her uncanny sense of timing, Maria has just awoken and is crying upstairs.

I enclose a snapshot of the house. The upstairs is just three bedrooms. The downstairs has a living room, a dining room, and an office (or fourth bedroom) under the upstairs, then a single-story, rectangular extension for the kitchen, a bathroom (literally—there's no shower), and a large utility room. I love it.

October 26, 1988—to Larry Weller

I've been dying to tell you that I'm singing in a choir again. Not just any old choir, but the cathedral choir, a professional choir. Get this—I get paid to go out WITHOUT THE KIDS and sing beautiful music. Michael agreed that I was owed one activity per week absolutely kid-free, and this is what I lucked into. I just can't get over it. I am not one of the best singers, but I'm working on it. It's been a very long time since last I concentrated on pitch and blend. Lucky for me, I still sight-read reasonably well, and I count better than most of them (why are singers generally such bad counters?).

[18] Steve was a member of the NVOT (Northern Valley Regional High School in Old Tappan) "gang" who attended Holy Cross, then transferred to the Wharton School of the University of Pennsylvania. By the time this letter was written, he was a highly successful businessman.

Worcester is great. I really love this city. It's cool, breezy, and hilly. There are half a dozen parks on hills that offer panoramic views of the city. And it's rather poorer and less snooty than Cambridge. Michael is very happy at Clark so far. If that continues, and if he gets tenure, we may just be set for life. Clark's very generous sabbatical policy should take care of our remaining *Wanderlust*. (I'm itching for a visiting professorship in Heidelberg or Britain.) We are so very, very fortunate.

I am heartbroken over your admiration for Dukakis. Even without the abortion issue, I am utterly turned off by the guy. Michael thought the most telling moment of the debate was when Dukakis couldn't think of a hero. That fits with the political-type people's assessment of the guy—he is inhumanly self-assured and confident in his own judgment. I don't think he is a flaming liberal—I don't think he has that kind of ideological fervor. But he is surrounded by advisors who are flaming, wild-eyed ACLU [American Civil Liberties Union] types who really do think abortion rights should extend to cover babies born with handicaps and that the churches should be muzzled on any issue affecting public policy. If you think no one is as liberal as Justice [William] Brennan, you haven't met Susan Estrich or Laurence Tribe.

George [H.] Bush also strikes me as a man who lacks ideological fervor, but at least he's more or less surrounded by advisors of a more conservative bent. I have never heard anyone accuse him of being "Hitlerish" before. Do you really think he's that bad? He always strikes me as rather a pleasant, easygoing guy who, if anything, is a little too anxious to avoid controversy.

How would I find out whether our street is named for the Shelby of undisturbed bed drilling fame? I suppose I would have to read old newspapers to find out when and under what circumstances the street was named. Now, that would be a fun project. I already find myself looking forward to grandmotherhood, when I will have more time for interesting projects of that sort.

Did I tell you I got new contact lenses? They are gas-permeable hard lenses. It's like having a new pair of eyes. They're great. My eyes never burn or itch. I forgot what it was like to have eyes that don't always bother you.

December 20, 1989—to Katy Whisenant

Well, I'm finally plowing through all the cards, writing thank-yous. Most of them are pretty straightforward. But your note—I hardly know where to begin.

I can never thank you enough for being here for Thomas' funeral. Your friendship is one of the most treasured blessings God has given me. When I think of you—how funny you are, how thoughtful, how loyal, how plain-speaking—I just want to thank God for having made such a person. I suppose if I were a saint, I would see all human beings in this way, but the truth is I don't. Friendship with you is like a foretaste of the communion of saints.

Thomas is already doing a good job of keeping me on the straight and narrow. It's not contemplating Our Lord's wounds or the Virgin at the foot of the cross that moves me to do my norms.[19] It's the feeling of shame that my infant son is gazing at me and wondering why his mother is so silly that she thinks typing newsletters or folding laundry is more important than prayer.

We will be having a pre-Christmas party with the Hardys and Swopes on Saturday. Our families have become quite close. The kids have a blast together, though I fear Maria is going to think all the other little girls in the world are named some variation of Theresa.

I asked Michael about your dispute over whether Jesus knew He was the Second Person of the Trinity incarnate.

This doctrine, that "Christ's soul possessed the immediate vision of God from the first moment of its existence", has the force of a teaching that has not yet been finally pronounced by the Magisterium but "whose truth is guaranteed by its intrinsic connection with the doctrine of revelation". As a proof from the Fathers, the author (Dr. Ludwig Ott) quotes Saint Fulgentius—"It is ... quite irreconcilable with

---

[19] Spiritual practices that Ruth followed as a member of the Catholic group Opus Dei. For more on norms, see p. 55.

the integrity of the faith to assume that Christ's soul did not possess a full knowledge of its divinity." [20]

Hope that helps. [21]

February 18, 1991—to Larry Weller

... Sarah just grabbed my glasses—she's entered a new developmental phase. It makes it much more difficult to eat, write, type, etc., with her on my lap.

We've seen several good movies lately. We thoroughly enjoyed [*The Hunt for*] *Red October* and *Henry V*. I wish I could play his pre-battle speech at Agincourt every morning. Nothing like it to get you ready to meet the day (come what may).

I got a *wonderful* letter and tape from Joe Sireno. Reading his letter, it seemed like just yesterday we were standing on the stage at Norwood Presbyterian performing *Canterbury Tales*. Do you remember punching me in the nose? My children love to hear that story. (I still win the "I won't blink" game.) [22]

I've been busy lately. I spoke at Boston College, Columbia, and a small college in Worcester (Assumption, the Catholic college that's not Holy Cross). I'm scheduled to speak at Brandeis and Brown in a month. Oh—I forgot—Amherst [College] on March 3. Keeping the household in order gets a bit challenging, but I still thrive on having too much to do.

[20] Ludwig Ott, *Fundamentals of Catholic Dogma* (Rockford, Ill: Tan Books and Publishers, 1974), p. 163. The comment of Saint Fulgentius may be found in *Patrologia Latina* (ed. Migne) LXV, Epistle 14, question 3, paragraph 26, column 416.

[21] Katy commented later on this letter: "I could feel Ruth chastising me for being gushy about her and saying she saw Christ in everyone like Mother Teresa. Of course, the letter was ten years ago, and I have noticed in more than one person that cancer goes a long way helping one see Christ in everyone. The dispute she refers to is because I had related my distress on hearing the silly director of religious education at our parish ask the RCIA [Rite of Christian Initiation for Adults] class if they thought Jesus knew who He really was."

[22] While Ruth and Larry were in the wings waiting to go onstage, Larry suggested they pass the time by playing a game: he would bluff at punching Ruth in the nose, getting very close, and Ruth would have to try to resist blinking. She won, but Larry misjudged the distance and ended up giving Ruth a hard punch in the nose just moments before their entrance. They had to go immediately onstage and sing and smile as if nothing had happened.

April 3, 1991—to Larry Weller

It was really nice of you to call on my birthday. As I mentioned, I had been mentally composing my next letter to you. I always think of you when I read or see books or movies about the British Empire, heroism, individual versus national integrity, patriotism, etc. [The movies] *Gallipoli* and *Breaker Morant* fall into those categories. On top of those, I just finished two Le Carré spy novels: *Looking Glass War* (ugh) and *A Perfect Spy*. They are both rather bleak, in different ways. I have *Russia House*, but I'm beginning to think I've maxed out on Le Carré's disenchantment with Britain's post-empire blues and his notion that politics is an extension of prep-school shenanigans.

Michael's first book is in the bookstores!!! It's called *Other Selves: Philosophers on Friendship*. He also had a paper accepted for a very prestigious international conference on Bertrand Russell. I think financial security is within a few years' striking distance. I can't wait.

Living with Cancer

October 17, 1991—to Larry Weller

Thank you so very much for the exquisite edition of *Andersen's Fairy Tales*. You make me quite nostalgic for those good and sweet moments out of a youth which was not uniformly so.

Recovery from surgery has been almost embarrassingly easy. Chemo starts on Wednesday. It'll be two Wednesdays in a row, then two Wednesdays off, from now until spring—that seems fitting, somehow. I'll feel blah and miserable during the blah and usually miserable (wet, no *snow*) winter and then pick up just as things start getting green.

The children love the illustrations, especially Maria, who goes into transports over little mermaids, elves, and princesses.

I am singing in the choir again. Some funding suddenly materialized, so our director scheduled a concert for November 3. The two principal pieces will be R. Vaughn Williams' Mass in G Minor and a Bach motet, "Jesu, meine Freude". Then there will be several shorter pieces, all of which are really lovely and a treat to sing. I hope chemo doesn't mess up one's vocal chords.

Hope all is well with you. I just like to remind you that I pray for your father's repose every day and for your well-being.

November 25, 1991—to Tim Henly

I was so happy to receive your letter. I've been meaning to write to each member of the NVOT gang but am making such slow progress that I'll be through chemo by the time I succeed. Luckily, the news spreads at a faster rate.

It certainly came as a BIG surprise to me when I was told I had breast cancer, especially since I had shown the lump to my obstetrician over a year ago and had been told it was nothing to worry about. I've never been a litigious person (and I hope I'm still not), but this episode actually cries out for a lawsuit (which, in due course, will be set in motion). Perhaps I shall end up rich, and won't that be a curious turn of fate?

The mastectomy was no big deal. Lucky for me, my ego was never tied too closely to that anatomical dimension (perhaps I'd have had a little more humility if it had). In any event, the surgery went smoothly and there was no recovery needed, as far as I could make out, since nothing hurt.

Chemo is rather a different story. It is just plain unpleasant. I have so much help from our friends in Worcester—even the members of the philosophy department at Clark have been fixing meals and dropping them off. The chemo really only puts me back totally for two or three days, but I have to take it a little easy for a week or so.

I have great hopes we will be seeing you and Carrie in January. It will depend on a combination of my chemo schedule and Mike's degree of panic about being behind deadline on his book.

I will keep off political and controversial topics. What do you do with your spare time? Do you have spare time? (So few people seem to these days.) I'm still managing to sing for money in the cathedral choir of Worcester. We sing a most wonderful repertoire, and the other singers are so fine that I can't believe I actually get paid to do it. The conductor is the epitome of the highly strung sensitive Italian artist who periodically resigns because of the boorish, philistine insensitivity to aesthetics of our Irish, working-class bishop. It's comical.

Mike's and my favorite weekend pastime (after hiking, when possible—rarely—and visiting friends—frequently) is to rent videos. We just saw Steve Martin's *L.A. Story*. It was very much to our taste. Have you seen it? Of course, we are faithful Steve Martin fans, even when he is excessively goofy. It was a movie that made it possible for me to see how a person could love L.A., a state of mind that has hitherto been unimaginable to me.

P.S. Do you really think of Operation Rescue civil disobedients as "thugs"? Mike has been arrested. I don't think of my husband as a thug. These people sincerely believe it's wrong to kill innocent humans. Wouldn't you do the same if you knew people were being killed legally?[23]

Christmas 1991—to Nancy T

It's been a long while since we've been in touch, but many things bring you to mind.

I hope life is going well for you. It seems we only get in touch now to relay major news. This time our news isn't so great.

I was diagnosed with breast cancer in September. I've had a mastectomy and started six months of chemotherapy. It's no picnic (as you well know), but it's not the end of the world either.

[23] As president of Massachusetts Citizens for Life (MCFL), Ruth kept that organization neutral as regards the Operation Rescue (OR) movement of civil disobedience. But she found the argument behind OR sound and, with others in the Worcester area, compared OR with instances of justifiable civil disobedience in Worcester's past, such as helping runaway slaves escape to Canada through the underground railroad or running U.S. federal marshals out of town when they arrived in Worcester to capture runaway slaves and bring them back to slavery in the South.

Mike is under a lot of pressure, having to write his book (for tenure) and having my illness totally upset the timetable. On the other hand, if you needed an excuse for an extension, this one is hard to beat.

The children take it all in stride. As long as I don't look sick, they don't really take it seriously. I lost my hair—that has been a source of amusement.

I have total peace that God will bring good out of this experience, whatever the outcome. Still, I'd appreciate the spare prayer. I have a great devotion to the priest on this prayer card[24]—he has such a funny smile. I try to make the sentiment of that prayer my own.

I trust you already know about the birth of our daughter Sarah. She was born almost exactly a year after Thomas, the son who died of SIDS. We celebrated the second anniversary of his entry into heaven two weeks ago. How quickly the years fly by.

1992 [date indeterminate]—to Theresa Hanley, president of Massachusetts Citizens for Life (MCFL)[25]

MCFL has continued to operate at about the same level for too many years. The organization is too preoccupied by special events that serve merely as moral boosters or (limited) public witness. There is not enough progress in education, public relations, membership, recruitment (of activists), chapter development, or political involvement. There is a need for a breakthrough to a new level of effectiveness. Such a break-through cannot happen with MCFL's current governing structure.

---

[24] A prayer card for Monsignor Josemaría Escrivá, which included a prayer for his beatification and a petition for his intercession which read as follows: "O God, You granted your priest Josemaria countless graces, choosing him as a most faithful instrument to found Opus Dei, a way of sanctification in daily work and in the fulfillment of the Christian's ordinary duties. Grant that I too may learn to turn all the circumstances of my life into occasions of loving You and of serving the Church, the Pope and all souls with joy and simplicity, lighting up the pathways of this earth with faith and love. Deign to glorify your servant Josemaria and, through his intercession, grant me the favor of ... (here make your request). Amen. Our Father. Hail Mary. Glory be to the Father." (After the beatification of St. Josemaria on May 17, 1992, the prayer was changed accordingly to "Deign to canonize your servant, Blessed Josemaria".)

[25] This letter represents Ruth's ideas about how governance of MCFL should be reformed, which she outlined for Theresa Hanley, who succeeded her as president.

I see three major flaws in the current structure of MCFL.

I. The board is not functioning as a board ought to function.
  A. Board meetings tend to be opportunities for like-minded persons to catch each other up on news and haggle about small points of disagreement. This is a waste of time. This characteristic of the board has prevented some excellent persons from serving on it.
  B. The board fails to limit its scrutiny and tends to issue new mandates monthly. The board should decide on broadly stated, long-term goals and leave the execution of those goals to the staff. Quarterly meetings would be sufficient to keep the board informed of the organization's progress.

    (Goals should be of this nature: Increase budget by 10%. Increase membership by 3%. Increase database of identified pro-life voters by ten thousand names. Increase public awareness of MCFL through free media appearances, paid advertising, etc. Schedule 50% more LEAP [Life Education Awareness Project] appearances in schools, etc.)[26]

II. The MCFL bylaws create a two-headed monster by vesting executive authority in a president who is an unpaid member of the board. It is impossible for the executive director to take charge of the organization and move it forward when he or she lacks the authority to do that. Human nature being what it is, persons are always giving in to the temptation to complain about the executive director's decisions to the president, who then feels bound inappropriately to interfere.

The bylaws should be rewritten to create a single unpaid executive (I suggest [MCFL] eliminate the president and allow the chairman to assume the full powers of that office). The board would then hire the executive director, charging him with the full responsibility to effect the goals of the organization.

III. The board is too big and contains too many people who are not actively contributing to the organization. It would be

---

[26] The Life Education Awareness Project, created by Ruth, involved developing outlines for pro-life talks on set topics and effective presentations in schools and parishes.

better to return to the thirty at-large members. Chapters desperately need more contact with the organization. The office of chapter director has failed to produce the kind of contact that is needed. The kind of contact that is needed must come from the staff. Most local pro-life persons have much better things to do with the small amount of time they have for pro-life activities than to attend monthly board meetings.

March 6, 1992—to Tim Henly

One strand of my neo-conservatism arises from the conviction that the government tends to be inefficient, ineffective, and (at worst) downright corrupt. While regulation may in theory be wonderful, in fact it all too often ends up as you experienced. I'm not saying I oppose all government regulation, but there's definitely a point at which regulation becomes counterproductive.

I had my last chemo two and a half weeks ago, so I am feeling like a normal human being again. It is so good to feel well—after feeling slightly and vaguely ill for so long, you forget how great it is to feel normal. These days, I'm constantly ecstatic just to be able to taste and smell normally, etc. I wish I could stay in this state and not take it for granted again, but that's human nature.

April 3, 1992—to Larry Weller

I had my last chemo in February, so I am feeling just fine again. I look like a marine these days after initiation—about one half inch of hair sticking straight up. It's comical.

Michael read a paper at a convention in San Diego. To celebrate the end of chemo, we felt justified in making a holiday of it. My father-in-law came up to Worcester and stayed with the boys. Maria and Sarah went to stay with friends.

San Diego is pretty, especially in the spring. I gather it's pretty dry and brown at other times of the year, but it was green like Edinburgh while we were there. We walked all over the city—not the California thing to do. Streams and rivers have cut hundreds of gulleys, ravines, and canyons throughout that part of the country, which makes for interesting, attractive terrain. The (very few) old buildings are nice, but other than that, everything looks new, glitzy, and trendy. It was nice to return to stolid Massachusetts.

We did not tune into the opera broadcast that Saturday, but I'm glad to know I'm not the only one who gets sentimental listening to music.

Actually, these days I get sentimental doing just about anything. I'm continually being reminded of the fact that I have had a most wonderful life—much more wonderful than it seems most people get. My friends who have teenagers describe the (what sounds to me) rather bleak experience of raising teens these days. Most of these kids seem not to have anything like the opportunities we had to be involved in music and drama.

January 6, 1993—to Donald Shea, principal of City View School

Thank you for your concern regarding my son Michael's non-participation in the health program.

After reading the notice from Michelle Montavon, I must reiterate my decision to withhold Michael (and all my children) from this health program.

There is virtually nothing of academic merit in this program. My husband and I will see to it that Michael knows everything he should know about human reproduction, adolescence, AIDS, and drug abuse.

As for the rest, I consider it a waste of the students' time and the taxpayers' money. If my husband and I cannot impart to Michael a sense of self-esteem, I seriously doubt a few hours of lessons will remedy the problem. As for "recognizing feelings, decision making, managing stress", etc., these sound like topics more suited to group therapy than for a public school classroom.

I hope you understand that this decision does not reflect on our overall high regard for City View School and its staff.

July 15, 1993—to Massachusetts Senator John F. Kerry

I am well aware of your long-standing advocacy of tax-funded abortion on demand. Every educated person I know, including those who are pro-choice, understands perfectly well that a fetus is a living organism, some kind of animal, and that it belongs to the species *homo sapiens*.

These assertions (viz., that a fetus is a living thing and that a fetus is a member of the species *homo sapiens*) are not opinions: they are facts. According to the pro-life paper *MCFL News*, you claimed a fetus was not alive. Could you offer a definition of "life" to explain that belief? Could you propose a definition of "living thing" that would exclude a human fetus but would include something like, for instance, a tapeworm (which we all may desire to kill, should it take up residence in our bodies, but we could hardly want to kill it if we did not understand that it was alive)?

I would like to point out that the only "belief" pro-lifers of necessity hold is that human rights exist. That is a very simple statement, but its implications are great. If human rights truly exist, then it follows that any entity that is (a) living and (b) human must possess them.

You have made it perfectly clear that you think it is a good thing to permit doctors to kill human fetuses. I don't see how this is consistent with your frequent rhetoric regarding human rights.

All this aside, I am disgusted by the extreme provisions of FOCA [Freedom of Choice Act]. You know perfectly well that the supporters of this bill seek to abolish parental notification laws, that they resist all meaningful restrictions on third-trimester abortions, and that they have litigated from here to the hereafter to prevent informed consent laws from taking effect. Right here in Worcester, members of NOW [National Organization for Women] protested outside Saint Vincent Hospital because that institution does not permit abortions to be performed within its walls. The protesters were very up-front about expressing their conviction that institutions that refuse to perform abortions should forfeit *all public funding*. You certainly are aware that FOCA would have this effect. I cannot understand how any rational person could support a bill that would put Catholic hospitals out of business because they will not kill unborn humans. That does not sound very "pro-*choice*" to me. Wouldn't you agree that such a measure deserves the epithet "pro-abortion"?

I hope you will consider abandoning your extreme pro-abortion position and at least tolerate those of us who believe in human rights and who therefore choose to refrain from participating in the deliberate killing of innocent humans.

July 15, 1993—to Senator Edward M. Kennedy

The Founding Fathers had it right: the greatest threat to liberty is a meddlesome government. This is especially true when many persons look to the government to solve problems caused by human vices. Such problems have never, will never, and can never be solved by governments.

The futile attempt of government programs to compensate for the effects of promiscuity, illegitimacy, drug addiction, and lack of self-control (the list goes on) simply provides the conditions needed to expand the power of government to restrict the productive activities of citizens who possess the civic virtues.

I used to consider myself a liberal Democrat. Then I moved to a city and saw the disastrous effects of government welfare programs. If a tyrant had set out deliberately to reduce his subjects to a state of abject poverty and powerlessness, he could not have equaled the "success" of the Great Society programs.

Congress should not receive one penny more in tax revenues. If tax revenues were paid to the government according to merit, the IRS would be paying back taxpayers for the millions of dollars wasted over the past decades. No, worse than wasted—these tax dollars have been used to sustain programs that have destroyed individuals and families, making them gutless, hopeless dependent pawns of politicians who deceive them into thinking their destroyers are their benefactors.

There is no way to understand how any human being who is not brain dead could think that a raise in taxes will reduce the deficit. It's not as if this attempt has not already been tried (and tried and tried and tried ...).

Congress should do us all a favor and cut spending.

August 19, 1993—to Ivan and family[27]

I am sorry. I apologize. It has taken a very long time for me to write to you.

We are happy to hear that the tape recorder works well. We hope you and your family enjoy many hours of music with it. I am sending this letter alone. But in two or three weeks, I will send a little package with a tape for you. I hope it will arrive safely.

We have enjoyed the summer very much. We spent one week in the mountains of New Hampshire with the Swope family. (They are the friends we visited with you.) We had a wonderful time in the mountains. We walked to the top of Mount Washington. Do you remember the fancy white hotel with the red roof? Mount Washington is the mountain you saw behind the hotel. It is the highest mountain in our part of the United States.

We are returning to New Hampshire for one more week. When we go to New Hampshire, we rent a house with the Swopes. The house has four bedrooms. We are five adults (we bring the daughter of another friend who is fifteen; she watches the little children who are too small to hike) and ten children. It is very noisy, but a lot of fun.

We go to Mass each day with all the children at a beautiful little church called Our Lady of the Mountains. It has a very beautiful statue of Mary holding the child Jesus with the mountains in the background. Most of the people who go to daily Mass are old people with white hair. It is quite a sight when we troop in with all our little ones. We have been going to the same place for our holiday for four years.

---

[27] Ivan (whose last name I cannot recall) was a fifteen-year-old xylophone-playing conservatory student from Saint Petersburg who stayed with us for several days at the time of Sophie's birth, as part of an exchange program. We were delighted to discover that he was a devout Catholic praying about the possibility of becoming a priest. We helped him purchase a tape recorder to take back to Russia, so that he could listen to music easily.

When we return, it will be time for the children to return to school. Young Michael did not do well in school last year. He does not understand math. I will teach him at home next year. That is a little unusual, but if it is what the parents want, the government has to permit it, provided the child passes certain basic tests.

Michael, Max, and John will play soccer (Europeans call it football) in the autumn. Max, John, and Maria will still be at the grammar school that is just around the corner from our house. Sarah and Sophie will be at home with me. (The baby's full name is Anna Sophia, but we call her Sophie for short.)[28]

Bishop Harrington will be retiring in December, so we will be getting a new bishop. We are praying for a man like the Pope who will speak out against the hedonism and materialism that is undermining the strength of America.

I pray for you and your family every day. May God bless you, your family and friends, and your great nation, which has suffered so many trials.

September 18, 1993—to Larry Weller

I was chagrined (I think that is the word I want—a mix of embarrassed, mortified, shamed, pained, and sorry) to have to cut short your phone call. My life has been terribly complicated by the decision of my best friend to run for school committee. I had planned a civilized, calm autumn: now I'm smack in the middle of a heated political race, closer to the candidate than I have ever been before, with matters of friendship mixed in with the more usual factors of positions on issues.

Three of our children have returned to school, but Michael is being homeschooled. Michael is math-illiterate. The poor kid gets the glazed look of a trapped rabbit when confronted with mathematical expressions. So I am joining the newest of the new waves: homeschoolers. I think it will actually be fun. Michael and I get along quite well—he is a smart aleck, and I get a kick out of his sense of humor.

[28] Anna Sophia is Ruth's seventh child, conceived after chemo, born on April 16, 1993.

For example, I am making him use an old-fashioned reading primer[29] to learn how to answer questions about a story in complete sentences based on what is actually in the text. The stories are very moralistic (I think this is quaint and cute, and I want him to see that education wasn't always as warm, tolerant, fuzzy, and amoralistic as it currently is). Anyway, yesterday's story was about the dire consequences of laziness. Questions go like this: Question: Was it not wicked for George to fish instead of completing his lessons? Answer: Yes, it was wicked for George to fish instead of completing his lessons.

After about a half a dozen questions of this type, there is a question which asks whether there is indolence in heaven. The story does not actually say anything explicitly on this topic but implies that God does not look favorably on those on earth who waste their time. Michael (affecting humility? or a "just the facts, Ma'am, nothing but the facts" attitude? I'm not sure—but really meaning to point out the presumption of such a question) answered, "How would I know whether there is indolence in heaven?" How would he indeed.

I reread one of my favorite novels recently, *The Second Coming* by Walker Percy. I'm sure I have bored you before with my enthusiasm for Percy—some people like him, but most find him maddening.

Anyway, this book is, among other things, about the decline of Western civilization, its love affair with death. The main character is coming to understand a significant event from his youth—an apparent hunting accident in which his father shot him in the ear and wounded himself in the chest. As the book opens, the main character repeatedly relives this episode, each time remembering more clearly what happened, finally realizing that what had really happened was that his father had tried to kill him and then commit suicide, but botched both.

I make a point of praying for each of my close friends every day, but not just praying—also thinking about the significance of their friendship in my life, kindnesses done to me, wrongs I have done, etc. I think about you and I think about your father every day. I have this conviction that I was a source of conflict between you. (Is this true?)

[29] The McGuffey Readers, first published in the nineteenth century.

This book served to bring to the foreground of my mind how odd it is that the subject of his death has been totally unexplored territory. Have I done you a disservice by never asking what you made of him? Have you understood what he was about?

These topics seem to me related to what you experienced in eastern Europe—the sense of life and optimistic confidence that life is going to get better. The opposite seems to me to be true in the U.S.A. We have all the signs of a culture that is going down the tubes, and fast. There seems to be a kind of death wish at the core of virtually every aspect of life here. I would love to understand why this is the case. Can it be reversed? Has there ever been a culture that began to decline, then turned around? Or is this merely the illusion of decline? (No, this I feel certain of—my children's peers are less civilized than we were as children.)

What a depressing letter! I wish I had your knack for writing interesting, cheery news. How lovely the visits of your nephews must have been. I understand completely the relief you felt at the end of the day. Mothers long for the same every day starting at about 4 P.M. My friend Katy and I call it the Arsenic Hour (it's either you or them, but someone's going to get it in the tea).

However, we somehow drag ourselves through it, through dinner, through the bedtime bedlam, then collapse at the close of the day after maybe writing a letter (like this one) or reading a chapter or two. But it is a great life. As far as I can make out, everyone has the burden of finding a large part of the day a grind. Just because you experience this in a business suit does not make it more pleasant. In fact, it seems to me to make it less pleasant, because business suits are uncomfortable. A surprising number of people find the money they make adequate compensation for this experience of drudgery. I don't think I would.

Housewives have lots of physical work and drudgery and the psychologically difficult task of listening to children fight, cry, and whine. But we have more free time to think our own thoughts and converse with our friends than most people ever do. I cannot picture a job that would be more appealing to me than this.

Here's another piece of funny news—I've been asked to be a participant on a local cable TV news talk show—the host wants to do a local version of the McLaughlin Group. He said I could be their Eleanor Clift (over my dead body, I felt like saying—more like Pat Buchanan in drag). I think this will be lots of fun. You know how I have always loved to argue. But who'd have thought back at NVOT that one day I'd be the orthodox Catholic right-wing Republican?

September 1993—to Robin Russin and family

We rented *The Player* a few weeks ago, and, naturally, our thoughts turned to you.[30] We really enjoyed it. (Despite some gross plot flaws, like—why make so much about the Ice Lady? How did she so easily transform into perfect pregnant wifey? Did he or did he not already realize when he was choking the hapless writer that he had the wrong man? Was it just rage at the prospect of being exposed as a paranoid? Or did he still think he had the postcard author? If the latter, there should have been a much bigger reaction when the fax arrived in his car indicating that the harasser still lived. Etc.)

Anyway, after thoroughly enjoying the movie and talking about it for a good half hour, we realized that not one of us (four college-educated adults) had the slightest idea who wrote the script. Yours is truly a hidden profession. Anyway, the movie moved us one small step forward—now we realize at the end of every movie that we have no idea who wrote the script.

We had a marvelous summer—two weeks in the White Mountains with our favorite other family. Between us we had ten children; for the second week my nephew joined us, and we brought along a fifteen-year-old babysitter so we could hike without the babies. It was brilliant. Everyone did what he liked—little kids swam in the nearby pond, babysitter perfected her tan. The adults hiked, and the older children agreed to hike in return for ice cream, miniature golf, Attitash Alpine slides, and other worldly delights. One essential lesson for successful parenting is not to scruple about bribery. It works.

[30] After earning his degree at the Rhode Island School of Design, Robin embarked on a screenwriting career in Hollywood.

We climbed Mount Washington twice, Franconia Ridge, and three other mountains we had long wanted to climb but couldn't with little kids on backs. Mike and I are within striking distance of our wedding weights and measurements. That's an accomplishment (with the exception of my abdomen, which after seven babies has taken on the characteristics of a new state of matter somewhere between liquid and colloidal suspension).

This September is different—I am homeschooling young Michael. Michael is what you would call mathematically challenged. The poor kid just doesn't get certain key and very basic concepts (like how there are many ways of naming the same quantity: fraction, percent, decimal, etc.). We are using a very traditional curriculum that's been around for a century (predating the current homeschool craze).[31] Contrary to what you might expect, this is not being done for moral or religious reasons. We figured that this is about the last chance Michael will get to learn basic math before it starts having irrevocable consequences, closing off courses of study that require proficiency in math.

We also watched *Husbands and Wives* recently. I loved that movie. I think it got a bum rap because of [Woody] Allen's private disasters. But I don't think I have ever seen a more true-to-life portrayal of the weird currents of attraction, flirtation, and infidelity, as well as the strangely strong satisfaction that comes from a permanent, though clearly imperfect, union.

We continue to be horrified by your man in the White House [William Clinton]. Everything he does seems to us to be disastrous. We expect him to increase the size of the deficit, drive the economy into recession, and increase inflation and unemployment. I suppose you expect him to do the opposite. This is a measure of the elasticity of the human mind. Let's make a point of commenting on what really has happened come the next presidential race. But remember, you cannot blame Clinton defeats (should there be any) on a Republican Congress. And remember that Reagan, while he increased the deficit (admittedly a bad thing), did manage to decrease inflation and increase growth and employment—and this despite a Democratic Congress.

[31] The Calvert curriculum, designed by the Calvert School in Baltimore.

Does this count for nothing?? Will you hold your guy to the same standards?? Let's see.

I'll enclose a few snaps of the family. I'm slowly adjusting to the idea of having as many girls as boys. And I am making a conscious effort to root out any signs of ditsiness in my girls. Maria has a clear tendency to light-mindedness—clothes, hair, jewelry, etc. She seems to me like a creature from another planet sometimes. I never cared about such things as a little tomboy.

Hope you are all well. As always, you are in my thoughts and prayers much more often than the frequency of my correspondence indicates.

October 11, 1993—to Fr. N.[32]

I left a message at the rectory about 1 P.M. on Sunday. I called again about 5 P.M. I'd rather talk to you in person, but I don't want to let a week or two elapse before I deal with this in some way.

I tried to get it out of my system talking to Patti M. and (over the phone) to Mary Mullaney. I tried to sit down and work on something else. I was in tears all the way home following the CCD teachers' meeting. I could hardly compose myself enough to talk to Patti in the car (she gave me a ride home). I rarely cry. I am very accustomed to disagreeing with people, arguing for opposing views. I do this all the time, usually without taking it personally. I am even used to having people make uncharitable assumptions about me and misinterpret everything I say; that is, I am used to it when dealing with ideological adversaries. I guess I am not used to it when dealing with people I think of as being on the same side. I was crushed by what you said to me yesterday morning.

I have interpreted a lot of what you said as an outburst of pent-up frustration and resentment. I want to know whether that's how you view it or whether you really think I am as much in the wrong as you made it sound yesterday. Let me give three examples of what I mean.

First, have I ever said an unkind or critical word about Judy N.? I don't think I ever have. My two older boys attended her First

---

[32] A priest in Ruth's parish at the time.

Communion classes. I intend to have John Henry attend her class. I have no recollection of ever having criticized her, her teaching style, or anything about her. Why, then, did you make this remark: "I would take one Judy N. to ten of you"? (I think you did not mean me in particular but meant "you" as a group of us whom you referred to as rigid, conservative Catholics.)

You did make that remark. If I ever said or did anything to deserve that remark, I sincerely want to know. If I didn't, then I guess I want some kind of explanation for why you said that to me. To my knowledge, I have never criticized any of the CCD teachers or said that they are incompetent to teach CCD.

Second, you spoke about "you" in the plural, a group of us at Saint Paul's who are "so rigid". You spoke (as if these things were all related) about how no one but a handful of us like the long solemn Mass, how Joe Policelli refuses to play "On Eagle's Wings", and how this is driving people out of the Church, that this will destroy Saint Paul's.

It is a fact that some people do like the solemn Mass. That is what attracts them to Saint Paul's. There isn't another parish in the city that offers that kind of Mass. Surely there is room for one parish of that type? Yet you made it sound as if it were wrong for us to like the solemn Mass because others find it too long. Do you really think this?

You said that Saint Peter's is the future of the Church, where they have folk Masses and everybody laughs and sings and has a good time. Then you gave as an example the fact that M.T.[33] complained repeatedly about how conservative the preaching is at Saint Paul's, about how he wanted you to preach about contraception being OK, the need for a married clergy, and ordination of women. You said he finally left Saint Paul's in frustration. You seemed to be implying that you and Monsignor Jim were engaged in some elaborate balancing act between the demands of "us" conservatives and those like M.T.

Is that what you perceive yourself as doing? Would you preach that there is nothing wrong with contraception and abortion if that's what the congregation wanted to hear? Do you refrain from saying things

[33] A professor from a local Catholic college.

142

like that only because you think it would outrage people like me? I don't think so. I think you understand your role as being called to preach what Christ teaches through His Church.

It seemed to me you were expressing exasperation at me as the representative of some group that is driving people out of the Church. I don't think that's fair. I would like to know if that is what you really think.

Finally, I brought up the example of the Cheffers sending their children to the Benedictine sisters for CCD. I gave that example because I think it is a shame. I think it points to a problem. Obviously I don't think the sisters' CCD program is the ideal, or I would send my own children there. It certainly would be a lot easier, seeing as that church is just around the corner from our house, and so the children could walk there on their own.

I also gave the example of some friends of mine who are a long, long way from being what you would consider "conservative" and who attended Saint Paul's before they had children. They now belong to Blessed Sacrament because (the wife told me) they believe there isn't an adequate CCD program at Saint Paul's. At this point, you said that was bull——, and you said to me, somewhat pointedly, "If that's how you feel, then go ahead, go to Blessed Sacrament." You said this as if I had threatened doing likewise, which I certainly did not and would not do.

I left the CCD building reeling. I had always thought you were, on the whole, favorably disposed toward me and in general agreement with my concerns about how little real learning is going on in CCD. This exchange made me feel as if that impression had to have been self-delusion, that in reality you thought I was very misguided and seriously lacking in simple justice, let alone charity.

So I guess I want to know what you really think. I'm still stuck with the conviction that Catholic education is failing, at Saint Paul's as well as just about everywhere else. I still don't know what to do about the religious education of my own children, and I don't know what to make of what you said to me.

A few weeks ago, you preached a homily from the text "If your brother wrongs you, go and speak with him in private." That is what I am doing (though to be fair, it is not entirely in private since Patti M., Mary Mullaney, and my husband have all listened to me pour out my perception of what happened).

I know I am sometimes plainspoken to the point of being rude. I know I have a very high opinion of my own intelligence and competence. I know I intimidate people who find open disagreement threatening or difficult. For all these failings, I probably deserve censure from my parish priest. But I do not think I deserve the kinds of criticisms you levied against me yesterday.

Christmas Letter, 1993

Here's the update on our family: our youngest child, Sophie, was born April 16. Actually, her full name is Anna Sophia, but she's too little a morsel of humanity quite to fill that name yet. Sophie has started crawling, pulling the houseplants over, and swallowing whatever she finds on the floor. What fun! I'll be a nervous wreck until we get through this lethal stage.

Michael, son no. 1, turned twelve this November. He is being schooled at home, at least for this academic year (seventh grade for him). So far it is working out well. He is getting a more solid grasp of basic math. It has rather altered the household schedule, though, since the younger girls and I basically have to stay put each morning. All the errands and shopping have to be squeezed into the early afternoon hours, before the other three get home from school.

Max is having a great year at school—he got straight A's on his report card, his intramural football team won the school's Super Bowl, and the soccer team he and Michael played on were undefeated this season—eighteen straight games!

John Henry is in second grade now, doing well. He also had a good soccer season. He has an insatiable appetite for stories about sports heroes.

Maria, in first grade, has learned to read. This means I can no longer get away with my old ploy of skipping paragraphs out of children's books that bore me since I have this eager-beaver new reader trying to catch all my mistakes.

Sarah (three years old) is herself, a bit irrepressible and a few decibels above normal. But she's cute, and she says very funny things. She has a very vivid imaginary life. Each day at dinner she gives a detailed report on all the mischievous behaviors of the children in her "class". We are told in all seriousness about what Sarah's teacher said and did to reprimand each girl and boy (but never Sarah). You would swear Sarah had actually been to kindergarten or nursery school, but she never has. Where does she get these ideas? We haven't a clue.

This is tenure decision year for Mike. That about sums up his life 'til June. He absolutely must (and will) finish his book (Aristotle translation—not best-seller material) by the end of the academic year. I expect a wretched spring.

I'm still singing with the cathedral choir (which is also our parish). I'm also still quite active in pro-life work, speaking to high school students and doing debates at colleges. Something new—I got involved in an interesting city-wide election because my best friend was running for school committee. She won, upsetting all the expectations of the local pols. It was great fun.

We ended 1993 with some difficult news: my cancer has returned, to the right hip and backbone. Conventional medicine cannot cure metastasized breast cancer, so my years are numbered (in single digits). So far, Mike and I are (no doubt supernaturally) accepting of whatever God has in mind. We've gotten somewhat used to His ways not being our ways.

Christmas 1993—to Larry Weller

Thanks so much for your last letter. I wanted to write sooner, then thought I'd see you at Thanksgiving, then realized too late our stay in New Jersey was going to be too brief (arrived 5 P.M. Friday, departed 7 P.M. Saturday, with a turkey dinner and joint birthday—young Michael was born on my father's birthday—party fit in, then a return to Worcester to avoid the Sunday traffic hell).

Our Christmas visit will be almost as brief—arriving Sunday night (twenty-sixth) and returning Wednesday the twenty-ninth. Please let me know if you will be free one of those days. Monday will be the day when all my brothers will be in Norwood, so Tuesday or Wednesday would be better, but I'll squeeze time out of Monday if necessary.

Please don't imagine I teach Michael according to the quaint, somewhat excessively moralistic, tone of the McGuffey Readers. I'm, if anything, much too easy on this kid (who is really lazy, but unabashedly so, which I admire). I do try to make him work hard for at least three hours a day, but then he gets to do pretty much what he likes. Still, I am confident he is learning far more than he would in a classroom.

I just started reading William F. Buckley's book *Windfall*. Even the prologue left me breathless. This guy really lives in high gear. I try in my very small way to be like that—deliberately cultivate varied interests, observe some sort of discipline maintaining them, have a schedule, try to make the most of what time you have at your disposal, etc. Buckley is a master at this. He also writes well, and I agree with him most of the time. Plus, he's obnoxious and utterly self-confident, traits which I often find endearing.

Before this, I just finished reading a most interesting novel, *In a Dark Wood Wandering*. If you ever have a long daily commute on the train again, this is worth attempting. It follows the life of Charles d'Orléans, through the vicissitudes of the Hundred Years' War.

Yes—we won all that we wanted (and then some) on Election Day. My friend, who had been dismissed as unelectable by the newspaper in town, came in fourth (six are elected; twelve ran). She beat two incumbents—unheard of in Worcester. What's more, she is not Worcester born and bred—another unheard-of accomplishment in this very provincial town. We were ecstatic. I love politics. It is a great competitive game with real stakes, but if you lose, there's always another election coming up so you can try again.

You make a legitimate complaint about *The Second Coming*. Naturally, many problems resolve themselves if you fall in love. But this convention points to something beyond itself. For that matter, the reality points beyond itself. Love irresistibly leads one to think in terms of absolutes and eternity.

The current Pope writes about this all the time. He is always trying to get modern man (that shortsighted, hedonistic idiot) to think about the fact that human beings are created in order to love. What does that mean? It doesn't mean that we are meant to find someone who pleases us; rather, we are meant to give ourselves to someone else. All human loves involve the giving of oneself and receiving of the other as a gift. All loves are like this, but romantic love paints the clearest picture of it.

Most people, when they receive the gift of another person, perceive that this gift implies a Giver. This can be sensed very completely and clearly, or dimly. But I think that is why love is so often portrayed as a redemptive force. It forces the mind and heart to think in terms of what is forever. People who are in love think, speak, and act as if death cannot separate them. Why should this be the case? Either it is a silly illusion, or it is, in fact, the case.

It cannot be that however you spend your life, it is all the same in the end. You put it this way: "We are it, and we can only try to make the most of it in whatever manner we consider appropriate." If that were true, then Hitler would have lived as noble a life as Mother Teresa, or anyone else, for that matter, since there can be no good, better, best if all we end up is dead.

Percy is trying to get blind people to see some very basic truths. He's trying to point out the absurdity of thinking that man is merely a product of the material world. He tries to focus the mind of his reader on the fact that is so obvious and pervasive in this world that we lose sight of it—that something is wrong, that we are not what we know we ought to be, that we are missing an essential part of the puzzle.

This truth used to be called Original Sin, but modern man can't wrap his little mind around that big concept any more. So Percy points out little baby steps of the truth—most apparently happy people seem to be mindless idiots who fritter their lives away in meaningless distractions. Less happy people seem to have a firmer grip on the true situation of man in the universe, but these kinds of people quite often end up killing themselves and others. Something is clearly wrong. Christianity purports to explain what is wrong and what is to be done about it.

This is turning into a treatise. I hope we find time to talk about it after Christmas. I got a note from Tim saying Marg is pregnant. Another amazing example of how adopting a baby is followed by conceiving a baby. I sure hope all goes well for them.

January 6, 1994—to Katy Whisenant

Did I tell you this funny story? A friend of mine has a son John Henry's age, very like him in spunky boyness. They attend CCD together, taught by these funny, very pious, very old Benedictine nuns.

Anyway, Martha's son, Patrick, came home wide-eyed the other week to tell his mother most solemnly that in CCD they had learned "the first half of the Act of Conception".

(I want to send this to *Reader's Digest*, but I'm afraid too few people would get the joke in this pagan age.)

Listening to NPR [National Public Radio], I heard back-to-back the new federal condom ads (you know you're in trouble when the *government* is trying to appear hip and slick) and then the report on federally funded fetal experimentation.

GET ME OUTTA HERE!!!!

I got up at 5 A.M. so I could do the dinner dishes from last night and put away the piles of clean folded laundry that are burrowing into every corner of the downstairs. Instead, I'm tapping away at this computer. Now it's time to get back to practicing the virtue of order. (Do the dishes!)

January 17, 1994—to Ivan

Thank you for your letter. Congratulations on the excellent news of your decision to become a priest. We consider ourselves truly blessed to have met you, a brother in Christ and now also to be one of His priests.

We keep you and your family in our prayers. Each day, I say the prayer card of Blessed Josemaría and ask him to obtain blessings for you and all the members of your family. My husband told me that your father has been in a hospital for the mentally ill for many years. Did we understand that correctly? I especially pray for him and for the sadness that must cause for your family.

I follow the news about Russia with great interest. We know your nation is undergoing terrible hardships. I am trying to learn more about Russian history. It is a mystery of God's providence why some countries (like Russia) have suffered so much while others (like the United States) have been blessed with peace and wealth. We (the United States) no longer deserve God's favor.

Tomorrow, our entire family will travel to Washington, D.C., with the Swope family (the people whose home we stopped at in New Hampshire). There will be an enormous demonstration against abortion. It is called the March for Life, and it happens every year on the anniversary of the day our Supreme Court legalized abortion. This happened twenty-one years ago. There will be about a hundred thousand people at this March. But despite all our efforts, most people in America prefer comfort, convenience, and sexual license, and they do not want to obey God's laws.

We also have some sad news. Back in 1991 it was discovered that I (Ruth) had breast cancer. I had surgery and went through chemotherapy. Last month, we found out that the cancer has come back in my spine and hip. There is no known cure for breast cancer once it has spread like this. Most women die within five years.

I am not afraid to die. But it will be a terrible hardship for Michael, left alone with six children. And the children will suffer much sadness. I want whatever God wants from this situation. But I also pray Blessed Josemaría's prayer card for my own cure, if it is God's will.

You asked to know more about Opus Dei. Let me tell you a little, and you can ask more specific questions in your next letter. From his youth, Josemaría understood that God was asking something very special from him, though he did not know what. Josemaría set about preparing himself as best he could to respond to God's call. In 1928, Josemaría received from God an understanding of what he was supposed to do—found Opus Dei.

Opus Dei is a way to bring people closer to God through their daily work. It is also a way to help these people be more apostolic, to bring Christ to others.

What Opus Dei does is very ordinary. Members agree to follow a plan of life that includes prayer, daily Mass, weekly confession, Rosary, etc. They go to a weekly meeting for spiritual formation. Once a year they make a retreat, and once a year they attend a five-day workshop to learn more about the faith.[34] Through this formation, they are helped to grow closer to God and to live out their faith. The goal is not one specific thing—to educate young people or to feed the hungry. Rather, the goal is to strengthen each individual so he or she will bring Christ into the world in that particular place. I hope you are able to be in contact with members of Opus Dei in Russia.

Monsignor Mongelluzzo from Saint Paul's Cathedral was delighted to hear of your decision to become a priest. He sends his regards.

I am sending a box of a few T-shirts and things. Michael's sister and her husband work in marketing for two large corporations (Colgate and American Chicle). They are always receiving these kinds of shirts and things—more than they could ever wear. I thought they might amuse you.

If there is any particular item you could use, please let me know and I will try to send it to you. Many years ago, it was a custom in Catholic churches in the United States to recite the prayer to Saint Michael the Archangel for the conversion of Russia. In the 1970s, that custom was dropped by most people. But I make it a habit again to pray that prayer after Mass for the intention of an end to abortion in the U.S.A. and for peace and prosperity to return to Russia.

[34] This remark pertains to "supernumerary" members of Opus Dei. The celibate members of Opus Dei, "numeraries" and "associates", attend when possible a longer annual workshop, lasting about three weeks.

January 26, 1994—to David Lionett[35]

Here are some pamphlets that address the pro-life issue from the perspective that I think is of most interest and importance today. Given the [*Planned Parenthood v.*] *Casey* decision, where Justice [Anthony] Kennedy unexpectedly sided with a pro-*Roe* majority, it is inconceivable that *Roe* will be reversed in the foreseeable future. That means pro-life energies will become more concentrated on efforts to reduce the numbers of abortions in ways that do not actually prohibit abortion.

Problem Pregnancy is a remarkable organization. It cannot be rivaled for human interest stories. One story involves a girl who jumped out of her bedroom window and ran away from home just to avoid an abortion her parents were determined she should have. Her little girl is in grade school now, she is happily married to that baby's father, and they have younger children as well.

Another story involves a young woman scheduled for a late abortion. Late abortions are performed over two days: on the first day, a plug of super-absorbent seaweed (called laminaria) is inserted into the cervix. It gradually expands and opens the cervix. The girl returns to the clinic on the second day for the actual abortion procedure (which is gruesome).

This girl changed her mind on the morning of the second day. She was taken to an area hospital for the removal of the laminaria. This action was very risky and fraught with danger of lawsuits for the medical professionals involved, but they took the risk and the baby was born a few months later, perfectly healthy.

I'd like to talk about ways in which women could be given more information and make a more informed, more authentic "choice".

Another issue which ought to be addressed is the opposition that has been and will continue to be mounted to Clinton's plan to include abortion as part of any basic health care package. This issue will cause a long, drawn-out, messy fight that could help torpedo Clinton's entire health care proposal.

---

[35] A politician and the host of a local talk radio show, *In the Lion's Den*. Ruth was a guest on his show on at least two occasions.

Chris Derr will accompany me. She has been a volunteer at Problem Pregnancy for many years. She has provided temporary housing for many of their clients. She is currently providing day care for one client so she can finish school. Chris has nine biological children and one adopted child.

I appreciate the invitation to be on *The Lion's Den*. It has been a pleasure getting to know you and to argue as an ally on at least some conservative issues.

January 28, 1994—to Katy Whisenant

Another snow day. Hari-kari looks good. I went outside to shovel just so I could get away from the kids.

Leone called yesterday. Therese had called her. It was so nice to hear her voice. She told me of an amusing idea she had had for a little drama featuring Blessed Josemaría berating John Henry Newman for being so lackadaisical about getting canonized. She envisioned Blessed Josemaría trying to stir up some national rivalries, urging Newman to intervene for a miracle if only to uphold the honor of England, seeing how this son of Spain was already light-years ahead of him.

Anyway, Leone resolved to get the Oratorians[36] on my case with a novena. She felt sure Blessed Josemaría's good manners would persuade him to stand aside while Newman played a little catch-up ball.

Joyce phoned me yesterday, all grateful for the photocopies. She also urged me to look further into bone marrow transplants, which I am doing, though it is actually more pleasant just to think that everything is settled and all I have to do is brace myself to go over the hump of the roller coaster. BMT would mean reopening some percentage chance of a medical cure (but at what cost!).[37] Nevertheless, I do not want to

---

[36] The congregation of the Oratory which Blessed Newman joined after becoming a Catholic.

[37] This refers to a radical and risky treatment, where such high doses of chemotherapy are given that they even destroy all of the patient's bone marrow. Prior to treatment, some healthy bone marrow is extracted and preserved. After chemotherapy, these healthy cells are reinjected into the patient, in the hopes of regrowing the bone marrow. BMT implied many months lost from weakness and a compromised immune system.

be guilty of premature acquiescence, so I am dutifully calling around to various cancer institutes trying to find out what is really known (very little, it seems).

My sister is visiting tomorrow, armed with a stack of papers about breast cancer, bone marrow transplant, and alternative cancer therapies. She also seems determined that I should try other experimental approaches.

Our visit at the Hardys' was great fun.[38] We arrived late Wednesday afternoon. Tom and the older children were still out—they had gone skiing in Pennsylvania (taking advantage of the snow day). That night we had a pleasant visit, the adults just talking. We managed to turn in at a reasonable hour (Paul was by this time quite sick with bronchitis and needed sleep).

The next day, four adults managed to get to Mass. Then we went bowling with some outrageous number of children. That was a big hit. The three men engaged in charming macho competitiveness. I broke 100, which is something of an accomplishment for me.

That evening we played Tom's favorite game—Monopoly. I beat him into the ground. Most satisfying. I always thought of Monopoly as a staid, boring game, but not when Tom Hardy plays it.

Then next day was the March. Again, we left all the little children with Jan, Diana, and Paul at home. We had a great time, though we were all pretty numb in the foot by the end. It was a very pretty day, though—intense blue sky, clean white snow, and the even more startlingly white Capitol buildings. What a shame such beauty should give rise to such evil.

We borrowed the Hardys' car to visit the Caseys, not returning home until about midnight. We should have called it a night, but instead, we stayed up way, way too late, talking about our dysfunctional families. Jenny is the only one who comes from a "normal" family, though even there, some very odd dynamics exist.

---

[38] Paul Swope had rented an RV so that both families could travel together to the March for Life in style. There had been a big ice storm in Washington, D.C., closing the government and businesses for days. The front lawn of the Hardys' house in Bethesda had such a hard-packed sheet of ice on it that we parked the large RV right up on the lawn.

The next day was the most lunatic. We piled into the RV and drove out to Luray Caverns. The trip was wonderful—beautiful scenery, mild, springlike temperatures. The caverns were impressive. The children had fun. But when we returned, the Swopes left immediately to visit Paul's sister and brother. We then borrowed the Hardys' car to go visit Mike's brother and sister-in-law. We went from there to visit one of Mike's high school buddies, not returning 'til midnight. Paul met us as we came in the door, saying he wanted to be on the road by 10:30 the next morning. This meant we were all supposed to get up go to Mass at 7:30 A.M. I thought this was utterly insane but was too tired to argue.

In the meantime, Mike had made arrangements to have breakfast at 9 A.M. with his high school friend who is now a Legionary priest working in D.C. Again, I thought this was insane.

We woke up at about 7:15. Sophie had a fever and was very fussy. I refused to go to 7:30 Mass, not willing to take her and not willing to wake up one of the Hardys and dump a sick baby on them.

Mike and the Swopes went to Mass, but by the time they returned, Mike and Paul had had the one falling out of the trip, all over Paul's determination to depart by 10:30 A.M. Lucky for us, Tom Hardy saw that there was a problem, asked me to state the problem, then turned to Paul and told him he was being nuts. At that point, everybody relaxed. I went to a later Mass, Mike went to see his friend (Father Rich Gill), and we left all happy and friends again by 11:30 A.M. All this heartache for the sake of one hour!

It's time to get lunch for these kids. Hope all is well in sunny Texas.

February 8, 1994—to Janet Villas

Thanks for the angel book. I've seen that book about and have been intrigued by it. It's a beautiful book. Very nice of you.

Today I'm going for CAT scans. My doctor is not in favor of bone marrow transplants (BMTs), but I felt I ought to go to [the] Dana-Farber [Cancer Institute] for a second opinion. Dana-Farber requires all these additional tests.

My doctor is convinced that BMTs don't actually help women with metastasized breast cancer (although it does work for other types of cancer—isn't that odd). She also says that some women will "perk along" (her phrase) for quite a number of years with metastasized breast cancer. Of course, most won't. But again, the odd thing is that they have no way of knowing or predicting which women will go along just fine for a fairly long time and which will die in short order.

Another thing I've figured out is that you don't, as a rule, die of cancer in the bone. That just causes pain and limits movement (as it progresses). What kills you is when breast cancer spreads to the liver, lungs, or brain.

So, today I'll find out whether there are already metastases in those organs which have not yet gummed up the works enough to cause symptoms.

Enough on that for now. We're going to get more snow today. Probably a snow day tomorrow. Oh no! Winter has worn out its welcome. Too bad spring doesn't arrive until late May (Rogers and Hammerstein weren't kidding).

Michael is playing indoor soccer this month. He's doing much better in math these days. I hope I won't be homeschooling him next year, but the three relevant persons don't agree on where he should go to school.[39]

Brace yourself. I'm going skiing next week. Our dear friends, the Swopes, have decided that I must experience the thrill of downhill skiing before I die, so they are taking the three boys and Mike and me up to New Hampshire next week. What fun. Hope I don't break my neck.

I pray for you each day. I know you're doing the same for me. It's funny that the prospect of dying does not bother me that much. I really do believe that whatever God wants is going to turn out best. If He wants me to die before getting out of my thirties, then I trust that good will come of it. I pray that all my friends will come to have a

[39] Janet, besides being one of Ruth's best friends from high school, was also Michael's godmother, which explains the extra information on Michael in this letter.

strong faith, that my sister will be reconciled to the rest of the family, that my children will grow up in the faith—that sort of thing.

I'll ask you again to say this particular prayer card.[40] This is the guy who ought to be looking out for me. He also has a reputation for blessing people who say this prayer card faithfully. I'd love to see that work for you!

February 19, 1994—to Emil and Elaine Pollak

Perhaps you have by now heard the rather bad news that my cancer has returned. It's in my hip and backbone, so while it does not affect my life at all at this point, it is virtually certain (barring a miracle or something pretty darn close) that I will die of breast cancer in the next three to ? years. Apparently it is not really that much of a problem as long as the cancer stays in the bone. Metastasized breast cancer becomes lethal when it spreads to the brain, lungs, or liver. There is no way of predicting when it might do that.

Anyway, our best friends, the Swopes, decided that I absolutely had to experience downhill skiing before I die, so they footed the entire bill for Mike and me and our three boys to join them and their two older children in Nordic Village for four days of non-stop skiing. It was great. We skied at Wildcat [Mountain], where they have the free (!) lift for the baby beginner's slope. This way we were all able to take our time getting confident before shelling out the bucks for a lift pass.

By the end of the first day, young Michael and Max were doing jumps. The next day, they started doing moguls. Needless to say, the old folks took to it a little slower, but by our last day, I was happily skiing the beginner slope all the way from the top of the mountain to the bottom without falling.

We literally skied every free moment and then collapsed exhausted at 8 P.M. in front of the TV to watch the Olympics. Perhaps you also heard that we had to take Max to the North Conway hospital (nothing serious), where we met Dr. MacLaren, a friend of yours.

[40] The prayer card for Blessed Josemaría Escrivá.

If only there were a university somewhere near the White Mountains, we would be looking to move in a minute!

I'm giving a pro-life talk at Columbia in March.[41] Last year, they needed a police escort for the pro-life speaker—Act Up showed up. I would actually enjoy such a lot of hoopla, but I expect my appearance will be very tame.

February 1994—to Dr. Susan Love [42]

A former patient of yours urged me to call you. The number she gave me was a private line, and I was reluctant to leave a message.

I was diagnosed with breast cancer in the fall of 1991, with three positive nodes, no metastasis. Metastasis was detected in December 1993, in my lower back, my right hip, and a spot on my skull.

My oncologist prescribed tamoxifen, which I am taking without serious side effects. She does not recommend a bone marrow transplant. She is persuaded that a BMT does not offer the hope of a significantly better outcome for metastatic breast cancer than does standard hormone therapy followed by chemo as needed.

I have called the NIH [National Institutes of Health] and spoken with a Dr. Riesberg (who works with Dr. Joyce O'Shaughnessy). I have called the Dana-Farber Institute, 1-800-4CANCER, and the National Cancer Institute. So far, I have not encountered a physician who holds a different view of BMT. All seem to agree that there is no good evidence that BMT offers the hope of longer survival rates.

On the other hand, somebody must believe that BMT is potentially effective, since there is so much news about it on TV and in the papers. The Massachusetts legislature just passed a law requiring HMOs [health maintenance organizations] to cover the procedure.

I am trying to decide whether or not to pursue the possibility of BMT through Dana-Farber. I am thirty-six. I have six children, ages

---

[41] Columbia was Emil Pollak's alma mater.

[42] Dr. Susan Love is a noted breast cancer researcher and surgeon who later became head of an institute known as the Dr. Susan Love Research Foundation.

twelve down to nine months. I feel obliged to investigate BMT to discover whether it might offer a chance of longer healthy survival. If the data do not indicate the chance of a better outcome, I would not pursue BMT.

This is what perplexes me. My oncologist admits that 15% of women with metastatic disease will be disease-free five years after BMT. But no one is disease-free after five years on tamoxifen. My doctor seemed persuaded that these 15% would have been doing well, up and about, even without BMT. This seems counterintuitive to me.

I also want to know what happens to the other 85% of BMT recipients. How many are dead after five years? How many are in the terminal stages; how many are still up and about? Assuming one survives the BMT procedure itself, can a person be any worse off as a result of the procedure? And how do these results compare to more standard hormone treatment and chemotherapy?

February 24, 1994—to Mark Van Kooy[43]

We were in that area just after you, from February 15 to February 19. Paul Swope decided I had to experience downhill skiing before I die, so he took Mike and me and the three boys up to Jackson, New Hampshire. We skied mostly at Wildcat Mountain, directly across Route 16 from Pinkham Notch. We had superb views of the east face of Mount Washington. We had a great time. The boys took to it like they had been born skiing. By the day we left, they were going down expert trails, doing moguls and jumps. I skied much more sedately, but even I was able to go from top to bottom without falling.

I've continued talking to a battery of doctors regarding ABMT.[44] At this point, I've been convinced that there is really no reason to think that ABMT is likely to extend my life. My own doctor is convinced that many women who are doing well three to five years after ABMT would actually have been doing well anyway. She explained that the ABMT candidates are very selectively chosen and, she thinks,

---

[43] Mark Van Kooy is Ruth's older brother, a Family Practice physician.
[44] Autologous bone marrow transplant (a transplant using cells from one's own bone marrow).

disproportionately selected from women who would have responded well to less drastic therapies. What still has not been established (the studies are still too recent) is whether anyone is actually cured.

She also pointed out that of the approximately 15% of women who are disease-free three years after ABMT, not many had metastasis in the bone. On the other hand, as long as the disease remains bone-only metastasis, it progresses slowly and can usually be managed quite well for a few years.

So far, I am still feeling perfectly healthy. It would seem a shame to go and deliberately make myself deathly ill with chemo, and with so little likelihood of it changing the eventual outcome, I find myself unable to justify pursuing ABMT.

I'm writing all this to you because I want to be sure that I am not wimping out or missing something that offers a real (not imagined or wished-for) chance at living significantly longer. Given all the media hype about ABMT, I have been surprised at the lack of enthusiasm among actual MDs. I've spoken to people at the NIH, at Dana-Farber, and to the MD chosen to head up UMass [Memorial] Medical Center's soon-to-open BMT center. All of them have said they think it's unclear whether ABMT actually helps women with metastatic breast cancer, and since my disease is rather benign at present, they advise sticking with conventional hormone therapy.

Do you have any advice to offer on this? Am I missing something?

Hope you are all well. I'll be in Norwood from Friday, March 4, to Sunday, March 6. I was invited to speak at Fordham and Columbia. Nice excuse to visit the folks.

April 1994—to Larry Weller

My sister gave me a CD of *Lost in the Stars* for my birthday. I love listening to it. You and I listen to music very differently. I don't think I ever sit still and attend to a piece of music. I am always listening to music while I'm folding laundry, washing dishes, mopping floors, etc. Often, I put music on to drown out the noise of the children's squabbling and to give me something else to focus my attention on. Anyway,

I listen to musicals a lot now. It reminds me of yet another thing for which I am indebted to you and your family—introducing me to so many interesting musicals.

Speaking invitations just keep rolling in—I'm slated to go to Boston College, UMass Amherst, Clark, and Wheaton College in the next month. Unlike most other normal human beings, I just love these opportunities to defend what most people consider the indefensible.

I attended the Republican Party caucuses in my town and got myself elected to be a delegate at the Republican state convention. The only race of interest will be the primary, to determine which Republican will go down to ignominious defeat against Ted Kennedy (that charred and smoking ruin, as I believe [judge Robert] Bork or [commentator Bill] Bennett described him). The Republican Party in Massachusetts is a rather pathetic institution, conforming almost perfectly to the stereotype of country-club types. They really prefer to lose elections rather than let in grubby social conservative Reagan Democrat convert types like me and my friends.

May 1994—to Peter Blute, candidate for Massachusetts House of Representatives

I have been doing a lot of thinking about how to handle the abortion issue this political season. To get to the interesting point: many pro-life persons will be enthusiastically supporting Mitt Romney [for U.S. Senator from Massachusetts] while the same (or similar) people are opposing Kevin O'Sullivan. Kevin will most likely take a position quite similar to Romney's (with the notable exception of abortion in health care—I suspect O'Sullivan may support this highly unpopular and controversial measure). This seems to make pro-lifers appear inconsistent.

I want to articulate clearly how it is consistent for pro-lifers to support Romney (who is going out of his way to declare himself in favor of *Roe*) while at the same time opposing O'Sullivan.

People who are not brain dead realize that the opportunity to reverse *Roe* has come and gone. *Casey* should have been the opportunity to reverse *Roe*. Unfortunately, Anthony Kennedy did not do what he was expected to do, so we still have *Roe*. (I would not want to be in his shoes on Judgment Day.)

That being the case, it is defeatist for pro-lifers to hold their breath until a candidate comes along who pledges to reverse *Roe*. Romney is viewed as likely to favor whatever restrictions are possible under current law. And he would replace the most powerful pro-abortion politician in the country (after Hillary [Clinton]).

On the other hand, Kevin is a turncoat. Enough said.

As to handling the issue from hell, I think it is a good idea for politicians to spell out very clearly that we are no longer discussing whether or not women will go to jail for abortions (if the issue ever was that). The issue is not even whether or not abortion will remain legal. It will, for good or for ill. The issue now is twofold: can we preserve what little resistance still exists to the idea that abortion is just another method of birth control (the Planned Parenthood ideal), and can we take some tiny steps back toward a little more regulation aimed at encouraging women to think twice before aborting an unwanted pregnancy?

I hope a new political label will emerge—something like "supports reasonable restrictions". Pro-life politicians could say things like "*Roe* cannot be reversed, so there is no point in working to reverse it. I am not going to do that (even though I still think *Roe* was a mistake). But I don't think abortion is a wonderful thing. And I think many women who have had abortions actually agree with that sentiment. I think it is time to address the problems facing women with unplanned pregnancies and try to offer more information and more options to these women." And so on. This rhetoric would support passage of the wildly popular measures like parental notification, waiting periods, and informed consent.

I also think this kind of rhetoric can be used by pro-choice people who recognize that abortion is being abused—one out of four pregnancies cannot be bona fide crisis pregnancies. A 42% repeat abortion rate illustrates that many women are, in fact, using abortion as birth control. And so on.

No doubt you get great advice from real experts on how to handle this issue, but I thought I would throw my two cents in as well.

On a personal note, I know that you heard the news that I have metastasized breast cancer. I understand Robi has been trying to pass along some information to me. I appreciate that thoughtfulness. I have read every blasted article from every journal, and I feel confident I have an accurate picture of the (unfortunately, rather bleak) prognosis for this condition. However, for the time being, I feel as well as ever. I am going to be away from July 'til mid-August, but then I look forward to knocking myself out trying to up your percentage of the vote in Worcester.

September 14, 1994—to Ms. Walsh, teacher at City View School

I do not wish my son, Max Pakaluk, to participate in the health curriculum currently offered by the Worcester Public Schools. I would prefer that he receive instruction in some other subject during that interval. If that is not possible, please allow him to do independent reading in the library or another suitable place. My husband and I do not care if that results in a failing grade for that subject.

I understand it is the practice at City View to allow students to watch videos when they are unable to go outside for recess. Since we do not allow our children to watch TV during the school week, this seems an unfortunate inconsistency in their education. Would you please arrange some other activity for Max during these periods, perhaps independent reading or reading aloud to younger students or assisting another teacher?

If the video is educational, we have no objection to his viewing it.

Thank you very much for your attention to these matters.

September 27, 1994—to Larry Weller

By some minor miracle, I managed to learn the music for the Vespers service last Sunday. I fell asleep early on Saturday, then got up again around 2 A.M. and went over the music for about two hours. In fact, I knew the second alto part as well as the strongest singer and better than the two others (who had sung it before!). I found the Britten was not that big a deal, once you got the rhythms in your head. But I was in a state of mild panic over the Palestrina *Magnificat*. It was chock-full of exposed alto II parts that had unpredictable switches from F-natural to F-sharp and lots of somewhat unpredictable intervals. Nevertheless, I managed to sing the entire program without a significant mistake. It was a very beautiful service. I am so lucky to be able to sing with this group.

Our car seems to have died its final death today. It started overheating and making horrible clunking noises when I drove across town. Mike will take a look tonight, but I think this is the end of the line. Life is going to be complicated for the next few days.

Do please let me know the dates of your choir concerts. This last weekend's trip worked out quite acceptably. Knowing that I have rather limited time left makes me a lot more willing to abandon the laundry and housecleaning in order to do things like attend the concerts of close friends.

This is another very interesting question (like the interesting question of what is important to pass on to children as "family heritage"). When you know you have little time left to live, how should you conduct yourself? To a certain extent, I am glad that I have no burning desire to live any differently. I really enjoy the way my life has turned out. But I do feel it is important to spend more time with the people I enjoy being with.

The kids will be in from school in ten minutes. It is time to clean up the mess Sophie made while I have been preoccupied on the computer.

October 23, 1994—to Nancy

This has taken me a very long time to get around to, but ever since you mentioned the possibility of resorting to in vitro [fertilization], I thought I ought to send this little pamphlet to you.

Very few people understand why the Catholic Church opposes this procedure. I have on many occasions heard people express astonishment that the Catholic Church, which forbids contraception, sterilization, and abortion, should also oppose procedures aimed at enabling women to conceive children. These people assume that what drives the Vatican is this obsession to see Catholics reproduce like rabbits.

Very few people seem able to understand the subtleties of the Catholic position, that it is not a no-holds-barred push for ever larger families. This pamphlet helps to explain how all these positions are linked by a reverence for the dignity of human life and the conditions of conception intended by God at creation.

I hope it won't bother you that I've sent this. We are very accustomed to associating with friends and family members who don't agree with Catholic sexual morality, but I think the arguments are reasonable and persuasive, and I think you are the kind of person who would be open to thinking them through.

March 11, 1995—to Larry Weller

The children and I (sans Michael) spent a very pleasant weekend with Emil and Elaine. I was determined that our boys should get the opportunity to ski again, and Mike's schedule wasn't looking like it would make that possible. So I decided to take Emil and Elaine up on their frequent offers of hospitality and get the kids to a mountain to ski.

With extraordinary luck, we managed to choose the absolute best skiing weekend of this rather disappointing winter. The snow was fine, but the weather was sunny and mild. Michael and Max took to it again as if they had been born with skis. John Henry made good progress in a more cautious manner (funny—in most everything else, John just bombs along keeping pace with his older brothers, but in this he just can't do it).

Elaine and I had the chance to go cross-country skiing. That was great fun, the first time for me, but I hope not the last. We were skiing around that beautiful flat plain at the base of Mount Washington behind Bretton Woods Hotel. It was heavenly. Elaine is awfully good company.

I am looking forward to a three-hour choir rehearsal tomorrow. At last, it is time to rehearse for Holy Week services. I love the Easter

Vigil Mass, but even better than that is the Good Friday service. We always sing the same repertoire, but I love that, too. Catholics really do understand something about human nature in the way that there are certain songs and texts which are only sung once a year, but always on the same feast day each year. On Good Friday, we sing this very deep, basso-profundo-type piece by Rachmaninoff for the veneration of the cross. You would love it.

March 15, 1995—to Peter and Robi Blute

I have wanted to write to you dozens of times regarding all the exciting political developments. I think the American bishops have been very retrograde on the issue of welfare reform. My husband and I strongly support the measures aimed at requiring parents to take responsibility for the children they bring into existence. That translates into mandatory reporting of paternity, and mandatory child support paid by biological fathers (or public service from minors or the indigent). We also support cutting off cash benefits for women who conceive additional children after they are already on welfare. Let's face it—if they are on welfare, they are unable to provide for the children they already have. How can tax-paying families be expected to continue to support additional children conceived by such a mother? She is being allowed to engage in utterly irresponsible behavior at taxpayers' expense. That is not justice, not for the taxpayers, or for the mothers, or for their unfortunate children.

I am sick to death of the distorted coverage of the school lunch program. I can tell you from firsthand experience just what a manipulative and wasteful program it is. It is ludicrous to say the federal government is responsible for feeding school kids their lunch.

Please, eliminate a few federal departments. [The Department of] Education wouldn't be missed by any of the right sort of people. Defund the NEA [National Endowment of the Arts] and NPR—Republicans will never get anywhere as long as the opposition remains subsidized with tax dollars. I listen to NPR every evening, and the extent of their political bias is just mind-boggling. They should not get a penny of public support. Besides, their target audience is the very upscale liberal yuppie type. These people can easily make up the lost income in private pledges.

Peter, I could go on and on, but if you read *National Review*, you'll know pretty much where I stand on anything else. You are a credit to Massachusetts—one of the few elected officials who inspire true respect and confidence. Keep up the good work. And don't let the D.C. rat race eat up too much of your precious family time. Your marriage and your children are infinitely more important than any of this political stuff (fun though it may be). I pray for all (four!) of you.

March 24, 1995—to Dad Van Kooy

No need to apologize for our last phone conversation: it was civil. But it has just about come to be downright comical how opposite our political views have become.

To the end of continuing the conversation, I enclose an article from the *Economist*. I find that magazine to be extremely informative and more devoid of ideology than most.

I have read a book by an economist named Jacqueline Kasun of Humboldt [State] University called *The War against Population*. She documents very persuasively that it is impossible to find a correlation between population growth, birth rates, population density, etc., and poverty. In fact, she shows that most of the countries that have experienced the most spectacular economic growth and rise in standard of living have done so while also experiencing very high rates of population growth. She argues that one of the obstacles to economic development in Africa is underpopulation, since there are not enough people to generate the infrastructure of roads needed to promote trade.

No doubt you were aware of the conflict between the U.S. government and John Paul II at the Cairo conference on development. The Pope has rallied Muslim and other underdeveloped nations to resist what they regard as cultural imperialism: an attempt to force Western sexual mores—divorce, premarital sex, illegitimacy, abortion, etc.—on poor nations by tying aid to population control.

I am persuaded by the point of view expressed in this article—government policies are the most potent ingredient in the effort to lift third-world citizens out of poverty. The U.S. should lay off all this population control nonsense and focus on promoting economic development.

April 10, 1995—to Joyce Cunha[45]

Thank you for your card. Madeline McComish had told me that you were asking after me, and she gave me your number. I am grateful for your concern and for your prayers.

I'm interested in your decision to go to divinity school. What is leading you in this direction? I won't pretend to be enthusiastic about Harvard Divinity School—I joke with friends about not being able to decide which institution is more deserving of God's wrathful judgment: the *Boston Globe* or Harvard Divinity School.

My health has remained stable for the past year. I was diagnosed with metastatic breast cancer in December '93. In May '94 I was diagnosed with additional metastasis. I was switched to a different hormonal therapy, underwent radiation, and had a metal pin put in my right thigh (to prevent fracture). Much to my surprise, I have returned to virtually the same state of physical ability I had before I was diagnosed. I was able to hike in the White Mountains last summer (though no one lets me carry a backpack anymore), and I think we will try it again this summer.

None of this changes the fact that metastatic breast cancer is incurable and that I will in all likelihood die within the next year or so. For a Catholic, it is truly a blessing to have almost certain knowledge regarding the imminence of death. I have enjoyed—no, savored—these past two years more than any others of my life. My youngest child, Sophie, is now two years old. She has been among the most enjoyed children in human history. I have to admit the one thing I most frequently regret about my current situation is not having another baby.

[45] A former director of Mass Choice (now NARAL Pro-Choice Massachusetts) and a frequent adversary of Ruth's in abortion debates.

I have almost eliminated committee meetings from my schedule and let only speaking engagements take me away from my family. I have made greater efforts to make our family life peaceful, joyful, fun, and loving. I think I have had some (modest) success.

I do not feel afraid of dying or of being dead. I have to admit that every now and again, I actually look forward to getting out of this fray. If you are given the gift of empathy, you can imagine how painful it must be for us pro-lifers to live in this country. Imagine how frustrating it must be for us to see women viewing their own offspring as adversaries to be destroyed, throwing away the priceless gift God has lavished upon them to love and by whom to be loved. As Mother Teresa says, the greatest evil of abortion is the death of love in those who participate in it. I know those of you who are pro-choice do not see it this way. For you, the fetus is just not an entity to be accounted worth the requisite sacrifice.

Best wishes in your studies and in whatever follows from that. Thank you again for your concern.

June 7, 1995—to Ray Mariano, mayor of Worcester

I meant to write this letter quite some time ago. For all I know, this issue might already be resolved. But in the event that it is still being discussed, I want to pass along this episode which happened with my sons.

A couple of years ago, a good friend of my husband's and mine was sentenced to two and a half years at the Worcester County prison (not for any violent offense—he had peacefully blockaded abortion facilities). On several occasions, my husband took our older children (three boys, grades 2 through 6 at the time) to visit our friend at the jail.

We were a bit taken aback by our boys' response to life in prison. As parents, we set limits on our children with regard to television viewing. They are not allowed to play video games except on the weekend. They all have household chores, and I try to limit their intake of junk food.

Well, when we asked them what they thought of prison life, we were surprised to hear that what impressed them most was that the inmates didn't have to do any work and got to watch TV and videos, play arcade games or basketball, and work out in the gym, and they seemed impressed with the quantity and quality of the food. This was not what we expected, and it certainly wasn't what we wanted—imagine having young boys think that life in prison held a certain appeal!

I write this as a warning that perhaps conditions in West Boylston are not sufficiently awful to have the effect you are looking for. Adults understand the humiliation of being deprived of freedom, but I'm not sure that is so readily apparent to young people.

Rather than require that all students be exposed to the prison, perhaps it would be better to ask principals to make discretionary use of a prison trip for troublemakers. They could evaluate whether such a trip had a beneficial effect on the students.

Thank you for your attention to this matter. I think you are doing a great job and that Worcester is looking up.

July 5, 1995—to Tim Henly

Thanks for your last letter. Naturally, I was delighted with the Republican victories. More than that, I was delighted with the pro-life victories. Not a single incumbent pro-life Democrat was voted out of office. Obviously, the same cannot be said for pro-choice Dems.

I don't actually think of you as a Democrat as much as an anti-Republican. And I'm not so much a Republican as I am an ideological conservative—fiscal, social, defense policy, you name it.

So far I'm a bit perplexed by the presidential race. Phil Gramm strikes me as the obvious continuation of the Reagan revolution. For some reason I don't fully understand, he is not striking other people the same way. Dole seems too prone to compromise. I am of the school of thought that a bona fide revolution is needed to strip down the oversized central government. Such things are extremely difficult to accomplish peacefully, and the leaders of such an effort need a cast iron will and stomach, which Dole has not got.

Mike leaves tomorrow for Oxford University. He'll be there for a month, working out the last fine points of revisions on his book with his publisher. Meanwhile, back on the ranch, I'll be driving boys to end-less Little League all-star games. It's a lot of fun for me, though the girls get frightfully bored by baseball. I end up bringing along Barbie dolls and Pretty Ponies just to keep them distracted. If they stop win-ning, we'll be free to visit people. I'd like to head up to New Hamp-shire to see Emil and Elaine, but I'd also like the kids to see their grandparents. Unfortunately, we're talking three hours' travel in oppo-site directions. Maybe the boys will have a great season and settle the issue by keeping me chauffeuring 'til Mike gets back. Then we're head-ing up to the White Mountains, where we've gone for the past six years.

I just started reading some of P. J. O'Rourke's books. Even though he considers himself a conservative, I think you'd enjoy his books.

February 13, 1996—to Pamela McBride

I know June has told you about me. I apologize it has taken so long for me to write to you.

June told me you decided to remain in Thailand for your chemother-apy. My initial reaction was that you would be better served here, but after hearing more of the details, you were right to proceed as you have.

Chemo affects people very differently. I was never seriously sick from it, though I did get sick to my stomach for a day or two after each treatment. And I felt vaguely nauseous all the time. But what was more difficult for me was the toll it took on my psyche. I have never been a worrier, never subject to much anxiety or depression. But while I was on chemo, I would experience dramatic panic attacks: I'd be sitting comfortably on the sofa, and suddenly, my heart would start pounding, adrenalin would flow, and I would experience all the symp-toms of total terror. I would try to dispel the symptoms by telling myself there was nothing to fear, but it wouldn't work.

I'm confident that this was not suppressed fear of mortality. It was just a side effect of the chemo. And it went away within weeks of the end of my treatment. That is the aspect of my experience I most want to convey to you: life after chemo is great. No matter how sick, tired, and depressed you feel during it, you will return to feeling like your-self when it is over. I think some people begin to think that the way they feel on chemo is a result of the cancer, but it isn't. It really is just the chemo itself.

God willing, you will be among the thousands of women who are cured by chemo. The odds are with you. But another difficult aspect of breast cancer is the fact that you cannot know whether you are cured or not. This was resolved for me two years ago when I was diagnosed with metastatic disease. But that period of uncertainty was still a good time—it helped me become much more abandoned to God's will. Now, oddly enough, I am happier than I have ever been in my life. I have been blessed with two years of strength and continued normal health, despite the metastatic disease. Since I know it is almost certain (leaving always the possibility of something inexplicable or mirac-ulous) that I will die in the next couple of years, I have been able to savor every aspect of life (even some drudgery appears charming when you consider you won't be doing it for much longer).

I trust you will also find this experience brings you closer to God, trusting His sometimes inscrutable wisdom to bring blessings out of suffering. I would be happy to be of help, if there is anything I can do, besides praying for you and your family.

February 17, 1996—to Bishop Daniel P. Reilly, Diocese of Worcester

Marilyn Scola heads up the local Christian Coalition chapter. She has been a friend and ally of mine in pro-life activities for the past several years. Marilyn would like the opportunity to meet with you in order to promote clear communication and cooperation between Christian Coalition and the Worcester diocese.

With the emergence of the Catholic Alliance,[46] some misunderstand-ings and potential tensions have arisen between Christian Coalition and the Catholic community. Marilyn wants to answer any questions

[46] The "Catholic Alliance" was a Catholic branch of the Christian Coalition founded in late 1995 by Pat Robertson.

you might have about how Christian Coalition operates and what its mission is.

There are several good reasons to desire this kind of open communication and cooperation. You no doubt are aware that one of Christian Coalition's primary activities is the distribution of voter guides (see enclosure). While not perfect, they are a valuable resource. It is immediately obvious that they are much more simplistic than the NCCB's [National Conference of Catholic Bishops'] pamphlet for voter information. That has its advantages as well as its drawbacks.

Marilyn would like to be able to offer these voter guides at Catholic parishes. She would like to be able to say that you have no objection to such distribution (without implying any endorsement of Christian Coalition's platform or of any individual candidate).

More importantly, Christian Coalition will be developing a candidate survey to be used in the upcoming state representative and state senate races in November. They are free to use questions of local importance for these races. Would you be willing to appoint a representative from the diocese to assist in the formulation, distribution, and reporting of such a questionnaire? A united effort by Christians of various denominations could be very effective.

I am not myself actively involved in Christian Coalition or Catholic Alliance. I have acted more as a liaison between Christian Coalition and CMCFL [Central Massachusetts Citizens for Life]. I am impressed by the industriousness of the Coalition's membership. This is an up-and-coming movement with the potential to do great good. I hope you will be interested in meeting Marilyn Scola and paving the way for a good working relationship.

February 18, 1996—to Pamela McBride

I'm happy to answer any questions you have and in general just share what my experience with chemo was. I know it helped me a lot to talk with another woman who was the friend of a friend who had gone through mastectomy and chemo. By the way, she is still cancer-free, six years after the fact! And she had another baby (at forty-four!)

and managed to breast-feed him with the one breast. He is adorable and healthy.

I did not live a totally normal life on chemo. I spent a lot of time thinking and praying and reading. I did try to force myself to keep some normal things, even though I felt overwhelmed. For instance, I continued to give pro-life presentations at high schools. It was difficult, but I always was glad after the fact. Dropping the baby off at a sitter and getting dressed up and getting out of the house early in the morning often seemed impossible the night before, but I would just keep plugging away, and I found I was able to do it.

Catholic spirituality emphasizes "offering up" our sufferings. That can sound a little pie in the sky, but I found it very helpful. Jesus came from heaven to share our life. He even wanted to share our experience of pain, fear, loneliness, suffering, etc. When we experience these unpleasant things, it is helpful to think about Jesus alone in Gethsemane or in agony on the cross. We want to be like Him, we want to share His suffering with Him, to keep Him company, not falling asleep like Peter, James, and John. He will accept our patient endurance of trials and turn them into glory, like His Resurrection.

How to deal with the children is different. I never wanted my children to think that I was happy about the prospect of dying and leaving them alone. It is a difficult balance to strike—I do not know that I have gotten it right. But we talk a lot about heaven. My fifth child died of SIDS, so we are already accustomed to thinking about family members who are in heaven. I want my children to know that I trust God to arrange things for the best, even if it doesn't appear that way to us. My grandmother's mother died when she was nine. My mother's father died when she was seven, so I know children grow up OK even without a parent. It is sad and difficult, but not impossible.

But you are still in the category of women with a high likelihood of cure. So while it is good to think through the worst-case scenario, you have excellent reasons to focus on the hope that when chemo is over, you will be finished with this for good.

As for hair, I got a wig before my hair fell out. It all fell out quite abruptly over the span of a day or two about three weeks into chemo.

I was given doxyrubicon (Adriomyacin—I can't spell any of these things) the first time.[47] It was the most difficult drug. I am on chemo now, but it is a different combination, and so far (three treatments) my hair is OK and the nausea is minimal.

I hated each approaching chemo treatment, but I focused on how many were left to go. I resigned myself to getting sick for several days and kept looking forward to the last treatment.

You are in my prayers.

April 6, 1996—to Larry Weller

Oh, shame, shame, shame be heaped upon my guilty head. I foresaw your birthday coming, I was thinking of it on the day, I even called, but your Wagnerian message did not kick in. But I refused to mail a card until I had at least a disjointed note (alias, this) to enclose.

I hope you are well and enjoying this spring weather. Usually, spring is just cold, wet, and muddy up here, but we have had day after day of sunny weather in the fifties. Perfect spring weather (minus leaves and flowers—those have yet to emerge).

Meanwhile, I feel just great. Isn't that odd? I read today that there's a new cancer treatment getting ready for human trials that had remarkable effects on rats. Here I went and got so resigned to the idea that I was going to die shortly, and now I have to consider that I may most likely live into my forties. It's almost embarrassing.

I have been searching for my copy of *Ivanhoe*. I loved that book, but my memories are muddled. Right now I am reading David Donald's biography of Lincoln. My admiration for that man just continues to grow as the years go by.

We just bought young Michael a better trumpet. He still insists that he hates the trumpet, but he's losing credibility. He actually wants us to come to the high school spring concert because they are doing a couple of jazz pieces and he has some prominent solos.

[47] The reference is to doxorubicin, manufactured under the trademark Adriamycin.

We carried the telescope out onto the sidewalk last night to watch the eclipse. I kept trying to enter into the supposed terror felt by primitive peoples at the sight of an eclipse, but it didn't even seem a little spooky to me—just interesting. I wonder whether pre-scientific human beings spent a lot of time being frightened, since they had plausible explanations for so few things, or whether they just got used to it.

June 24, 1996—to Helen Alvare, the NCCB Spokesperson for Pro-Life Issues

In response to our phone conversation earlier today, I am writing a description of my experience with pregnancy following diagnosis of and treatment for breast cancer.

I was diagnosed in September 1991 with breast cancer. A mastectomy was performed, and two lymph nodes were found to contain one-centimeter tumors. Following the surgery, I underwent chemotherapy.

There was at the time of initial diagnosis no evidence of metastasis. I read every article I was able to procure regarding the likely outcome, and I understood that there was, in spite of the chemotherapy, still between a 50% and 75% chance that the cancer would recur.

The literature regarding pregnancy after breast cancer is somewhat limited, but it seemed to me (and my oncologist confirmed) that the likelihood of metastasis did not appear to be related to pregnancy. In other words, if metastasis was going to occur, it would do so whether or not I conceived and bore another child.

My husband and I decided that it would be better to live life with the hope that my cancer would not recur rather than cowering in fear. Even if my life were to be cut short by recurring cancer, we felt it would be a beautiful thing to give life to more children. Our daughter Anna Sophia was born April 16, 1993. As with my six previous pregnancies, all went well, and she was born healthy and at term.

In the fall of 1993, I was diagnosed with breast cancer that had metastasized to the bone. I began hormone therapy. I have had two rounds of radiation treatment, one additional course of chemotherapy, and

175

am currently on a third hormone therapy. My daughter is three years old.

I will almost certainly die of breast cancer in the next few years, as there is no cure for metastatic disease at this point in time. But, as I said before, there is no evidence to indicate that carrying Sophie caused the recurrence of my cancer. It pains me to think of women who have killed their unborn children in a vain attempt to preserve their own lives, only to find that they develop metastatic disease and die anyway. How much easier it is to face death with a clean conscience.

It is impossible to imagine why a physician would claim that a partial-birth abortion is necessary to save the life of a woman who had a medical history similar to mine. Even if a physician thought an abortion would enhance the woman's chances of survival (a belief not grounded in evidence), it is impossible to explain why the partial-birth abortion procedure should be preferred to another less cruel and gruesome method.

I hope this information may help increase support for a ban of partial-birth abortions.

May 9, 1997—to Bishop Reilly

I recently had a disturbing experience which I want to bring to your attention. In a meeting where two excellent priests of the Worcester diocese were present, I made this statement: "The magisterial teaching authority of the Church is preserved from error—that is, it is infallible—when teaching on matters of faith and morals."

I was stunned when both priests insisted that the Church has *never taught infallibly* on any matter of morality, but only on matters of the faith. I spent at least ten minutes restating what I understood to be the truth, and there is absolutely no doubt that both of them were convinced that the Church has never taught infallibly on any matter of morality. They insisted that this is what they were taught in seminary.

I made the distinction between those doctrines taught *ex cathedra* (of which we all agreed there were only two, the Marian doctrines) [and those not taught *ex cathedra* but infallible nonetheless]. I cited as two other sources of infallible teaching the texts of ecumenical councils as well as the ordinary Magisterium.

The priests granted that all three of these were sources of infallible teaching in the Church, but they were still of the opinion that no statement regarding the moral law fell into these categories. I cited the passage from *Gaudium et Spes* where abortion is listed along with numerous other crimes. They were not familiar with this passage (paragraph 27, where abortion, among other things, is condemned as an "offense against life itself" and "against the honor of the Creator"). I referred to the *Catechism*. They were not familiar with paragraph 2035, which clearly states that the Church's teaching authority extends over both matters of faith and morals.

I have been quite agitated about this exchange since it revealed a level of ignorance or miseducation that cuts very close to the heart of what is essential to Catholic belief. Which brings me to a request. Father [Richard] McBrien's recent article in the *Free Press* (regarding the appointment of Bishop Francis George to Chicago) ridicules the idea that what the Church teaches regarding matters of divine revelation is as true and binding as what the Church teaches regarding morality.

Now this is just one more in a long series of heretical opinions expressed by Father McBrien over the years. But this column riled me because of its proximity to the above-described experience. Ignorance, confusion, and rejection of authentic authority are wreaking havoc in the Church. I cannot understand why a writer who distorts, misrepresents, and undermines the legitimate teaching of the Church should be published by the diocesan paper.

It also seems to me that the competent authority (which appears to be you) should figure out why two priests who view themselves as orthodox and loyal to the Church should nevertheless be misinformed on what ought to be an elementary matter of Catholic belief.

Thank you for all the good work you have already accomplished in this diocese. I should thank you principally for having the wisdom, audacity, or inspiration (I'm not sure which word best applies) to appoint Father [Richard F.] Reidy as rector at the cathedral. The diocese could use a few more similarly intelligent, orthodox, energetic, and prayerful priests. I'd be happy to know you were praying for one of my sons to help in this matter.

October 12, 1997—to Larry Weller

Thanks for the autumn letter. Yes, the address works (it's the correspondent who is unreliable).

The western views have been beautiful since we moved in here, last December.[48] It seemed to me the summer sunsets this year were uncommonly gorgeous. This summer was much too short, though, and I have not been able to rise to the usual level of anticipatory excitement at the early morning chill in the air or the autumn aroma of whatever it is—damp leaves, wood smoke, etc. I feel a bit of dismay as I note how far, far south the sun's point of contact on the horizon has fallen.

Yes, it was awfully nice to see everyone. I hope there are more opportunities for similar gatherings.

Speaking of which, we are planning to bring our church youth group down to New York the day after Thanksgiving and stay 'til Sunday morning. One idea is to take them to see a Broadway musical. Do you have anything to recommend? Would Kenty? Remember, it's a church group. I want to steer clear of decadent and depraved. As a mother, I would never have given permission to myself (as a teen) to see some of the things we saw. But I think every American kid should have the opportunity to be totally bowled over by a glitzy Broadway show. I think we will also do the Statue of Liberty, Ellis Island, perhaps the World Trade Towers (Center—what's it called?). I also mentioned the Cloisters as a possibility. An early Mass at Saint Patrick's, then I think we're off to West Point Sunday afternoon. Can you improve upon these suggestions? You always knew New York better than I.

Maria has been bitten by the musical bug. She has taken to playing my CD of *Lost in the Stars*. I find it impressive that she likes the music well enough to listen repeatedly. Typically, kids her age only listen to shows they have seen. It makes me reflect upon how much I benefited from knowing you and your family. And here is my daughter,

[48] Ruth and her family moved to 17 Beechmont Street in Worcester in late 1996.

memorizing the lyrics to a show that no one else her age has ever even heard of, thanks to the Wellers.

Maria has a lovely singing voice. Today, I tried to teach her and her friends "Now I Walk in Beauty". As usual, I'm a little vague remembering the lyrics. Is it before, behind, above, beside? It makes me ashamed that I cannot remember clearly something we sang so many times.

Not a lot to report on the music front. On November 2, we will be singing a Duruflé Mass, as an actual Mass. That should be interesting. We were going to do the music more as a concert, but I suggested that we do it the way it was composed to be sung—as part of an actual Mass. I don't see why the faithful of this age should have to settle for short, wimpy little Masses with guitars or a few hymns when people of earlier generations were able to hear these glorious choral Masses.

The Cancer Spreads

February 20, 1998—to Larry Weller

I had a great time in Washington at the March for Life. I resolved as one of the first goals of my new job to get more high-school-aged kids to go to the March from the Worcester diocese. In the past, we have never sent more than three buses to the March. I managed to fill five buses. Boy, was I pleased with myself over that! The kids all had a great time.

Unfortunately, I had started a new chemo treatment just a week before the March. I have had such good luck with chemo treatments to date that it never occurred to me that I might have an adverse reaction to this one, but that's just what happened. One rare but predictable complication of chemo is that it drives your white blood cell count down dangerously low. This usually happens about a week after the chemo. Lucky for me, it happened after the March was over, after I had waved good-bye to the buses returning to Massachusetts and had made my way by Metro to a friend's house in Bethesda where I planned to stay for the weekend. Mike was driving down with the rest of the family to make a long weekend of it. Anyway, no sooner had we finished dinner than I found I couldn't breathe well, I had developed a fever, and my lungs were killing me. They had to take me to the ER, where it turned out I had pneumonia and my white blood cell count was down to 1.3 (it should be around 8 or 9). So I spent the rest of the weekend in Suburban Hospital in Bethesda. But I feel fine now. I've switched to a different chemo which agrees with me.

The bad news is the cancer has spread to my liver. I think that means I am pretty much a goner in the next year or so. Not that that comes as any great surprise. What is surprising is that my health has been so good for so long. I was skiing in New Hampshire last week. Very odd.

We will likely be in Norwood on Saturday, March 21. Is there any chance of a visit? We may arrive Friday evening. I have to be back by Sunday evening. Let me know if you have some free time then.

March 30, 1998—to Edward Fitzsimmons[49]

I have tried and I have failed. Repeatedly. I simply cannot record a letter on a tape cassette. For a while, I tried carrying around a little portable tape recorder. In odd moments, I would start chatting away into it, telling you news and responding to what you had said, but I would get interrupted so often that I would lose my train of thought and have to rewind and play back, doing this so many times that I inadvertently erased bits and pieces of the letter. Anyway—I give up. I cannot do better than another typed letter, which Marcella will have to try as best she can to decipher.

You have gotten my age a little wrong. I was born in 1957, making me a venerable forty-one this year. My class graduated from NVOT in '75. My son Michael was born in '81; he is now sixteen. Max turns fifteen this summer, John Henry is twelve, Maria is ten, Sarah is seven,

---

[49] Ruth's favorite teacher from high school, her senior-year English teacher. Edward had to retire after becoming almost blind from macular degeneration. He married a much younger woman from the Czech Republic and immigrated in retirement to Ostrava. The correspondence Ruth reestablished with "Fitz" in her final months gave her great consolation.

and Sophie will turn five in April. All three boys are musicians and athletes; two are good students (Michael is dead average in that department). The girls appear to be smart enough, though it's early to say. Maria is extremely pretty. Her face is similar to mine as a girl, but she has a much more open, smooth countenance (like Catherine Deneuve). Her eyes are truly enormous and round, unlike my squinty little slit eyes. And her eyes are an absolute true green, startling to see. Unfortunately, she tends to be a bit ditsy. I am trying to stamp out frivolous, idiotic girlish behavior and develop those personality traits in her that correspond to her unusual beauty. She also has a very graceful body.

Sarah, on the other hand, takes after her Polish grandmother, Mike's mom. She is very big and very solid. She has a personality and energy level to match—she is irrepressible. She is very affectionate and loving. Sophie is more like Maria, with similarly enormous, round eyes, though hers are blue. She has full, Slavic lips and a somewhat more exotic look than Maria's open, symmetrical, serene face.

I keep in touch with several of the gang from NVOT, most regularly with Larry Weller. He lives in Cranford, New Jersey. His mother sold the house in Old Tappan and lives near Sally and husband (a theater professor at Rutgers, I believe) and their adopted son, Geoffrey. Fran is still living in God-forsaken Nebraska. She also adopted a son, an Indian who apparently suffers from fetal alcohol syndrome. It sounds as if Kay is slipping into deep depression, taking little interest in the boy (Joel), Fran, or life in general. It doesn't sound good for the boy.

Larry is still singing in various choirs in New York City and New Jersey. He still works for Woodward-Clyde, traipsing around in tunnels and digging under bedrock. Larry, Russell, Emil, and I were all at a surprise birthday party for Tim Henly this past August. It was a lot of fun. We were a little surprised not to see Steve Patricola, who also stays in touch with various members of that group. But Steve and his wife recently adopted a baby boy and perhaps are still getting used to the rather different lifestyle of parenthood.

Yes, my eldest, Michael, now resists many family activities. He would far rather hang around with his friends than spend time with all of us. But my strategy has been to include their friends in what we do. We have moved to a much larger house, still in Worcester. It has a swimming pool. There is a rec room in the basement with a Ping-Pong table. So Michael's friends spend a fair bit of time here, which I like. Max seems to enjoy our company. He loves to talk to adults and seeks out conversation with me. My sister, Karen, lives in Boston. Max is very fond of her and spends overnight visits regularly. Karen is in law school, and Max finds legal argumentation very interesting.

I now work part time for the Pro-Life Office of the diocese. I go to speak at Catholic schools and to CCD classes in parishes. I enjoy this kind of public speaking very much. I also teach the confirmation class in my own parish. In fact, I am the director of religious education for my parish, which also happens to be the cathedral parish. I help run the high school youth group. I sing in the choir. It is a very nice parish with a great bunch of families. Our friends are similarly educated and interested in political, religious, and cultural issues. We have a monthly book discussion group. This month we read Richard Weaver's *Ideas Have Consequences*. Last month we read "The Hound of Heaven" and some poetry by George Herbert. We read Graham Greene's *The End of the Affair*, a great book, I think his best. Have you read it?

My cancer grinds inexorably on. It has spread to my lungs and liver. I am going to be on one form of chemotherapy or another for the rest of my life, which in all likelihood will not be that much longer. I don't complain, though. I have had a great life. I have known wonderful people; I have done interesting things. I have had many gifts and talents that made life lots of fun (singing, acting, public speaking, etc.). My husband is great. My kids are great. And I really believe the Catholic faith. This life is short, and it is merely the qualifying exam for the real thing.

I regret that I have not written regularly to you. Your friendship has been a great source of happiness. Now that I have completely given up the idea of trying to use the tape machine, I will try to correspond more regularly. I wish I could correspond in the way you find more enjoyable, but this will have to suffice (perhaps when I am confined to bed I shall master the taped letter).

March 30, 1998—to Laura Garcia[50]

Thanks so much for your letter. I hope Jorge's plane ultimately did arrive. (Unlike a plane Mike and I once went to meet to pick up a friend—after hours of waiting for the delayed plane, we found he wasn't on it after all because we had written down the wrong date. We picked him up the next day.)

I just had a CAT scan today. In a day or two I'll know the results. I think they could be dire. My doctor is looking to see whether the chemo I'm currently on has shrunk the tumor in my liver. If it hasn't, I think it means that she'll be looking for yet another chemo to switch me to. But I think the number of as-yet-unused chemo [drugs] is running low.

Then again, if it has shrunk the tumor, I think I'll be doing OK for a stretch. I told Michael I'd get a new pair of contact lenses in the latter case, since the ones I'm wearing now are ridiculously old and I simply can't see properly.

The weather here has been extraordinary. Last week, we had a snowstorm. We had to call off CCD classes. This weekend, the temperature hit eighty-eight, and we have had four days in a row like the most beautiful days of midsummer. Everyone has been ecstatic—it's amazing what this kind of weather does to people's moods.

I've been alternating between deep, painful unhappiness and a kind of serene joy. I try to remember that I should be glad of the opportunities to unite my sufferings with Christ. Then, when I actually feel miserable, this all goes right out the window. It's tedious.

Another odd thing is that for many years, it seemed to me as if I experienced very few emotions, all within a pretty reasonable range of intensity. There was the happiness caused by the children. There was exasperation when Michael was difficult, and contentment when things with him seemed on an even keel, and that was about it. Now, it seems to me my emotions utterly dominate my perception of reality.

[50] Laura Garcia is a philosophy professor at Boston College and was a frequent collaborator with Ruth at pro-life and pro-woman events.

This must be menopause.[51] It's interesting, occasionally pleasant, often horrible.

I'm loving my part-time job in the Pro-Life Office. What a trip it is to dream up schemes and then actually be able to pull them off. We moved the annual pro-life Mass to the feast of the Annunciation, invited the Catholic schools to send kids, and invited all the parish pro-life reps and priests—we had a full cathedral, and it was a great event.

I am looking forward to seeing you. I keep you in my prayers.

April 28, 1998—to Edward Fitzsimmons

I am using larger type and double spacing this letter. I hope that makes it easier for you to read. If this fails, perhaps I could try writing phonetically (I'm sure my attempts would be a source of amusement).

My cancer is getting worse. I don't realistically expect to live even a year more. Things could deteriorate very quickly; it's in my liver, and once it interferes with liver function, there's very little that can be done.

I am not afraid to die—not by a long shot. I go beyond just accepting what the Catholic Church teaches. Ever since I knew I had incurable cancer, I have thought long and hard about how I live my life and what I think death means. I have loved the life God gave me. There's no other life I would rather have lived. But I recognize God as the author of this life, as well as the author of the lives of all the people I love and the world, which is so beautiful and interesting. I want to see God; I want to see the One who thought all of this up. I cannot imagine that He will be less interesting and beautiful than all of the things He has made. And of course, I hope to see all the best people in heaven, anyway, even you, to whom I (and so many others) owe so much. This life is short. Eternity is—well, it's eternal.

I just finished reading *Silas Marner* by George Eliot. Somehow I missed reading that one before. I quite liked it. I liked it better than *Middlemarch*; that heroine struck me as a bit of an idiot.

[51] The chemotherapy Ruth was undergoing attacked her ovaries and produced early menopause.

I recently served as godmother to a young girl received into the Church. She is very bright and eager to learn. She had never heard of *Jane Eyre*. I recommended it as the best book on marriage ever written. It was deeply gratifying to hear her gush with enthusiasm for the book. Why don't high schools require good books? It's so much easier to get kids to like a book that is actually worth reading.

I am composing this letter at our computer desk on the second floor of the house. The window in front of the desk faces due west. It is a gorgeous spring afternoon—the sky is deep blue; the grass, illuminated by the long, slanting rays of late afternoon in northern latitudes, looks impossibly green. We have a large built-in pool—the kids are skimming the pool, eagerly awaiting temperatures high enough to make swimming possible. Worcester is bordered by hills to the west. From this window, even though we are in the heart of the city, we can see barely any houses—just tree-covered hills. It's very lovely.

I well remember seeing *Lion in Winter* for the first time. I've never read the play, but I've seen the movie two or three times. It is quite good. But with my religious proclivities, I much prefer *A Man for All Seasons*. Saint Thomas More is, of course, one of my great heroes. So excellent in learning, intelligence, in his professional and political ambitions, yet a man of integrity. I admire that kind of courage and virtue more than the radical, otherworldly virtue of a Saint Francis. Perhaps I shouldn't say I admire it more—just that it is more the kind of virtue I think a secular person should strive to imitate.

Our next-door neighbor's eldest daughter is finishing her first year at Providence College. She is quite happy there. We also have a philosopher friend who teaches there: Steven Swartz.[52] I've been there to give pro-life presentations two or three times—I am always impressed by the atmosphere of more or less happy, well-adjusted students who seem interested in learning. We are hoping our son Michael gets admitted there. He's not academically very strong, but he is an excellent musician and very good at sports. We are hoping something like that will help.

[52] A small confusion: Stephen Swartz was at the University of Rhode Island. However, we had a good friend in philosophy at Providence College, Philip Devine.

185

My birthday is March 19, close to your daughter's. My claim to fame is that my birthday is Saint Joseph's Day. I have always been devoted to that saint of the ordinary working person.

Yes, you were rather prescient when it came to our conversion to the Roman Catholic Church.[53] Of course, now that I am a Catholic, I think anyone who seriously reads history and who wants to join the church actually founded by Jesus of Nazareth would simply have to become Catholic. The Protestants have an utterly ahistorical view of reality. I have read just about every encyclical and apostolic exhortation written by John Paul II. I am very devoted to his intellectual and theological views.

May 22, 1998

Well, I got interrupted, and here it is—weeks later. That is fairly typical. It is Memorial Day weekend. My father is visiting. I have stopped working for the diocese. My health got very bad in early May: I could barely breathe at all. Had things continued, the next step was going to be to give me bottled oxygen with tubes up my nose. What a horrible prospect! I think quite literally I would rather die than walk around looking like some alien out of a [Steven] Spielberg movie. However, I also rather grimly suspect that once true oxygen deprivation sets in, you lose all consideration for matters of vanity and will do almost anything in order to be able to breathe.

Anyway, my oncologist started me on yet another chemotherapy, and—voila! In two weeks I was running up and down stairs again, as good as ever. It was a most dramatic turnaround. However, this too will pass. The cancer gets increasingly good at mutating to resist any given chemo.

Not wanting to seem maudlin, but this could be my farewell letter. I hope not, but just in case, let me thank you for your great friendship and for the world of literature and culture you encouraged me to

[53] Fitz made this prediction soon after Ruth and I were engaged, when Ruth introduced me to him.

186

know and love. Though I have been a very poor correspondent, you have been daily in my thoughts and prayers.

Naturally, I hope you will manage to return to the faith of your baptism. Really, what else could be true? There is no God at all? There is a God, but He hasn't bothered to communicate with us? There is a God, and He has communicated with us, but we don't know whether it was through Buddha, Mohammed, Jesus, someone else, or all of the above? The last possibility seems much more likely than the first two. Then it is a matter of figuring out which of the great religions actually seems to be most likely to be the true communication of God to man. I have no doubt that if you were to turn your considerable intellectual powers to this question, it would only be a matter of time before you realized there is no explanation for the Catholic Church's existence except that, in fact, the guy named Jesus from Nazareth really did die and His corpse really did rise from the dead and He really did walk around talking to those rather uninspiring eleven who somehow, after this experience, transformed the course of human history. And for the better.

Well, thanks again and farewell.

May 3, 1998—to Bishop Reilly

I have grown accustomed over the years to having my views dismissed as those of a "conservative Catholic" or even a "pre–Vatican II Catholic" (though, before Vatican II, I was a Presbyterian). But I have never before been dismissed as "Amish".

A successful bishop must possess the skills of a diplomat. You seem by temperament to be a pleasant and non-confrontational person. I am by temperament a controversialist, and I enjoy argument as a means of discovering the truth of a matter. So I will not attempt to express my opinion of the clergy conference at Blessed Sacrament in diplomatic terms; rather, I will state as clearly and straightforwardly as I can the principal errors expressed during the course of the evening and why it is (in my opinion) important to clarify these matters for all those who were present.

Dr. Thomasma[54] was presented as a reliable authority on ethical questions regarding fertility treatments and related matters. Since the target audience was priests, deacons, and pastoral ministers, it seems the presentation was intended to help them understand these issues in the context of what the Catholic Church teaches.

Instead, Dr. Thomasma started with the assumption that it was "Amish" to accept what even he identified as the straightforward teaching of the Church regarding in vitro fertilization. He proceeded to articulate during the course of his presentation many, many positions that are flagrantly contrary to authoritative Church teaching. During the discussion period, more erroneous statements were made. Not a single one of these erroneous statements was directly questioned, except by me. I think it is clear that the majority of those who attended left the presentation convinced that Dr. Thomasma had articulated a point of view that is consistent with Catholic teaching.

I have three sons. I experience serious reservations when praying for any of them to have a vocation to the diocesan priesthood. This is because I believe it is easier to pursue sanctity in the lay state than in holy orders, given the (poor) quality of seminary education, spiritual direction of priests, and continuing priestly formation. My experience at Blessed Sacrament increased the level of this concern. The priests of this diocese are misinformed on many points of Catholic moral teaching, and they are in turn misinforming the faithful on these points. I recognize that this statement sounds rather impertinent and arrogant. It is, nevertheless, true.

I am not capable of recording every erroneous statement made during the presentation on April 28. I have noted the most egregious errors, cited who said them, and commented [at the end of this letter]. I would enjoy the opportunity to discuss any or all of these points further with any interested persons. I am very keen on dialogue and (as you saw) not in the least reluctant to express what I understand to be true.

[54] The diocese had invited a bioethicist named David Thomasma to be the keynote speaker at the conference mentioned. Ruth attended, in her office as pro-life director. Questions she raised from the floor during discussion were dealt with dismissively by Thomasma.

188

I pray for you each day. Thank you for the wonderful things you have already done for this diocese. God grant you many years of similarly fruitful service.

"Moral truths cannot be known with certainty."

At several points during the course of the question-and-answer period, Dr. Thomasma asserted that moral truths cannot be known to be true absolutely. He even went so far as to claim that the deliberate killing of an innocent child could be viewed as a moral act if done to prevent the capture or likely death of other innocent people (the smothered crying child example and the scenario from the movie *Sophie's Choice*).

This point of view is wrong and is condemned as wrong in *Veritatis Splendor*. It is explicitly rejected in the *Catechism of the Catholic Church*. I attach tremendous seriousness to the articulation (unchallenged except by me) of this erroneous view by a man brought in by a diocesan committee to educate diocesan priests because I know by experience that many of your priests were taught this false view in seminary and still think it is true.

The Church is the infallible and authoritative teacher of both doctrinal and moral truths. Your priests need to have this point clarified. Moral truths can be known with certainty. The faithful are obliged to accept as authoritative those moral truths proposed to them infallibly by the Church's legitimate authorities. The Church's teaching about taking human life clearly falls into this category of infallible teaching.

(*Catechism of the Catholic Church*, no. 2035: "The supreme degree of participation in the authority of Christ is ensured by the charism of *infallibility*. This infallibility extends as far as does the deposit of divine Revelation; it also extends to all those elements of doctrine, including morals, without which the saving truths of the faith cannot be preserved, explained, or observed.")

"The Church does not teach authoritatively that in vitro fertilization is immoral."

Dr. Thomasma began his presentation by saying someone is "Amish" if he believes that what the Church teaches as true, is in fact, true.

My reading of *Donum Vitae* was characterized as "conservative", as if it were still a question open to debate whether in vitro fertilization violates the Church's tradition that every marriage act must express both the unitive and procreative meaning of the act.

Dr. Thomasma said, "I am unable to understand why in vitro fertilization cannot be viewed as complying with the Church's teaching on the necessary integrity of the unitive and procreative aspects of the marriage act." It is true: he appears not to understand it. That does not mean the teaching is not true. Nor does it mean that the teaching is not authoritative, requiring the assent of the faithful. Dr. Thomasma was dismissive of the authoritative weight of *Donum Vitae*. However, *Donum Vitae* is cited as the relevant text in the *Catechism of the Catholic Church*. If we are to accept the *Catechism's* teaching on the death penalty, why are we not similarly expected to accept the teaching on in vitro fertilization?

(*Catechism of the Catholic Church*, no. 2377: "Techniques involving only the married couple ... remain morally unacceptable. They dissociate the sexual act from the procreative act.")

> *"If the marriage viewed as a totality is 'unitive and procreative', an individual act of conception in a petri dish need not be viewed as morally wrong."*

Father B. articulated this point of view. This is precisely the argument that was raised and rejected with regard to the use of contraception in *Humanae Vitae*. It seems logically necessary that the argument applies with equal force to artificial means of conception. "To justify conjugal acts made intentionally infecund, one cannot invoke as valid reasons the lesser evil, or the fact that such acts would constitute a whole together with the fecund acts already performed or to follow later, and hence would share in one and the same moral goodness. In truth, if it is sometimes licit to tolerate a lesser evil in order to avoid a greater evil or to promote a greater good, it is not licit, even for the gravest reasons, to do evil so that good may follow therefrom." [55]

This is a serious error. The faithful are being misled by their priests into believing that in vitro fertilization is morally acceptable if their

---

[55] Paul VI, *Humanae Vitae*, 14.

intentions are good. Priests are putting themselves in serious supernatural danger by giving this advice.

"Manipulating body parts to repair, damage, or cure disease is morally right; therefore, it cannot be intrinsically wrong to manipulate gametes to conceive human life."

Dr. Thomasma articulated this position as a response to my point distinguishing between using technology to serve already existing human life and using technology to produce human life. Dr. Thomasma never explained why he did not view this distinction as persuasive. He continued to assume that no Catholic was bound to accept the Church's teaching that in vitro fertilization is wrong because it treats the human being as a commodity produced by the will of human beings rather than [as a new creature resulting from] the loving cooperation of spouses with God's plan for life. This position of Dr. Thomasma was not challenged (except by me) or corrected.

"Such fertilization entrusts the life and identity of the embryo into the power of doctors and biologists and establishes the domination of technology over the origin and destiny of the human person. Such a relation of domination is in itself contrary to the dignity and equality that must be common to parents and children." [56]

"The Church can dispense the faithful from the requirements of the moral law."

One priest (I think it was Father H.) said words to this effect: the beauty of the Catholic Church is that it articulates ideal moral principles but grants dispensations to those unable to comply with the law. A dispensation can be granted for something that is a matter of discipline, but the Church cannot dispense anyone from the moral law. Either Father H. does not understand that dispensations do not apply to the moral law, or he does not understand that the Church teaches that in vitro fertilization is morally wrong. But his statement was left unchallenged and uncorrected.

[56] Congregation for the Doctrine of the Faith, *Donum Vitae*, II.5.

"Conception is not the point at which the life of an individual human being begins."

Dr. Thomasma claimed that it did not make sense to view conception as the beginning of the life of an individual human person. He asserted that this ambiguous status of the pre-implantation conceptus arises from the fact that each cell in these early stages can be manipulated to produce a genetic twin.

First, that genetic manipulation is capable of producing a genetic twin does not imply that the original entity from which the cell is taken is not correctly viewed as an individual. Most likely, human cloning will occur [in the future]: that a cell from a human adult can be manipulated to produce a genetic twin of the entity from which the cell was taken will not imply that the adult was not an individual human being.

Second, such genetic manipulation can only occur if one has already resorted to in vitro fertilization in the first place. No one can manipulate developing human life in the Fallopian tubes. The Church has taught with perfect clarity and consistency that the conceptus is to be treated with the respect due to human life from conception. Dr. Thomasma was trying to come up with a way to view experimentation on early embryos as morally permissible, as long as it is done before the cells lose this ability to produce a complete individual, if manipulated to do so. This is utterly incompatible with Church teaching. This view was not challenged (except by me).

July 3, 1998—to Clare Fitts

It has been a very long time since I received your letter about your mother's death. What can I say? It seems to take a year or two for me to get around to replying to letters.

I appreciated your letter very much. And I appreciate all your prayers. My situation continues to be pretty grim, despite the fact I still look and act perfectly healthy. The cancer has spread to both lungs and to my liver. In late April, I was having trouble breathing—I thought the jig was up. But my oncologist switched me to a new chemo, and within two weeks, I was feeling as good as new. How odd! Now

I seem to be gradually losing ground again. I am hoping to be accepted for a clinical trial of a drug called Herceptin. The trial is being conducted at Beth Israel [Deaconess Medical Center]. There is a lottery for women like me—the next lottery drawing will be July 31.

I am not afraid to die. In many ways, I am sincerely looking forward to it. But there is still a lot of worthwhile stuff for me to do here, so either way, I am content that God has the best idea. Sophie is already five—I remember when the one thing I hoped for was that I would live long enough for her to have a clear memory of me. God has been very good to me.

I wish I saw Jennifer and Eric more often. During this past academic year, Sophie was in preschool from 8:30 to 2:00, so I worked part time for the Pro-Life Office of the diocese. It was lots of fun. I spoke to about 2,500 students (no kidding!). Now the office has hired another woman; she has lots of experience with Project Rachel.[57] She's bright and articulate, and her children are grown. I'm hopeful she will carry on the work I was able to get started.

John Henry is playing for the Joe DiMaggio all-stars—his last year in Little League. He hit *ten* home runs in regular season play. I hope he has as good a time on all-stars. How I have loved Little League and soccer.

Michael now has a driver's license. Max turned *fifteen* this past week. John Henry is taller than I am. A lot of time has gone by.

I would love to see you and your family (and the new baby!). There seems to be so little spare time. Unlike heaven, where there will always be plenty of time. How nice.

July 4, 1998—to Henry Van Kooy

I'm still feeling quite good—the lungs feel as if they are filling up a bit, though still not as bad as they were when Mark and Dave visited. I'm off 5-FU [chemotherapy drug] for two weeks, starting again on July 27. The next lottery for Herceptin will be July 31. Then August,

---

[57] Project Rachel is a ministry of the Catholic Church for the spiritual and emotional healing of women after abortion.

then September, then I get it automatically (six strikeouts is deemed enough).

We're off to New Hampshire on July 17 for a week. We had such a nice time with Dave and Kathy in Montreal. We're thinking of a trip to Jersey in August, though where to stay is now a bit of a problem. Dave and Kathy have suggested a visit to the Currys'. That would be a lot of fun. We also have friends in Highland Park. I suppose we could camp out at 20 Ver Valen, though it must be getting less and less homelike as time goes by.

July 13, 1998—to Michael Pakaluk

Hope your audition went well and that you are pleased with your ensemble assignments. We had an uneventful trip home.

I went down to the cellar to get your shorts to mail to you. This is what I found in the bathroom: two T-shirts of yours; two pairs of wadded-up, dirty socks; one pair of briefs; one pair of shorts; and six (!) damp towels on the floor—including one of the blue towels I expressly told you never to use. Forget the shorts.

As I said in the car regarding your making us leave late—I have let you get away with a fair amount of inconsiderate behavior. You have a habit of placing the blame everywhere but with yourself. It is not as though I enjoy doing things that seem petty and meanspirited (like not mailing your shorts). But I feel I must try to get you to see that when you are inconsiderate, you should admit it and apologize.

If you or Max want to call home, you should use our phone card. Dial 1-800-860-6000. Wait 'til the voice requests your home phone and PIN. The voice will then request the number you wish to dial. Just dial your home phone number again. Do not use this account to call your friends. We get a printout of every number called, the date and time of the call, and the phone number of where the call originated. You cannot hide a call. Also, be careful not to let anyone else get this account number.

Sorry this is not as pleasant a letter as it might have been. Please call or ask Max to call as soon as you know when your concerts will be.

Remember to say your prayers morning and evening. Don't do anything utterly brain dead. Have fun.

July 13, 1998—to Maria Pakaluk

Just a very quick note before I dash off to John's game. I hope you have already settled in and have made a few friends at camp. The other girls on the bus looked very nice. I'm sure you'll have lots of fun.

Did you know the Cheffers are away at the cape this week? And Flannery and Clare are going to New Jersey to see the grandparents on Wednesday. This was the perfect week for you to be away.

We will be picking you up and heading to the Pollaks' on Friday. Let me know if there are things here I should pack for you to have in New Hampshire. I'm sure you'll need more clothing—warm clothes, hiking stuff, etc.

Remember to say your prayers morning and evening. Try to be cheerful and happy even if you are not wildly enthusiastic about an activity or the food or whatever. You must begin trying to master your emotions and behave in a considerate, pleasant way no matter how hot or hungry or tired or bored you are.

It is very odd to have only three children around the house. Dad gets home tonight. I'm sure he will miss seeing you.

July 13, 1998—to Edward Fitzsimmons

Not dead yet. Actually, I'm still feeling pretty darn well. I completed another six weeks of 5-FU (that is really the name of this chemo). It still seems to be keeping the cancer at bay. Once a month I enter a lottery for a very promising treatment that will be FDA [Food and Drug Administration] approved at the end of 1998 but is not ready yet in sufficient quantities for all the women who could benefit from it. The next lottery drawing is July 31.

The sobering reality is that the cancer is in both lungs as well as in my liver. If it starts spreading in the liver, I will probably not live very long. In fact, it's a little unusual to have lived this long with metastatic breast cancer in the liver—I've had it there since December. Oh well. One day at a time.

I was sorry to hear of Bonnie's death. I know how much she meant to you. I will have a Mass said for her. It can't hurt, and who knows?

We'll be visiting Emil Pollak this weekend. He and his wife, Elaine, and two children, Alyssa and David, live three hours north of us in Littleton, New Hampshire, just west of the White Mountains. Every summer for the past eight years, we have spent a week in the White Mountains with another family, very close friends of ours (from our pro-life and Catholic circle of friends). We try to see Emil and family during the week. He is a very happy cardiologist, with a very down-to-earth, friendly, affectionate wife and two energetic and interesting children. He lives in a positively enormous house—twenty-three rooms! It is very grand; it was rather neglected when they bought it, but he has done a fine job of renovating and restoring it. They have a power boat and water ski in the lake nearby. They all ski all winter long (which in New Hampshire lasts from November to April). They usually manage a snorkeling vacation to the Caribbean each year, and Elaine's family vacations off the Maine coast each year. I believe she takes the kids there while Emil works. He puts in the long hours of a doctor but seems able to find enough free time to have a real life. He very deliberately chose to practice in New Hampshire because it is possible there (unlike in the New York metropolitan area) to be a doctor and still live like a human being.

Yesterday, I drove three and a half hours west to drop the two elder boys, Michael and Max, at a music camp at Oneonta, New York. This is the first time they have been away on their own (as opposed to staying with family or friends). The music camp looked great, and the campus and town are very picturesque. Naturally, they don't appreciate it and would prefer to be hanging around Worcester going to the movies with their friends. I trust they'll come to thank us for these sorts of things. (But maybe they won't.)

The sun is setting as I type, and the sky is vivid pink and violet. Very pretty.

Mike just got home from a conference on civil society in Los Angeles (where there's not much of it). He gave a paper on the natural-law view of civil society. This is the up-and-coming topic in political science—even liberals are waking up to the idea that individuals linked only to a Big Brother government doesn't make for a very healthy or pleasant society. But they are deeply suspicious of any institutions that place constraints on individuals based on culture, religion, heritage, custom, etc. It seems to me that little by little it is becoming clear that human beings cannot flourish in a vacuum of infinite choices. Most people simply are not self-starters and benefit tremendously by having someone or something else tell them what they should do. The trick is to have the right amount of compulsions while allowing self-starters the freedom to blaze their own path.

I finished reading Thomas Hardy's *The Return of the Native*. It was interesting, but rather too pat to be believable. I also recently finished *Brighton Rock* by Graham Greene. Did I already tell you this? I loved the book—very creepy. Greene is rather heterodox in many views, but he has a deep sense of how radical and unconventional grace truly is. The book ends with the heroine confessing that she wishes she had committed mortal sin and killed herself so as to accompany her very sinful lover into the next world to be disposed of in the same way as he is. The tired old priest says words to this effect: "I cannot absolve you, but come back soon. Come back tomorrow. You cannot conceive, I cannot conceive, the appalling strangeness of the mercy of God."

This has become one of my all-time favorite lines from literature. It is so true. Life is very, very strange, but too often for mere chance, it seems clear that all works out for the best.

Some friends of ours from the parish get together once a month to read and discuss a book. Two months ago, we read this book called *When a Pope Asks Forgiveness*.[58] Or something to that effect. The Jan Huss apology took up an entire chapter. It is very admirable that this Pope [John Paul II] is so willing to admit that the human beings who have occupied the Vatican and magisterial offices of the Church have

---

[58] Luigi Accattoli, *When a Pope Asks Forgiveness*, trans. Jordan Aumann (Staten Island, N.Y.: Alba House, 1998).

frequently been very flawed. He seems very keen to reunite the various branches of Christianity which share virtually every article of faith but are canonically separated. I hope he succeeds.

July 16, 1998

Well, I got interrupted—and here three days have gone by. Friends came over to swim on Tuesday afternoon, and then our parish priest came for dinner that evening. He is a wonderful fellow—forty (young for a priest these days). He went to Holy Cross, then Boston College Law School, then practiced law for several years. He's an accomplished rock and ice climber. He's only been ordained three years. It is a great pleasure to have a pastor who is extremely intelligent and utterly orthodox, but athletic, normal, energetic, and very appealing to the young people. Our boys think he's the greatest thing on two legs, and our girls simply adore him.

Wednesday (yesterday) we took a trip with the parish to Battleship Cove in Fall River. Every Wednesday in the summer our parish organizes an outing for the kids. It has been great fun, and it exposes some of these inner city kids to scenery and historical sites they would otherwise never see. This was a great trip—the kids could explore virtually every inch of a battleship, a submarine, and two destroyers. By some miracle, no one fell overboard or plunged headlong down one of the very steep stairways.

Today I'll be doing laundry and packing for our week in New Hampshire. We don't yet have any travel plans for August, though I'd like to try to get to New Jersey to see my brothers and a few other friends, including Larry.

Have I mentioned the course my husband teaches on Aquinas at the parish? Once a week, about twelve people get together to read and discuss passages from the *Summa*. So, in yet another way, you are regularly in our thoughts as the generous donor of the esteemed volumes.[59] This has been going on since February. It was designed as a

---

[59] Fitz loved Saint Thomas Aquinas' *Summa Theologiae*; often when a dispute arose he would resolve it by opening one of its volumes, saying, "Let's go to the source." He gave his volumes to us when he was going blind.

Lenten program, but everyone wanted to keep on reading and discussing. It's great fun.

July 28, 1998—to Emil and Elaine Pollak

Thank you for such a pleasant (though too short) visit. It was great to see you both, looking happier and healthier than ever, and to see your children, who have entered into that phase when they grow too quickly for us to keep up with mentally. It was also great to see your parents, Emil, after all these years. Thanks also for so generously towing the kids around on the tube.[60] When do you get your turn?

Elaine, my husband interrupted us when we had embarked on one of the great taboo subjects of modern times. I wish I could have had endless time to answer your questions. As it is, I'll give a brief answer and encourage you to read the photocopied articles I've enclosed.

I converted to the Catholic faith by being intellectually convinced that it is, historically speaking, the Church founded by Jesus of Nazareth. My mind works in rather a simplistic, straightforward way. I had become convinced that the most plausible explanation for the existence of Christianity was that, in fact, Jesus of Nazareth had risen from the dead. Someone who rises from the dead is obviously qualified to tell the rest of us what life is about and what we are supposed to be doing. It seemed clear to me that Jesus trained the twelve Apostles and told them what they were supposed to do to. Historically speaking, it seems clear to me that the Church they founded still exists—it is the Roman Catholic Church.

Anyway, having concluded the above, it followed that what the Catholic Church teaches is what Jesus required of me. The Church teaches that contraception distorts the meaning God intended for the marriage act. Intercourse is a human action somewhat similar to smiling or shaking hands—it has a true meaning. If you smile and shake hands with someone and then turn on him and stab him, it is pretty well understood that your smile and handshake did not signify hostility; rather, you used a gesture of friendship to deceive.

---

[60] Emil would tow the children on a tube around the lake with his power boat.

199

Similarly, intercourse means something. It means, "I love you, and you alone, completely and for the rest of my life." God intended this kind of love to be the context where new human life would arise. The Church has taught for centuries that it is an offense against God to use the sex act for the individual pleasure or intimacy of the couple while at the same time frustrating the life-giving power of the act.

Anyway, we adopted this way of living, though I don't claim that I embraced it with wholehearted enthusiasm at first. It is the sort of truth (like fidelity in marriage) that you understand and appreciate more fully as time passes and you accumulate more life experience.

That's rather a long answer to your question whether pro-lifers use contraceptives. Many pro-lifers do use contraceptives, though the Catholic ones don't. Oddly enough, there is a growing movement among Evangelical Protestants who are adopting the Catholic view of contraception.

The rest of our vacation in New Hampshire was lovely, as always. On Friday, we headed out to hear Michael and Max perform at their music camp. It was extremely impressive. Max got so much out of it, he asked to remain for the next two-week session. So we'll be heading out to Oneonta again on August 15 for more concerts. Michael was eager to get back to see his friends.

I saw my oncologist on Monday. Fluid is accumulating in my right lung. I am supposed to have surgery to get rid of it. As a result of that decision, my next round of chemo has been postponed. Meanwhile, I am on the waiting list for the lottery for a new drug, Herceptin. The next lottery drawing will be July 31. It appears to be a very promising drug. Naturally, I hope I win the lottery this time around.

Again, thanks for your hospitality. I hope we see you again before too much time goes by.

August 24, 1998—to Claire Fitts

I have begun this letter only to be interrupted so many times. I will not leave this computer desk until I have printed this letter and put it in an envelope with a stamp!!!

My health has tottered to the brink. My lungs are a wreck—I can barely get up a flight of stairs without a rest. Now my liver has begun to enlarge, causing a lot of discomfort (OK, sometimes it is downright painful). I cannot tolerate narcotics, so pain relief is a very complicated affair.

But some potential good news—I am starting a clinical trial of a drug called Herceptin at Beth Israel tomorrow. This treatment has been unusually effective for women in my condition. I hope it does me some good, as I have had every chemo known to oncologists and there isn't much more to do.

I spoke with Jennifer the other day. She is expecting no. 6 and is still ambulatory, several weeks past her usual confinement to bed rest. How nice it would be for her to get to the end of this pregnancy without that unpleasant complication.

Mary Beth recently gave birth to her seventh, a girl named Monica Mary. It is nice to have another spate of newborns in the mix. With Sophie five (!) I feel the lack of a bona fide baby. You are so lucky to have your little one. I also see now how much less labor intensive and exhausting motherhood is once the age of the children shifts toward the teenage spectrum.

I am relieved to have lived to see Sophie into kindergarten. Whatever happens, I am quite grateful for the great life I was given with so many more blessings than most people ever get. I am even just a little bit impatient to see heaven, being—I suppose a true believer and also hard to please, I figure if the fallen world is this pleasant, what could heaven be but irresistible?

How I wish there were time and opportunity to get up to Maine again, but not for now. Thank you for your prayers and friendship.

August 26, 1998—to Larry Weller

Well, I've been putting off and putting off writing this letter. Naturally, I hope you know it's not for lack of thinking of you or appreciating your faithful correspondence. I never even wrote to thank you for your birthday card and present.

Thank you.[61] We had one other Capercaillie tape, called "Blood is Strong", I think. I love their music. I don't know why it doesn't bother me that I do not understand the lyrics. It sounds pretty enough even when incomprehensible.

I had a Mass said for you on your birthday. For your intentions. That can't mean a whole lot to you, but it's a very good Catholic thing to do. Now I am finally sending you this CD—another friend gave me a copy, and I really like several of the arrangements. I hope you also like it.

Yesterday, I started receiving a cancer treatment called Herceptin. It's still in clinical trials, but it has had very good results for a significant percentage of women so far. It is basically the only thing left—I have had every other chemo known to oncologists. I am in pretty awful shape—my lungs are so bad I cannot walk upstairs without taking a wheezing break. My liver has started to enlarge, which is unpleasant and uncomfortable, not to mention a sign that things have taken a turn for what is usually fatal within a matter of months. So, either Herceptin is going to work well for me, in which case I'll be around for a while longer, or it won't, in which case I think it's time for me to start writing somewhat melodramatic letters like this.

I don't want to seem melodramatic, but I don't want to exit this life without telling you how much your friendship has meant to me. I have had so many years to think about what a blessed youth I had, largely because of the almost-fairy-tale romance we had. I have also had many years to ponder why my identity went AWOL during freshman year. It was, I conclude, sinful self-will and self-absorption, pure and simple. Perhaps it was necessary for me to learn just how selfish I could be and just how badly I could hurt people by following my own inclinations rather than what is really true. Anyway, as a result of the debacles of that year, I became serious about Christianity and ended up marrying Michael, the one person who has proved capable of forcing me to admit when what I want to do is, in fact, wrong.

And you have remained a good and valued friend in spite of it all. Thanks for that.

[61] Ruth is thanking Larry for the gift of a CD of Scots Gaelic folk music by the band Capercaillie titled "Crosswinds".

Your sister, Kenty, wrote me such a sweet letter. I would like to write to her, though I misplaced her address.

You see I have also sent you some things, the chief thing being the Northern Masque ticket and money box. It obviously has no real value but enormous sentimental value. Someday, someone should interview all the relevant parties and write an account of the masque—it was such an amazing phenomenon.[62]

I also include some recent photos of Fitz. He looks and sounds extremely happy with his wife and life in general. He's another one I pray for a lot. Is this ever odd—his first (and according to the Church, only) wife is dying of breast cancer. If she dies before him, I think he plans to marry in the Church. The heavy ironies here are a bit much, but it would make me happy to see him reconciled. It would seem very wrong for a man named Edward Peter Fitzsimmons and educated by Jesuits to die without all the smells and bells and Catholic hoopla.[63]

I recently read an article about the third [water] tunnel project in Manhattan—the largest water supply tunnel in human history, or something like that. Have you had any dealings with that? It sounded like your kind of project.

September 2, 1998

Can't say I'm any better. I'll end this so Mike can print it and mail it. I'll try to write a fair number of these. If I fail, please do me the favor of thanking the gang [at NVOT] on my behalf for their friendship. I will keep you in my prayers.

September 10, 1998—to Laura Garcia

I seem to be coming (at last) to the end of the rope. Over the past month, my lungs have gotten so bad that I cannot even walk across

---

[62] Ruth marveled throughout her life how high school students on their own—without adult initiative or guidance—had formed and run a theatre company, each year putting on several performances of plays and musicals.

[63] Fitz's marriage was regularized, and he was reconciled to the Church the following year.

the room without having to sit down and catch my breath as a result. My liver has begun enlarging because of tumors. It's uncomfortable, but not (yet) downright painful. Lucky for me, I am still getting by on nothing stronger than ibuprofen.

I have had three treatments with Herceptin so far. It's impossible to say yet whether it is having a beneficial effect. This seems to be a bit of a horse race—which will win out, the cancer or the Herceptin.

Naturally, it is difficult to live in this state—still here but unable to do anything. Friends are being wonderful, bringing meals and doing laundry and cleaning. But it's that constant monitoring, coordinating, and tidying up that it seems only mothers can do which isn't getting done.

I am a little worried that Herceptin will work just well enough to keep me alive in this state—that seems like a nightmare. But I've tried up to now to avoid overreacting to imaginary scenarios ...

September 10, 1998—to her children

Dear Sophie,

I want to be sure to leave behind for you just a few words for you to ponder as you grow up. A mother cannot have favorites, but no one minds if the baby of the family gets slightly special treatment.

Everyone knows that I think you are the only natural stoic among my children. My mother was a stoic, and I took after her somewhat in this regard. I admire it a lot. But don't let it substitute for Christian hope and joy.

You have been a beautiful blessing in this family. You are so adorable and perky. Even gruff Michael softens up around you.

In the year before you went to preschool, I was still strong enough to walk a bit. You were my little companion (or burden, as I nearly always carried you piggyback) on many walks out at the Wachusett Reservoir and Boynton Park. I was extremely happy during these walks.

I once got a phone call from a woman who had had local breast cancer. She was pregnant and afraid that having her baby might cause the cancer to return. I told her I did not think it would make a difference—the cancer either comes back or it doesn't. But even if it did make a difference, I told her I had you under the same circumstances, and looking at you I could say without hesitation that I would happily die in order to have brought forth such a creature. I still mean it. Of course, I would mean it regarding any of my children, but in your case it is very clearly true.

Dear Sarah,

After your brother Thomas died, I was determined to have another baby as soon as possible. My arms felt so empty without a baby. God was very good to me, and I was pregnant again within about a month after his death. You have heard many times the funny story of your birth—how I could not wake Dad up and how you were almost born before I got to the hospital. You were born eleven minutes after I arrived at Saint Vincent's. I felt no real pain during your birth. It was the easiest of all my births.

I spoiled you rotten as a baby. I don't think I ever let you cry. You were the best sleeper of all my babies—you happily snuggled down and fell asleep for two naps a day and slept through the night. From very early, I called you the "death-wish baby" because you were so adventurous and always heading straight for something dangerous. I remember once seeing you head right for the cord that attached to the vacuum cleaner. It [the cord] was plugged into the electric socket but had fallen out of the vacuum. I nearly tackled you to keep you from putting that live current right in your mouth. You climbed up on things all the time. In general, you showed right from the start something characteristic of you—you did things wholeheartedly, with a lot of enthusiasm.

You were also and continue to be a most affectionate, loving, sweet child. I love the way you are so friendly and open to people. You have a big heart. Never lose that quality. You brought so much happiness and emotional healing to me after the sadness and emptiness of losing little Thomas. You were a great gift and blessing from God for your mother.

Dear Maria,

Maria, I don't say nice things to you often enough. Forgive me for being harder on you and more critical than I should have been. It is, of course, because I am relatively so unemotional and you are much more emotional. But I should have risen above being annoyed by that, being the adult. Too often, I failed to do that, and I am sorry.

You are so physically beautiful. I love to look at your face. You have such an open, beautiful face, and your eyes are truly a wonder: the color is unearthly, and their size and expressiveness are remarkable. Very quickly, you had better learn to value how your physical appearance will turn boys' heads. Try not to let that make you vain. Don't use it as a weapon to hurt or conquer boys. But keep in mind the power you will have to attract their affection. Don't underestimate this, or you could break hearts unwittingly.

Dear Michael,

Your birth was one of the greatest things that ever happened to me. For the first time in my life, I had to put the needs of someone else ahead of my own preferences almost constantly throughout the day. And though it was a little difficult to get used to, I loved it. You were a good baby, easy to take places, easy to please, very cute and endearing.

As my firstborn, you have always had a special spot in my heart. I love looking at you, at how handsome and athletic and graceful you are. You have a funny mix in your personality—you can be pretty mean, picking on your siblings. But you also have a very sweet streak in your personality, the characteristic that enables you to make friends so easily and to be a loyal friend.

You are very talented. Dad and I probably valued academics too much—it's obviously not everyone's strength. I hope you didn't suffer too much as a result of that mismatch in values.

You don't seem to have a lot of natural piety. Rather, you seem to be by nature a bit of a skeptic. Naturally, I worry about that. Please don't ever abandon your Catholic faith. Even if it's only out of respect for your mother, try to keep in mind that the Catholic faith is what made me the kind of wife and mother I was. Without the Catholic faith, I doubt very much I would have had six children, I doubt I would have stayed home full time with you guys, and I even doubt I would have had the patience and forgiveness to stay married to Dad. I would have been much more obsessed with professional and material success and much less able to put aside little frustrations and annoyances. If you ever want to know how selfish and self-absorbed I was before becoming a Christian, ask Uncle Dave.

So even if it seems false at times, please stick with the practice of the faith.

Dear Max,

There is one particular story from your childhood that I treasure. At one point, after I was diagnosed with metastatic cancer, Dad had been explaining how sick I was and how I might die. You kids went to the Mount Carmel fair, and you came home with that cute Scottish bear—Bear McGregor, I called him. I could tell that you had set your mind on bringing me something special to show me that you cared. It has always touched me so much, that endearing determination to do something special for your mother.

You became the most interesting conversationalist of the children at a young age. Perhaps as the years go by, others of your siblings will become more thoughtful and reflective, but you were already this way when you entered double digits.

You have spoken openly with me about how I look at my approaching death. You know I think I have been blessed far more than the vast majority of human beings. My life has been great in every category that counts. Beyond that, I understand that this life is short and that heaven is the point, so why not get on with the main point. And, of course, I trust that the way God arranges life is always the best way.

But there was another interesting moment that had to do with heaven and you. At the very end of the Lavalle tournament this year, the rather disappointing year, I went back to the van ahead of everyone else. You were the first to appear walking toward the car, the sun illuminating you from behind. You looked like an angel, all burnished gold, so strong and graceful. Suddenly I realized someday you too would be in heaven, that Max would be in heaven, glorious and eternal. It made me almost start to cry with happiness. I am crying now as I type this, not very characteristically. You just walked out the door to wait for Kevin Menard to pick you up for the soccer tournament. Before you left, you were very solicitous to be sure I was OK, that I wouldn't need anything, that I would be OK on my own. I love you for the way you are so thoughtful and for the way you want to show that you care.

Dear John,

What can I say, John? You have been such a sweet, affectionate son. I love the way you just spontaneously put your arms around me and hug me. From the time you were a baby, you have been such a sweet, chirpy, affectionate soul. (With a temper—none of us is perfect.)[64]

---

[64] It seems that Ruth's strength gave out. These are perhaps the last words she wrote.

AFTERWORD: Our Life After Ruth

Michael Pakaluk

A woman in the mothers' Rosary group in which Ruth prayed described the time in late 1993 when Ruth told everyone that her cancer had metastasized. Ruth said to her friends, "I'll tell you everything I know about my cancer and the treatment, but after that, let's not discuss it any further; we can talk about something else instead." Ruth then explained her condition and the chemotherapy that was planned, and also how it was now certain that the cancer would be fatal and that she would likely be dead in two or three years. After explaining all this, at which time the Rosary was about to begin, Ruth clapped her hands and said, "Right—now let's pray for Michael to find a young wife to marry."

Although Ruth confided to her friends that she had entrusted her children to Mary, the Mother of God, to take care of them and raise them after she was gone, and she had peace that everything would work out for the best, she also said that, for her, "The worst suffering is the fear of dying while my children are still so young. What are the chances my husband could marry again with six children? Neither grandmother lives nearby. No siblings are nearby or able to help raise my children. I hate the idea of my children growing up without a mother."

Ruth was especially concerned that her youngest daughters would grow up without a mother. When Ruth died, Sarah was eight years old, and Sophie only six.

Less than three months before she died, I had a conversation with Ruth where she expressed such concerns very vividly. We were alone and embracing, and when I looked at her I felt moved to give voice to something that I hadn't said before. I told her that she was such an amazing woman and so extraordinary that I couldn't even think of finding anyone like her or falling in love with anyone else. Ruth smiled and said, "I think that you should remarry." Not knowing really what to say, I prattled on foolishly about how one of the happiest times in my life was when I was away in Oxford for the summer, studying and writing twelve hours a day, and how it would be great to devote myself further to scholarship. Such silly ideas were no doubt worrying for Ruth. But she calmly said in reply, "For the sake of the girls, I think you should remarry."

It was clear, however, that she was uncomfortable about something and, as it were, pushed me away, so that we no longer embraced. She clasped her hands together on top of her chest and paused as if to take a big breath. Then she looked up at the ceiling and said, "I find it interesting that Catherine Hardy is moving to Cambridge." Catherine Hardy was the eldest daughter of our friends Tom and Jan Hardy mentioned in the biographical introduction above. Catherine had been studying at the University of Pennsylvania but had recently chosen to attend Harvard University for graduate school in economics. I recalled that Tom was going to help her move soon into an apartment in Cambridge and that he had mentioned that he wanted to stop in and see Ruth afterward.

This thing that Ruth said seemed very strange, so I asked, "Why is it interesting that Catherine Hardy is moving to Cambridge?" "Because", Ruth replied, "for a long time I have had the thought that Catherine Hardy would be good wife for you, and now she is moving to Cambridge." Ruth did not need to say that by "now" she meant, "Now that I am dying." She gave this explanation as if revealing some kind of intimation that was, in turn, confirmed for her by Catherine Hardy's move. We had met the Hardys when they were living in Arlington, Massachusetts, back when I was in graduate school, but not long after that they had moved to Washington, D.C., where Catherine had attended the Oakcrest School and then the University of Pennsylvania. So throughout the years of Ruth's sickness, Catherine was in Washington or Philadelphia, and when Ruth was at the point of death, it happened that Catherine was moving to the neighborhood.

I didn't give much thought to this strange statement, yet neither could I dismiss it. Ruth didn't say things lightly. One also should understand that, by this point in Ruth's life, Ruth's friends and I had seen so many astonishing things in connection with her that we were almost ready to ascribe prophetic powers to her. As one of Ruth's friends joked later in this regard, "If Ruth told me that my husband was about to die, I would take out an insurance policy and buy better makeup!"

At Ruth's funeral Mass, Catherine by chance ended up seated next to Ruth's spiritual director, and, as mentioned, she was with her mother and beside me at the gravesite when I made the remark, "Until death do us part".

After Ruth died, I was in agony for many weeks, of course. I don't have the skill to convey the pain of those times, nor do I wish to revisit it. As I explained to my class at Brown, when I resumed my lectures there, it felt as if the heart had been ripped right out of my chest and I was walking around with a gaping wound. I had lost not only Ruth but also half of my life, because Ruth had been my companion in everything since I was twenty years old. She was the only living witness to most of my life, a kind of testament to and living connection with all of my experiences and memories, going all the way back to college. When she died, it was only I who had lived through them.

I spent countless hours in Mass and in prayer weeping, meditating upon Ruth and the gift that she was to me, and my loss. Yet it seemed to me that I had to try, at least, to draw a limit to this: I should drink deeply of grief, but that grief, like everything else, needed to come to an end. I decided that after a certain point, I would no longer willingly grieve. It seemed to me that six months should be the limit, which took me to March 1999.

In late February a colleague who was a visiting professor in philosophy at Harvard, Mary Louise Gill, invited me to participate in a Greek reading group on Aristotle's *De anima* that she was forming and that met on Friday afternoons. The time was free for me. This would be for me the first new commitment I would undertake since Ruth died. So I told Mary Louise that I would be pleased to attend. This was a huge step for me. It was no more than an informal reading group, but in my own mind I regarded my traveling to Cambridge for that meeting as the first step I would take in a new life that was to begin after grieving. To be sure, I did not expect to be entirely successful in this attempt to start a new life, but nonetheless I thought it was time to try to embark on it.

Since I was going into Cambridge for these meetings, I thought of what Ruth had said, and it seemed to me that at least I ought to meet with Catherine Hardy. This was not something I was especially looking forward to. My memory of Catherine from visits with the Hardys was of an ungainly and seemingly somber girl hauling stacks of math books with her as she went into another room to work for hours on homework. Besides that, I knew nothing about her and presumed it was likely that she would be some kind of artificially pious person, which I would find unpleasant. Furthermore, I certainly would never have contacted her with any romantic intentions, as she was at least fifteen years younger than I, and I believed, probably as a result of my happy marriage, that the only healthy romantic relationships were between couples roughly equal in age. Nonetheless, I found Catherine's address on Harvard e-mail and wrote to her, and we arranged to meet for lunch before the Greek reading group. This was March 5, 1999.

I met Catherine in front of the philosophy department building, Emerson Hall, at the base of the stone steps in front. As she walked down the stairs, I saw that her appearance was different from what I had imagined. She had beautiful long and flowing blond hair. Her face was very appealing, somewhat boyish, it seemed, and uncomplicated. She looked nothing like the gawky kid with the math books from my memory. Catherine suggested we go to the crepe shop for lunch. To get there we had to walk by Saint Paul's Church. Here, a first "test" suggested itself to me: "Should we stop for a visit to the Blessed Sacrament on the way?" Catherine said that that was a great idea, and so we went and prayed together before the Blessed Sacrament—this was the first thing that we did together.

We both enjoyed the lunch so much that I asked if she would like to go with me to hear the Boston Symphony the following evening—I had subscription tickets—and she said she would be delighted. We enjoyed that so much that we went to a pub afterward and stayed up until the early morning hours talking.

We met after the Greek reading group in this way on Friday afternoons for a few weeks, fell in love, and soon realized that this was so. Catherine accepted my proposal on May 7, 1999, and we were married in Saint Paul's Cathedral in Worcester on August 15 of that year.

On May 14 of the following year we were blessed with a son, Joseph, who brought much healing to the family. There have since followed Nicholas, Gregory, Elizabeth, Mark, and most recently, Blaise Francis (born December 14, 2009). Catherine successfully defended her dissertation in economics at Harvard exactly one week after Blaise was born. Soon thereafter, Catherine and I accepted joint offers from Ave Maria University, where we both now teach and work.

The dissertation took as long as it did (eleven years) because Catherine as a twenty-two-year-old consented not simply to my proposal to marriage but also, implicitly, to raise Ruth's children. There were some rocky patches at first, especially for John Henry and Maria, who were entering young adulthood and were the most emotionally vulnerable. Michael and Max were mature enough and had strong enough faith to see them through the trial. Sarah and Sophie, from the moment Ruth died, were yearning for a mother, any mother: regarding any woman unknown to them who happened to enter the house, they would immediately ask, "Is she married? Is she a Catholic?" and, if the answers were right, they'd look at me, asking with their eyes, "Then why don't you two get married?"

But here is a brief update on the children. Michael attended the Hartt School of Music, got a master's degree from the University of New Mexico, and now leads the music program at a high school in Lompoc, California.

Max went to Harvard College, worked a couple of years as an editor at National Review Online, received his J.D. from Harvard Law School, passed the bar exam, and has joined a major law firm in Boston.

John Henry followed Ruth's and my example and in his junior year of college married Kasia Iwanicki, the daughter of Polish immigrants, whom he met in classes at Thomas Aquinas College. Kasia's mother also died of breast cancer. John expects to receive his master's degree in accounting from Bentley University in 2011 and has already accepted a job with a Big Four accounting firm in their Boston office. In November 2009, he and Kasia had their first child, Eva, and, on February 9, 2011, their second daughter was born, named Ruth.

Maria followed in John Henry's footsteps and had a brilliant academic career at Thomas Aquinas. She married a classmate from college, Sam Almeida, who is the son of a classicist and is studying to become an engineer. They are expecting their first child.

After attending the Trivium School and being homeschooled by Catherine, Sarah is attending Ave Maria University, studying literature and classics.

Finally, Sophie, the "most enjoyed child in history", also attended the Trivium School and is now a Freshman at Ave Maria University, interested in studying philosophy.

SELECTED TALKS
by Ruth Pakaluk

Contrition and Sacramental Confession

Contrition is sorrow for our sins and failings. Sometimes it is easy to have contrition for our sins and failings. When you are overwrought for one reason or another and you snap at one of the children, and you see a look of real hurt—that can really make you contrite. Or if you give in to self-pity or self-delusion and eat that second piece of chocolate or even the whole box of candies—then it is really easy to feel contrite.

But sometimes it is hard to feel as though we are rising to true contrition for our faults and failings. This is especially so if you have been going to confession regularly and it seems that you say the same old boring things over and over—that you lack patience, or generosity, or that you show stubbornness, and so on. Then it is hard to feel as if there is any real contrition there. So how should we deal with this?

First of all, do not attach too much significance to "feeling" contrite. The fact that you recognize that something in your life is causing you to fall short of what God wants, and the fact that you do something to remedy it—namely, you go to confession—is itself an indication that you have contrition. At least, we can take Jesus' word for it that such actions, uninspiring though they may be, will be acceptable to God the Father. The parable of the prodigal son reveals this in one of those almost comical details that one sometimes sees in the Bible. Jesus says that the boy finds himself disgusted at how low he has sunk; he realizes that even being a hired hand on his old man's estate is better than this; and he starts off, rehearsing the rather contrived and probably not very heartfelt or sincere "Father, I have sinned against heaven and before you ..." [Lk 15:18]. The gospel makes this point very clearly. In Jesus' telling of the parable, He has the boy starting to repeat what he had been rehearsing as soon as his father comes into view. We should be confident, then, that even very self-interested, very imperfect contrition will be accepted, and will be responded to with overwhelming generosity, by our heavenly Father.

But of course, we would like to rise to "perfect" contrition. Perfect contrition, as the old theology books tell us, "arises from a love by which God is loved above all else" (*CCC* 1452). Well, if that were how we loved God all the time, we probably would not be needing contrition very often. Sin is desiring something more than we desire God. Since God is the source of our being as well as our happiness, it is obviously really stupid to desire something created more than we desire God. Yet that is the human condition.

Often we do not even realize that we are desiring something created more than we desire God. For instance, you have been really organized for three days in a row: you are caught up with the laundry; every room has been dusted and vacuumed; the checkbook is balanced; you have already baked a cake for tonight's dessert; and you have even said your prayers and gotten to Mass today. You feel as if you are just really corresponding to God's will and that everything is great. Then, say, a pipe bursts in the basement—all over the clean laundry—and you cry out like Job, "Why me, O Lord?" It is very easy to get attached to our picture of what we think God's will is rather than accepting what it really is. We get attached to our own schedules and pleasant lives and then find we get upset, impatient, frustrated, and angry when things happen that upset the routine. But as Blessed Josemaría [Escrivá] says: "God does not want our wretchedness, but He is aware of it, and indeed He makes use of our weakness to make saints of us." [1]

We might wonder why God does not just give us perfect contrition and all the virtues all at once, because we ask for them and, in a sense, want them. But God has all the time in the world: He created time. And He wants us to do as much as we can on our own, most of the time—which means we have to learn one little lesson at a time, making what usually appears to be very minimal progress over tons of time. But we should try to get used to this.

Lent is a good time to work on perfecting our contrition. It is worth contemplating the extreme—almost insanely extreme—suffering of the

---

[1] Josemaria Escriva, "The Christian's Hope", *Friends of God* (New York: Scepter Publishers, 2003), no. 215.

crucifixion. The Church teaches us that a pinprick suffered by God incarnate would have been sufficient to redeem the human race. But would it have been sufficient to get through our thick skulls? I doubt it. God loves us so much that He chose, willingly and, in a way, *happily*, to suffer in the ultimate extreme, so as to do two things: to convey to us the depths of His mad love for each one of us and to give us some inkling of just how bad sin really is.

To conclude, here are some practical reflections.

We might wonder what keeps us from going to confession. There are really no excuses for not getting to confession in Worcester, since confessions are heard every day after the 12:10 Mass at the cathedral; every Monday, 4:30–6:00, at Saint Joan of Arc; and every month at this recollection.

Perhaps we are tempted to think confession does no good. Simply forget this: the Church, speaking for Christ, tells us it does good; ergo, it does good. It would, of course, do more good if we were making good examinations of conscience; if we felt we saw clearly what God wanted us to work on; if we diligently worked on particular faults and failings; and if we could give an honest, accurate account to the priest of those occasions when we fell. But even if we cannot do all of that, or even any of it, we can at least ask God for the grace to improve in our preparation for confession, our appreciation of the sacrament, etc. Just do it.

It is also a temptation to conclude that we are hopeless. No one is hopeless. Today's gospel—ask, seek, knock—applies perfectly to frequent confession. Jesus, through His Church, promises that confession is the source of the very graces we need to grow closer to God and to overcome our habitual faults and failings. Jesus will give our confessors the graces to help us as we need. (Note: Often what we need is not what we want or what we are looking for.) And Jesus has promised great rewards to those who persevere, precisely when it seems as if nothing is happening.

Let us ask Mary to help us meet Jesus in the sacrament of confession.

Life of Piety

The dictionary defines "piety" as reverence for God or the devout fulfillment of religious obligations. As the third definition, it has the dutiful respect or regard for one's parents, ancestors, and so on. Piety was considered a virtue by ancient Greeks and Romans. It had to do with showing the appropriate gratitude and sense of indebtedness to one's parents, one's family, and one's country, as well as to the gods.

The key aspects of piety are some outward expression of an inward awareness of indebtedness.

We speak of a "life of piety". What is that? The word "pious" has been tainted by the all too common experience of its caricature. None of us wants to be "pious" in the sense of showing a pinched, morbid, joyless performance of religious duties. But for us to live a life of piety, we have to find outward expressions of our love for God, for Our Blessed Mother, and for the angels and saints, which fit our personality and our character. We do not want to playact or assume a false identity.

For instance, in Mexico many pilgrims climb the stairs of the basilica dedicated to Our Lady of Guadalupe on their knees. You might want to do that—if you were there—but most of us would feel rather odd climbing up the stairs of Saint Paul's Cathedral in Worcester on our knees. It doesn't fit. Many of you have friends or have at least seen people who pray in the Pentecostal style, praying in tongues. Or as in *The Power and the Glory*,[2] praying with arms outstretched.

You get my point: the outward form is not in itself the important matter, but having suitable outward forms is essential. And why is that? Because we have bodies! We must use material things to

[2] The 1933 film starting Spencer Tracy.

communicate, to express, to make real our inward, immaterial states of mind and heart.

Piety, as mentioned above, has to do with a sense of indebtedness to those who are responsible for one's existence. For a Christian, this virtue makes more sense and attains a deeper meaning than it could have had for the ancients. They could, of course, have a sense of being indebted to a creator God, but Christ came to reveal that God is more than just the author of the created world. From the Christian revelation, we know that God is our Father in reality, through the divine life infused into our souls at baptism. We know God is our Father in the sense that He created the human race in His image; we know He is a Father who continues to care for all His children; but we also know that, through Christ, God has poured His own life into us. This is so hard to believe, but Saint John states it as clearly as anything ever stated in Scripture: "See what love the Father has given us, that we should be called children of God; and so we are.... Beloved, we are God's children now" [1 Jn 3:12].

Divine filiation is the truth of the faith which Blessed Josemaría [Escrivá] considered to be the foundation for the spirituality characteristic of Opus Dei. Blessed Josemaría defines a life of piety thus: "The piety which is born of divine filiation is a profound attitude of the soul which eventually permeates one's entire existence." [3]

Thinking about the reality of divine filiation should give rise to a life of piety, to outward expressions of an inward frame of mind, by the obvious implications of the truth that God is our Father, because, after all, what should be your mind-set, if the all-powerful, all-loving Creator of the universe is your Father? "Over the years, I have sought to rely unfalteringly for my support on this joyous reality. No matter what the situation, my prayer, while varying in tone, has always been the same. I have said to him: 'Lord, you put me here. You entrusted me with this or that, and I put my trust in you. I know you are my Father, and I have seen that tiny children are always absolutely sure of their parents.' My priestly experience tells me that abandonment such as this in the hands of God stimulates souls to acquire a strong, deep,

[3] Escriva, "Getting to Know God", *Friends of God*, no. 146.

and serene piety, which drives them to work constantly and with an upright intention." [4]

"Practical ways to increase our life of piety"

There are a million devotions: pick one to start. Get good at a few. "Growing in supernatural life is not a matter of piling one devotion on top of another." [5]

Start with the Mass. "A man who fails to love the Mass fails to love Christ." [6] We are children of God most profoundly because God the Son is our brother; He became one of us and died so that the Blessed Trinity could communicate the divine life to us. The act in His life when this reality was accomplished is, of course, the death of Jesus on the cross. At Mass, that moment is again present. Blessed Josemaría called it the moment "where time blends with eternity". [7] So at the moment of consecration, there is Jesus, and not just Jesus, but Jesus in the act of giving Himself for our salvation. This is the whole point of His life; He is the whole point of our life; so clearly, the Mass should be for us a real high point. How do we respond to this reality? "We must make an effort to live the Mass with calm and serenity, with devotion and affection." [8]

Are we distracted? Are we straining at the bit, eager for Mass to be over with? Are we planning the day's errands, or the menu for dinner? . . .

Perhaps you have the experience that this truth, that Jesus is really there, doesn't always make you feel pious. You don't feel like sitting there in rapture in close proximity to your Lord and Savior. Well, that's a good opportunity to tell Him just what is bugging you. The point is not to imitate somebody else's sentiments. God made you. He dreamed up your personality, with all of its strengths, weaknesses, and quirks. He wants you to love Him with *your* heart, not somebody

---

[4] Josemaría Escrivá, "Getting to Know God", *Friends of God*, no. 143.
[5] Josemaría Escrivá, *Christ Is Passing By* (New York: Scepter Publishers, 1974), no. 142.
[6] Ibid., no. 92.
[7] Ibid., no. 94.
[8] Ibid., no. 92.

else's. So if you find yourself sitting at Mass, distracted or feeling obtuse, just tell Our Lord that that's the way you feel and ask Him to change it, if He would prefer things to be different.

A good second place to improve in living piety is giving thanks after communion. Everything said above obviously still applies, only more so. "If we love Christ, who offers himself for us, we will feel compelled to find a few minutes after Mass for an intimate personal thanksgiving, which will prolong in the silence of our hearts that other thanksgiving which is the Eucharist." [9]

Why is it so important to give thanks after communion? Think about the reality. The Creator of the universe, your savior, the man who loves you and died a tortured death to get this point across, is now physically present in your body. That has to count for something.

It is a *strange* reality. The people who left Jesus after hearing Him talk about His flesh being food and His blood being drink were reacting in a pretty understandable way. After all, why on earth should the omnipotent Creator of the universe want to be consumed by us?

A few human experiences help us grasp the significance of this truth. Think of how ravishingly cute a three-year-old can be and how parents often say, "You're so cute, I could just eat you up." There is some deep truth in that experience, of loving someone so much that you want him to be part of you. This is even more explicitly the case in marriage. The biblical phrase for the marital act, being "one flesh", is an accurate way of expressing the inward yearning that finds outward expression in marital love.

Jesus loves us in that same way: He wants us to be joined to His very being, as much as this is possible. When we receive communion, the most cursory reflection on the magnitude of what is really going on should motivate us to want to spend that time when Jesus is physically present within us talking to Him. For about ten minutes, we should try to act in accordance with what is really the case. And if we don't "feel" the appropriate sentiments, tell Him that.

[9] Ibid.

Another devotion to adopt is the visit to the Blessed Sacrament: stop in the church and visit Our Lord for a few brief moments during the day. We should not neglect little gestures of love, for instance, greeting Jesus in tabernacles as you drive or walk by [the church]; placing images of Our Lady in rooms of your house, to think of her as you do your work; kissing your scapular as you put it on or take it off; and so on.

Service to others should be an overflow of piety: these are also our brothers and sisters; Jesus died for them as well.

Cultivate a devotion to Mary which involves expressions of affection just like those you show for your own mother.

Sanctifying Ordinary Work

"Introductory remarks"

This talk is on the topic of sanctifying ordinary work, which is a central theme in the spirituality of Opus Dei. Thus, this talk both concerns what Opus Dei is about and is an example of what Opus Dei does.

First, what Opus Dei is about. The founder of Opus Dei was a Spanish priest, now beatified, Blessed Josemaría Escrivá de Balaguer. When he was still a young man, he began to experience intimations that God was asking something special from him. For many years, young Josemaría pursued his studies, was ordained to the priesthood, studied canon law, and ministered to the sick and destitute as a parish priest in Madrid.[10]

On October 2, 1928, Blessed Josemaría experienced a revelation from God of what it was he was supposed to devote his life to. From what

[10] [Saint Josemaría actually obtained his doctorate in civil law (out of deference to his father's request, before he entered the seminary), and he was not a parish priest but the chaplain for a community of nuns in Madrid.]

he says about this experience, it is clear that he understood that God wanted him to devote his life to developing the path of holiness for people in everyday life.

In an interview published in a book, *Conversations with Monsignor Escrivá de Balaguer*, Escrivá says: "The Work was born to help those Christians, who through their family, their friendships, their ordinary work, their aspirations, form part of the very texture of civil society, to understand that their life, just as it is, can be an opportunity for meeting Christ: that it is a way of holiness and apostolate. Christ is present in any honest human activity. The life of an ordinary Christian, which to some people may seem banal and petty, can and should be a holy and sanctifying life." [11]

So this is the central message of Opus Dei, that *all* Christians are called to attain holiness—not just priests, monks, and nuns—and that the ordinary activities of daily life are the raw material that most ordinary Christians are supposed to use to sanctify themselves and sanctify the world around them.

Opus Dei exists to help laypeople do just that, to sanctify themselves through their ordinary work and to sanctify the world around them through that work. Another way to say this is that Opus Dei's purpose is to help you see your ordinary, daily work as the means for drawing closer to God and for serving God and mankind.

As I said, this talk that I am now giving is also an *example* of what Opus Dei does. It is nothing very complicated or mysterious. Opus Dei provides spiritual formation—like this talk—to remind, encourage, and teach us more about how we are to sanctify ordinary work. That is Opus Dei in a nutshell.

This does not sound so radical now, but it certainly did in 1928. One of the remarkable signs of the authenticity of Opus Dei is that many of its theological insights about the laity were articulated for the Church Universal in Vatican II.

[11] José María Escrivá, *Conversations with Monsignor Escrivá de Balaguer* (New York: Scepter Publishers, 1968), no. 60.

"What does 'sanctifying ordinary work' mean?"

What do we mean by this phrase, "sanctifying ordinary work"? We should understand that sanctity for us is not found in strange or exotic activities. Rather, it consists in treating all the activities of daily life and work as opportunities to love God, to serve God, to glorify God, to serve mankind, to advance the salvation of the world, and to convert sinners.

"Why do this?"

Why should we try to sanctify our ordinary work? Well—one might ask—why not? What *else* are you going to do? "Vanity of vanities"— that's what life is like otherwise. But, most importantly, sanctifying ordinary work is what Jesus wants: "You, therefore, must be perfect," he says, "as your heavenly Father is perfect" (Mt 5:48). And this is also what the Church is asking us to do this at this time: "By reason of their special vocation it belongs to the laity to seek the kingdom of God by engaging in temporal affairs and directing them according to God's will. They live in the world, that is, they are engaged in each and every work and business of the earth and in the ordinary circumstances of social and family life which, as it were, constitute their very existence. There they are called by God that, being led by the spirit to the Gospel, they may contribute to the sanctification of the world, as from within like leaven, by fulfilling their own particular duties."[12]

As John Paul II puts it: "In particular the lay faithful are called to restore to creation all its original value. In ordering creation to the authentic well-being of humanity in an activity governed by the life of grace, they share in the exercise of the power with which the Risen Christ draws all things to himself and subjects them along with himself to the Father, so that God might be everything to everyone."[13]

[12] Vatican Council II, *Lumen Gentium*, 31.
[13] John Paul II, *Christifideles Laici*, 14.

First of all, we need to do our work well. Blessed Josemaría writes, "If we really want to sanctify our work, we have inescapably to fulfill the first condition: that of working, and working well, with human and supernatural seriousness." [14] "That half-finished work of yours is a caricature of the holocaust, the total offering God is asking of you." [15]

Then we should do our work as something we are doing for God. Think of Mary doing housework—yet it was for Jesus. Take seriously the solidarity that Jesus wills to have with all of us: when we serve our family, we serve Jesus through them. Serve them, then, for Jesus' sake. See them as gifts of the Creator to us.

Think also of Jesus working as a carpenter until he was thirty. He must have experienced drudgery, things going wrong, impatient customers, less-than-ideal working conditions. If he thought it was worth his time to stick with this kind of work, there must be something to it.

In general, do your work with love and with a supernatural outlook.

"Practical tips"

Some simple practices help us to sanctify our work. A morning offering is a good idea, to offer up all of our work for the day to God— and then we should renew this intention throughout the day. It's also helpful to dedicate certain parts of the day to different intentions or to dedicate tasks to individuals or intentions.

Think of those everyday tasks that are a real drag: standing in the cold at the gas station pumping gas; pulling the wadded-up, dirty, wet sock right side out; clearing the gooey, matted hair out of the drain catcher in the tub; listening to five screaming children at once. We should try to put extra love into these [tasks] especially.

Finally, it's good to use material realities to stand for supernatural realities. When you go upstairs, think of heaven. As you pass through a doorway, think of Christ's Resurrection, opening the way into a new

[14] Josemaría Escrivá, *The Forge* (New York: Scepter Publishers, 2002), no. 698.
[15] Ibid., no. 700.

life. A phone ringing can stand for God's call to us to follow Him more closely. As you buckle a seat belt, think of God's protective grace and greet the guardian angel He has given you.

The Eucharist

The feast of Corpus Christi is approaching. This is a good time to reflect on the greatest of all the sacraments: the Eucharist.

Why did Christ give us the Eucharist? After all, isn't He present in the souls of the baptized, along with the Father and the Spirit? Why isn't that spiritual presence more than enough? Let's start with a very basic observation about human nature. We need our bodies: our souls, in the normal course of things, need our bodies. And we need physical contact with other human beings. We are not disembodied spirits. For a human being to become "more spiritual" does not mean to disregard or disdain the body and other physical realities. Rather, it means to bring our bodies, our entire being, and all physical reality, under the reign of Christ.

Let me illustrate this point. You have probably heard of the diagnosis "failure to thrive" common among orphans in institutions or among children of teen mothers or other stressed-out or inexperienced care-givers. Basically, a child that is not held in someone's arms for a certain amount of time each day will quite simply fail to grow properly, even if that child receives all the proper amounts of food and rest. This same truth about human nature carries on throughout life. We need human contact to develop as human beings. Solitary confinement is usually regarded as a most extreme punishment or even torture. Letters are great, phone calls are great, but they can rarely effect the same level of communication and shared love as being together in person. By supernatural grace, of course, God can infuse human and supernatural virtues, but He does not do this as a rule; rather, He expects us to use the natural means built into our nature. Thus, he relies on us to be with the ones we love; He relies on us to share our lives with them. Usually, quality time is quantity time—with our loved ones. That is what builds human relationships.

Jesus knows this about us, through His having created us, because He knows our innermost thoughts, and through His having shared our human life. He even gave us the example of wanting His closest friends, Peter, James, and John, to stay with Him and keep Him company during His agony. He knows we need to be physically with the person we love in order best to grow in that love. That is one reason why He left us this great sacrament of His physical presence.

Another reason is simply to draw us closer to Him and to increase our faith. Blessed Josemaría [Escrivá], in a homily on the feast of Corpus Christi in *Christ Is Passing By*, says, "The miracle of the holy Eucharist is being continually renewed and it has all of Jesus's personal traits." [16] What are the greatest of God's miracles? We tend to think of the big and splashy ones: creation; the destruction of Sodom and Gomorrah; the parting of the Red Sea; the raising of Lazarus. But recall the cure of the paralytic: what is the greater miracle *really*, to restore him to health or to forgive his sins? Ontologically, it's forgiving sins. But in the Eucharist one finds the great miracle of transubstantiation. The hiddenness of it all is astounding, the divine condescension. God will not force our love. "Perfect God and perfect man, Lord of heaven and earth, [Jesus] offers himself to us as nourishment in the most natural and ordinary way." [17] Why does God bend Himself so low, wait so patiently, and make Himself so accessible and helpless? "Jesus hides in the Blessed Sacrament of the altar because he wants us to dare to approach him", Blessed Josemaría remarks.[18] Would we dare approach Him if we could see Him in his glory? I doubt it. If we could see Him in His humanity? Maybe not.

Reverence of the Eucharist requires an act of faith. When we see so many people pass by the tabernacle without a second glance, when we see people receive communion and then go right back to talking

[16] Josemaría Escrivá, *Christ Is Passing By*, no. 151.
[17] Ibid.
[18] Ibid., no. 153.

or joking, it is hard to believe that here is the one who called the entire universe into existence.

Summer Vacation: Good Use of Time

My topic is summer vacation and especially, what are we to do with our free time and times of recreation? How do we make good use of the summer?

I thank God that I had a happy childhood. This is very important, one's memory of a happy childhood. One of the best things you can do for a child is to reinforce his or her innate sense that life is full of wonder and beauty.

Children see something magical in nature. As kids become teenagers or college students, they often lose this sense of the mystery of nature, the sense that the beauty of nature signifies something. Many people think this is a sign of maturity, but it isn't: it is a sign of obtuseness; sin deadens intuition.

We intuitively know that nature means something. Think of a gorgeous sunset or the rising of a harvest moon. Atheists and materialists dismiss this intuition as wishful thinking or an illusion, but it is in reality a deep insight into what creation is all about. As mature Christians, we should be deepening our sense of what the beauty of nature, the change of the season, and so on, tell us about God, about heaven, and about what we are supposed to be doing.

Some signs in nature are easy to interpret. Resurrection is represented by spring: new life miraculously springing from grey and brown dead earth. Nature in this case reinforces the belief that God is the Lord of life and has conquered death. Again, mountains signify the awe-inspiring majesty of God, His timelessness, the unchanging endurance of His promise, and so on.

So what does summer signify? Summer signifies eternal bliss in heaven. (No doubt, all the schoolchildren readily agree with this.)

What is it that is so beautiful about summer? The long, long days, with evening stretching out well into what really should be considered night. The hot, lazy days with blazing sun in a deep blue sky and huge cumulus clouds sailing across the sky. There is a sense of the infinite expanse of time, of the fullness of beauty. No deadlines, no final exams—all the effort and struggle is over and we're just meant to bask in the sun, smelling the fragrance from rosebushes in full bloom. Or gazing at the endless ocean, listening to the never-ending sound of the surf. And so on.

This is something like what heaven is going to be like. And it is good for us to get good at doing the things we are intended by God to do for eternity. And it is good for us to help our children and grandchildren acquire the conviction that they were meant for that kind of eternal beatitude.

What with the world being fallen and all, summer often doesn't keep its heavenly aspect right straight through to the end of August. Timelessness has a way of degenerating into chaos and ennui. So what can we do to make this summer more like a foretaste of heaven?

Summer is a time for recreation, the meaning of which word has been trivialized into "killing time", that is, doing something amusing that distracts you from the boring grind of "real" life. But in its origin, the word "recreation" has religious significance: literally, it is re-creation, a restoring and improving upon creation.

Rest and relaxation should not mean "vegging out", doing nothing. How many summers have we lived through, at the end of which we think about all the interesting and appealing places or people we could have visited, but somehow the summer just slipped away without anything getting done?

Blessed Josemaría [Escrivá] has this nice saying: "To rest is not to do nothing: it is to relax with activities that require less effort." [19] It is important not to view free time as empty time. Another apt Blessed

[19] Josemaría Escrivá, *The Way* (New York: Image, 2006), no. 357.

Josemaría saying: "People engaged in worldly business say that time is money. That means little to me. For us who are engaged in the business of souls, time is glory!" [20]

And sometimes recreation doesn't have to be less effort, but merely a different kind of effort—for instance, sports you don't normally have time for. Hiking is a lot more effort than lugging the laundry up three flights of stairs, but somehow it is rewarding and relaxing in a way that laundry never can be. Or just think about how much effort goes into traveling to see historical sites or cultural events. Or applying yourself to read worthwhile books: "An hour of study, for a modern apostle, is an hour of prayer." [21] "You frequent the sacraments, you pray, you are chaste, but you don't study. Don't tell me you're good; you're only 'goodish'" [22]

For mothers with school-age children, having everyone at home actually may leave you with less free time, but then it's your job to see to it that your children make good use of their free time. Don't let them drift aimlessly through summer, or they'll end up like this: "Dissipation. You slake your senses and faculties at whatever puddle you meet on the way. And then you experience the results: unsettled purpose, scattered attention, deadened will, aroused concupiscence. Subject yourself again seriously to a plan that will make you lead a Christian life."—Plan of life! [23]

Think realistically about how to fit prayer, Mass, the Rosary, etc., into your day. Don't go along thinking everything will work out: summer will be three-quarters over before you admit you have to change your routine.

Some practical tips to conclude. Put your interior life first: perhaps get out of the house early, before everyone is awake, to go to Mass or to pray. Try going for a walk to say the Rosary. Post a list of topics to study or books to read. Find a friend or two to read them with and

[20] Ibid., no. 355.
[21] Ibid., no. 335.
[22] Ibid., no. 337.
[23] Ibid., no. 375. "Plan of life" refers to following a set path of interior life and formation, involving especially the "norms of piety". See talk below.

discuss them. Make a list of trips you want to make, people you want to see. Post it on the fridge and see how many you can cross off in the course of the summer. Make the children stick to some kind of schedule. Don't let them sleep until noon. Make them do some reading and devote themselves to some educational activities. Maybe also make a list of some movies you've always wanted to see, and watch them all together. But don't overdo it.

Here is something very pertinent. In his encyclical *The Gospel of Life*, after laying out how bleak everything is and how much work has to be done to re-Christianize culture, the Holy Father [John Paul II] says:

> We need first of all to foster, in ourselves and in others, a contemplative outlook. Such an outlook arises from faith in the God of life, who has created every individual as a "wonder" (cf. Ps 139:14). It is the outlook of those who see life in its deeper meaning, who grasp its utter gratuitousness, its beauty and its invitation to freedom and responsibility. It is the outlook of those who do not presume to take possession of reality but instead accept it as a gift, discovering in all things the reflection of the Creator and seeing in every person his living image (cf. Gen 1:27; Ps 8:5).... Inspired by this contemplative outlook, the new people of the redeemed cannot but respond with songs of joy, praise and thanksgiving for the priceless gift of life, for the mystery of every individual's call to share through Christ in the life of grace and in an existence of unending communion with God our Creator and Father.[24]

Plan of Life

Having a "plan of life" means having a schedule or a system for working prayer and other aspects of the spiritual life into your daily routine.

[24] John Paul II, *Evangelium Vitae*, 83.

Many people adhere to the false notion that prayer should always and only be spontaneous. Now, spontaneous prayer is, of course, a good thing, and we should all aspire to live a life characterized by constant, heartfelt prayer. But the likelihood that one will attain to that level of prayer without first adhering to some system of regular, scheduled prayer is just about nil.

It is said that nothing of value can be gained without effort. That is not exactly true. The most basic and most valuable things in this life come to us as a gift—life itself comes from God through our parents. Our talents or strengths are usually inherited. Our laws and culture come to us through the efforts and sacrifices of our ancestors. And— the most excellent gift of all—salvation—comes as a gift from God. But to a large extent, the value of our lives is determined by what we do with the gifts we are given.

It is at this level—what we do with the gifts we possess—that it is true that nothing of value comes without effort. We know this is true in the natural realm: no one becomes a great musician on inborn talent alone. Everyone who wants to play an instrument must learn to do so gradually and systematically. There isn't going to be a single athlete in Atlanta who got to the Olympics without training.

The same truth applies in the spiritual life. To draw closer to God, to become more conformed to the mind of Christ, we must make a sustained and systematic effort to allow our lives to be transformed by grace.

As with most things, there's an upside and a downside to this. How nice it would be if the spiritual life were like winning the lottery—all at once, a complete and radical transformation of one's life. But how likely is it that one will win the lottery?

On the other hand, consider this. If you apply yourself each day and make a systematic effort to pray, it is guaranteed that you will make progress. It may be so slow as to seem imperceptible. But think about how a child learns to play the clarinet. At first, the sounds are atrocious, squeaky, and out of tune. But if the child practices just a little bit each day, in a couple of years he or she will sound pretty darn good. The kids who make no progress are the ones who never practice or who only practice when they feel like it.

Now, God has His ways, and whether you like them or not, you have to go along with them. In just about every aspect of life, God requires that we make sustained, systematic effort in order to improve. Why should it be any different in our prayer life? The person who only prays when he feels like it or "only when the Spirit moves me" is going to make about as much progress as the clarinetist who only practices when he feels like it. Not a pretty prospect.

That's one way to understand why we need a plan of life.

"How a plan of life helps us"

A plan of life gives us peace of mind. We all have days when it seems as if everything we do goes wrong: there's no bread to make school lunches; the car won't start; you make some phone calls about an upcoming event only to find that it's been postponed, and you have to call everybody back with the revised information. You totally lose it with your husband or one of the kids. You get to the end of the day, and it looks like a total wasteland. But if part of your plan of life is to get to Mass and say the Rosary, even if those two things were done in a bit of a blur, you can at least say to God: "Well, I did those two things for love of You." There are at least two good things you can point to in the day.

Blessed Josemaría [Escrivá] likened the plan of life to poles that are planted in the ground in Spain along mountain roads. In the winter, when the snow is deep, the poles stick out above the snow to show where the road is: "You must be constant and demanding with yourself in your regular practices of piety, even when you feel tired and arid. Persevere! Those moments are like the tall red-painted poles which serve as markers along the mountain roads when there are heavy snowfalls. They are always there to show where it is safe to go." [25]

We know that, in a sense, nothing we do on our own will accomplish anything in the spiritual life. But God has promised to honor our

---

[25] Josemaría Escrivá, *The Forge* (New York: Scepter Publishers, 2002), no. 81.

faithfulness: "Well done, good and faithful servant; you have been faithful over a little, I will set you over much; enter into the joy of your Master." [26] Well, if we persevere in our small way, in spite of everything, then God will reward our efforts by helping us along the way of sanctification, as well as by assisting those intentions we pray for.

Another way in which having a plan of life is helpful is that it shows that our devotion to God is authentic. Many saints and holy people have written that it is better to persevere in prayer without receiving what are usually called "consolations". Every now and again, most of us have been lucky enough to experience during or after our prayer an intense feeling of peace or even joy. Naturally, if this were to happen every single time we prayed, it would be no problem to pray. In fact, the problem would most likely then become how to make ourselves stop praying and get on with the work we have to do.

God clearly wants us to learn to persevere with our commitment to pray, especially when we really do not feel like doing it. Every great adult saint has experienced this type of trial. Every one attests that it is a most powerful time of inward growth. Now, if you are a religious in a community with a clear rule about what prayers to say and when, it is virtually impossible to avoid going successfully through just such a difficult stretch. But our vocation is in the lay state: we do not have a rule, and we do not have religious superiors telling us what to do with our spiritual lives. So if we do not have a plan of life, if we leave our prayer life up to chance, how are we going to reap the benefits of praying when the impulse to do so is absent?

Some people think prayer is a sham if it is done out of habit or merely because one has determined to pray. Let me read one of my favorite passages from Blessed Josemaría's writings. It can be very helpful. "In any case, if on beginning your meditation you don't succeed in concentrating your attention so as to be able to talk with God; if you feel dry and your mind seems incapable of expressing a single idea, or your affections remain dull, my advice is that you try to do what I have always tried to do on such occasions: put yourselves in the presence of your Father and tell him this much at least: 'Lord, I don't

[26] Mt 25:23.

know how to pray. I can't think of anything to tell you.' You can be sure that at that very moment you have already begun to pray."[27]

Again, this is similar to our experience in everyday life. When two young people first fall in love, they seem bent on doing as much as possible for each other. The great epics and poems of romantic love capture this desire to be tested, to prove one's love. Now, where does all this fervor go when it's time to get up with a teething baby or to be the first one up on Saturday morning to put out the garbage? But this is when love really shows its true colors. God gives young people the fervor of falling in love because otherwise the human race would probably come to an end. But the love God is really looking for, the love that is true and that counts, is the love of ten thousand mornings of getting up, being cheerful, listening to the kids when they come in from school like a thundering herd of elephants, and smiling at the husband when he comes in from work and refraining from rehearsing all the horrors of your day. It is these countless, repeated acts of self-denial that makes love deepen and grow.

The same is true in our relationship with God: "Every single day, do what you can to know God better, to get acquainted with him, to fall more in love with him each moment, and to think of nothing but of his Love and his glory. You will carry out this plan, my child, if you never, for any reason whatever, give up your times of prayer, your presence of God, with the aspirations and spiritual communions that set you on fire, your unhurried Holy Mass, and your work, finished off well for him."[28]

"What should our plan of life be?"

There are certain obvious basics: some time for conversation with God about the day-to-day events of your life, and the Rosary; daily Mass is always a good idea, and it can usually be fit into even a busy day. It's a good idea to talk to a good confessor or seek spiritual direction to keep yourself on the right track. Again, think how difficult it would

---

[27] [Josemaría Escrivá, *Friends of God*, no. 145d.]
[28] Escrivá, *Forge*, no. 737.

be to make progress playing an instrument or mastering a new sport without the help of someone trained to teach it.

Family Life: Summer Vacation

I begin with a quotation from *Familiaris Consortio*: "The family finds in the plan of God the Creator and Redeemer not only its identity, what it is, but also its mission, what it can and should do.... The family has the mission to guard, reveal and communicate love, and this is a living reflection of and a real sharing in God's love for humanity and the love of Christ the Lord for the Church His bride." [29]

We are composite beings, consisting of matter and spirit. As material beings, we are constantly subject to change. We do not experience reality all at once in its fullness, as God does, but rather we piece together our understanding of reality bit by laborious bit as we experience each moment of our lives. God made us this way, and He knows that, being as we are, we need a break every now and again from ordinary work. This is one reason why God built sleep into our daily life and one reason why God built the Sabbath rest into our weekly schedule. And it is why God in His wisdom created summer vacation.

Last year about this time I gave a talk on the topic of making good use of summer vacation. Those of you who heard it immediately realized this is a topic near and dear to my heart. Today's topic is more about living family life well, but with the particular application of how to do this in the summer.

Summer is a time for recreation. The meaning of the word "recreation" has been trivialized into "killing time", doing something amusing that distracts you from the boring grind of "real" life. But in its

[29] John Paul II, *Familiaris Consortio*, 17.

origin, the word "recreation" has religious significance—literally, it is re-creation, a restoring and improving upon creation.

Summer is the time of year when we should be sure to teach our children the importance of this God-given rhythm of life, alternating between diligent application to work and then refreshment of the soul through recreation. Summer is a time to teach children how to savor a slower pace, how to appreciate being outdoors, how to be with and get to know members of the family.

This life is a preparation for eternal life. It is worthwhile to stop and think about how you can make your preparation more deliberate. For instance, if you are preparing for an exam, you study the subject matter of the exam. If you are preparing for a marathon, you begin running long distances each day.

So if you are preparing for heaven, what should you be doing, actually? What is it we are going to do in heaven? Well, we don't have a manual or an instructional videotape called *How to Live in Heaven*. But we do know several things. First, we know we will contemplate God, seeing the ultimate expression of Truth, Beauty, and Goodness. So one safe bet for preparing for heaven is to become better at contemplating Truth, Beauty, and Goodness. Make a conscious effort to see God's creation as the expression of millions of tiny facets of His nature—the flowers, the trees, the feel of the wind, the blazing heat of the sun, the mountains, the rivers, the vast ocean, etc. Think about the people you love and admire. Think about the fact that God thought each one of them up. Isn't that clever? You owe God not only for your own existence, personality, talents, and gifts; you owe Him for everything you find amusing, amazing, and endearing about the people in your life.

In heaven, we will communicate with other people who are in heaven, as well as intercede for people still on earth. We should use the somewhat more relaxed schedule of summer to spend time talking to our children, spouses, friends, and neighbors, getting to know them better and being in a better position to intercede for them.

How to prioritize? Think in terms of what God expects from you. For those who are married, the first priority is your husband. In *Familiaris Consortio*, no. 18, the Holy Father [John Paul II] speaks about the family as the original "communion of persons" in human society. The family is not based on the relation of mother and child; rather, "the first communion is the one which is established and which develops between husband and wife." There is no communion of persons in this life more real or more complete than that of a husband and wife.

Of course, like most supernatural realities, this is a reality we do not always experience with tremendous clarity. Just as receiving communion does not always fill us with sensible experiences of charity and union with Christ, so also the sacrament of matrimony does not always make its reality felt as a total oneness of mind and will. Quite the contrary.

We must make the effort to deepen and improve the relationship we have with our husbands. Some obvious, time-tested pointers: don't greet your husband returning from work with a litany of complaints about what went wrong [during your day]. Save this for your sympathetic women friends. Make time for conversation with your husband. On retreat, I found an extremely perceptive point in C. S. Lewis' *Screwtape Letters*—that *we* tend to react to the *tone* of voice used by family members, but then we expect *them* to react only to our *precise words*. Don't do this. Be patient and trust that difficult times will pass.

After husbands come children. (Remember, not before husbands.) Then come parents and siblings, good friends, colleagues, neighbors ... the checkout clerk at the grocery store, even the driver cutting in front of you making a left turn at the intersection. Try saying to yourself, "See you in heaven (I hope)." Here's another apt saying of Blessed Josemaría [Escrivá]: "People engaged in worldly business say that time is money. That means little to me. For us who are engaged in the business of souls, time is glory!" [30]

In *On the Dignity and Vocation of Women*, John Paul II says, "The moral and spiritual strength of a woman is joined to her awareness that *God entrusts the human being to her in a special way*." [31] To fulfill this vocation, you have to think realistically about how to fit prayer, the Mass, the Holy Rosary, etc., into your day. Do not go along merely presuming

[30] Josemaría Escrivá, *The Way*, no. 355.
[31] John Paul II, *Mulieris Dignitatem*, 30 (emphasis in original).

that everything will work out: the summer will be three-fourths over before you admit you have to change your routine.

I conclude with a few practical tips.

Put your interior life first. Get out of the house early, before everyone is awake, to go to a Mass or to pray. Try going for a walk to say the Rosary.

Post a list of topics to study or books to read. Find a friend or two to read these books along with you and discuss them.

Make a list of trips you want to make, people you want to see, books you want to read. Post it on the fridge and see how many you can cross off in the course of the summer.

Improve your examination of conscience: Did I foster greater love and understanding with at least one member of my family today? Did I damage ... ?

Make the children stick to some kind of schedule. Don't let them sleep until noon. Make them do some reading and spend some time each day on some educational activities. Perhaps list some movies you have always wanted to see, and watch them all together.

Poverty

Poverty is an extremely important part of the Christian life, but also very difficult to figure out. Does Christ want all of us to give away our material possessions to the point of true material deprivation? Many of those who reject the Church point to the fantastic wealth and beauty of the great churches and cathedrals, as if this is a contradiction of Christ's teaching on poverty. What do we say to such people? And in our own lives, most of us live at a level of material wealth and comfort unimagined even by the greatest kings of ancient times. We live with greater security, wealth, and comfort than 99.9% of all the human beings who have ever inhabited this globe. How are we expected to live the virtue of poverty? What is this virtue?

"Christ's example"

First, to understand this better, let's look at what Christ did. After all, God became man so we could see who God is and what human beings are called to be like.

The Incarnation in itself is the most total and radical example of poverty and renunciation we could ever contemplate. "[Christ], though he was in the form of God, did not count equality with God a thing to be grasped, but emptied himself, taking the form of a servant, being born in the likeness of men" (Phil 2:6–7). We can never fully comprehend the degree to which Christ renounced wealth, power, beatitude, and glory in order to become one like us.

When Christ appeared among us, it is as if He desired to say in bold, neon lights, "Look at this. Wealth is nothing. Comfort, security, even keeping up appearances are worth nothing. All that matters is love."

Even though Joseph and Mary were people of very modest means, nevertheless, they had a place to live. They no doubt had furniture, blankets, and clothing. But God arranged it so that His Son would be born in a stable in some two-bit little out-of-the-way town. Joseph naturally had money enough to pay for a room at the inn, but God did not want that. He wanted the Holy Family to experience and illuminate a situation of total poverty—though not destitution. (They had shelter, they were not starving, and so on.) It was the bare minimum.

Mary's reaction was one of peace and serenity, not awkward mortified embarrassment. This is what we should imitate. Naturally, we do the best we can to provide in a fitting way for our families, but once we have done our best, we must accept with grace whatever lack of material means God has sent to us. There is no shame in lacking material possessions.

Christ tells us not to worry about material things: "Consider the lilies of the field, how they grow; they neither toil nor spin; yet I tell you, even Solomon in all his glory was not clothed like one of these" (Mt 6:28–29). The story of the widow's mite (Mk 12:41) is a good example of abandonment: the widow in faith gives her last penny. The parable of the rich man and Lazarus (Lk 16:19) teaches us that we must reckon carefully how we use our wealth. For the rich young man, his material goods get in the way of following Christ. Finally, the story of the rich fool in Luke 12:13 impresses upon us the futility of earthly treasure.

Blessed Josemaría [Escrivá] has some very strong words to say about these matters. "Gold, silver, jewels; dirt, piles of manure. Delights, sensual pleasures, satisfactions of the appetites; like a beast, like a mule, like a hog, like a cock, like a bull. . . . Honors, distinctions, titles; things of air, puffs of pride, lies, nothingness."[32] "Why stoop to drink from the puddles of worldly consolations if you can satisfy your thirst with waters that spring up into life everlasting."[33]

We should recall the Beatitudes. They indicate that detachment brings true freedom and the ability to possess without being possessed.

"Practically, what can we do?"

Be generous in giving: to the Church, to the poor, but especially in giving love and time to your family and those who need it. Do not obsess about material goods; try to practice abandonment to the will of God.

Get rid of excess goods: they are a weight on your soul. Radical poverty is liberating. We in the world have to adapt this principle to our own particular situation—*adapt* it, not *ignore* it. For instance, get rid of anything you have not worn in the last year. Get rid of extra dishes and pots. Get rid of papers and books! If they are of no value to someone else, then throw them away.

[32] Josemaría Escrivá, *The Way*, no. 677.
[33] Ibid., no. 148.

In general, do with less. Don't put yourself in temptation's way. (Avoid shopping malls!) Help your children in the same way, for example, by teaching them to reflect critically on television advertisements.

Ask Mary to give you the same spirit of abandonment she had.

"What is poverty, anyway?"

We tend to use the word "poverty" in at least three different senses: first, there is poverty in the sense of an actual lack of material necessities or comforts; second, there is the deplorable lack of spiritual goods; third, there is poverty of spirit, a virtuous detachment from created things. The worst poverty is spiritual poverty. "There is hunger for ordinary bread," Mother Teresa says, "and there is hunger for love, for kindness, for thoughtfulness; and this is the great poverty that makes people suffer so much." [34]

Suffering: Living Our Crosses

Why must we suffer? What does it accomplish? The sin of Adam and Eve was to put their will above God's. This is the essential sin— to prefer our will to God's will. You can understand suffering as the medicine needed to right the underlying problem. If a bone breaks and begins to heal crooked, it must be broken again and set straight. Similarly, we need to uproot our own will and realign it with God's. The experience of physical or spiritual suffering patiently endured for God's sake is a most effective way of realigning our will correctly.

"There is no love without renunciation." [35] The Persons of the Trinity live a life of perfect and complete self-giving. Man made in God's

[34] Mother Teresa [of Calcutta], *A Gift for God: Prayers and Meditations* (San Francisco: HarperOne, 1996), pp. 19–20.
[35] Josemaría Escrivá, *The Forge*, no. 760.

244

image is called to that same type of relationship. Self-giving did not hurt before the Fall. Now it hurts, but it is still our vocation, our essence as [persons] created in the "image of God".

Let's reflect on the different ways in which God asks us to suffer. There are of course disasters, such as a catastrophic illness, the untimely death of a loved one, accidents, and so on. Then there are disappointments in love: husbands who fail, relationships that fail, children who go astray, and parents and siblings who reject the faith. Perhaps most common are little sufferings that make up the day-to-day downward pull: tedium, minor aches and pains, irritations, cars that break down, soufflés that don't rise, rain when you plan a picnic, and other things like these.

For disasters, a natural question is: Why did this happen to me? There is a good and a bad sense in asking this question. The bad sense is [the one in which you] ask the question as if [you didn't] deserve the suffering—and someone else did. When you find yourself looking at things in that way, think rather about the millions of people who have suffered more and enjoyed less than you have. Rise above the natural inclination to self-pity. In contrast, the good sense [is the one in which you ask] the question [so as] to wonder: What does God want me to learn from this? What can I draw out from this experience? How can it bring me closer to God?

What *is* the point of suffering? We need to have faith that God brings good out of evil. We do believe this, but we should try to accept it at a deeper level. God really does bring the best out of the worst. Joseph was traded into slavery in Egypt, but God selected him as the chief steward of that empire. Moses was abandoned to die as an infant, yet God made him the liberator of Israel. The poor man Lazarus lived a life of destitution, but God lifted him up to the bosom of Abraham. Similarly, the tortures of the cross gave way to the joy of the Resurrection. Of course, we do not as yet see what we take on faith. But knowing as we do that the Resurrection is a fact, why don't we trust God more? Why do we think we know better than God?

> Listen to me, my child: you must be happy when people treat you badly and dishonor you, when many come out against you and it becomes the done thing to spit on you, because you are *omnium peripsema*, like the refuse of the world. It's hard, it's very hard. It is

245

hard, until at last one goes to the tabernacle, seeing oneself thought of as the scum of the earth, like a wretched worm, and says with all one's heart, "Lord, if you don't need my good name, what do I want it for?" Up to then even a child of God does not know what happiness is—up to that point of nakedness and self-giving. It is a self-giving of love, but it is founded on mortification, on sorrow.[36]

Did Christ ever not cure a sick person during His life on this earth? Usually He cured, but sometimes He did not: "And coming to his own country he taught them in their synagogue, so that they were astonished, and said, 'Where did this man get this wisdom and these mighty works? Is not this the carpenter's son? Is not his mother called Mary? . . . And are not all his sisters with us? Where then did this man get all this?' And they took offense at him. But Jesus said to them, 'A prophet is not without honor except in his own country and in his own house.' And he did not do many mighty works there, because of their unbelief" (Mt 13:54–58). What is different now? Do we lack faith? We should imitate the widow whose son Christ raised (Lk 7:11); the leper who came up to Christ, kneeled down, and beseeched Him, "If you will, you can make me clean" (Mk 1:40); or the faith of the centurion, or the tenacity of the Syro-Phoenician woman (Mk 7:25–30).

If God's will is that we continue to suffer, we might wonder whether God has stopped paying attention to us. But He hasn't: God knows what it is to suffer. He, after all, chose the cross. God went out of His way to experience suffering worse than yours. Also, we know that His favorite person is Mary: look what that got her—certainly not a reprieve from suffering.

How can suffering be redemptive, as we believe? It is redemptive because God makes it so. We could not actually do anything for God unless He made it so. It helps to take one's suffering to prayer: "There can be no doubt that for us who love Jesus, prayer is the great pain-reliever."[37] Prayer is a "pain reliever" both naturally and supernaturally.

A real form of suffering is when someone you love suffers. Christ, as He suffered, was beloved by His Mother Mary, and also by God the Father

---

[36] Ibid., no. 803.
[37] Ibid., no. 756.

and God the Spirit. For whom is suffering harder—the one who suffers, or someone who loves the one who suffers? Think about this, and offer up whatever is harder. Do not gloss over what is painful. Death is an indignity. It is something to be sad about: Jesus wept for Lazarus.

Finally, how can we help others suffer? We should, for our part, offer up sacrifices for them, and we should try to explain what it is to offer up suffering. In doing this, it helps to point to the cross.

Hope

Hope is a particularly fitting subject for the season of Advent, since hope is the characteristic attitude of this season: reliving the hope of God's chosen people yearning for their Messiah, as well as anticipating that definitive coming when Christ's kingdom will be fully established and every longing on earth and in heaven will be answered.

You recall, I trust—from my talk last spring on fortitude—the difference between human virtues and theological virtues: human virtues are those firm dispositions to do the good, which are acquired by human effort; theological virtues must be infused into the soul by God, and they are what dispose a person to be in relationship with God. The theological virtues are faith, hope, and charity.

The *Catechism* defines hope in this way: "Hope is the theological virtue by which we desire the kingdom of heaven and eternal life as our happiness, placing our trust in Christ's promises." [38]

We are accustomed to thinking of the importance of hope in adversity, and it is, of course, important. It is what helps get us through tough times. Viewed merely from a natural perspective, human life is utterly pointless. Many people claim to be thoroughgoing atheists and materialists, but I don't believe that many, if any, of them really are. If someone seriously believed that death is the absolute end of a person's

---

[38] *Catechism of the Catholic Church*, no. 1817.

existence—that there is no continuing personal existence, no God, no righting of injustices, and no compensation for the unequal distribution of suffering and pain of this life—then I cannot see why anyone would put up with the inconvenience of another day. Hope is more than a comfort: it is what keeps one from concluding that life is utterly meaningless: "When encountering the bitter injustice of this life, how the honest soul rejoices remembering the eternal Justice of its eternal God! With the knowledge of its own wretchedness, it utters with a fruitful desire that Pauline exclamation: *Non vivo ego*—it's not me living now! It's Christ who lives in me! And He will live forever."[39]

Hope is, of course, intimately linked to faith. By faith we believe that God really exists, that He has spoken to us, and that He took human form and suffered on the cross so that we could live united to Him forever.

Believing this, it is obvious that we have good grounds for entertaining the wildest, most extravagant of hopes. We believe God chose freely to undergo the most excruciating method of execution devised by human ingenuity and that He did this to show us just how much He loves each one of us. Furthermore, He promised that if we unite our sufferings to His, this will be a means of righting wrongs and expiating our own sins, as well as winning graces for others. Given that fact, how can we not be sustained by hope and consider that every obstacle, every disappointment, every pain—even to the point of agony—is, in reality, a great blessing; that from the vantage point of heaven, we will see the good that has been accomplished through our acceptance of every trial? Now, that is something that should give us a lot of hope—even anticipatory pleasure—while we are still slogging through it all down here in the fog. "In our poor present life, let us drink to the last from the chalice of pain. What does it matter to suffer for ten, twenty, fifty years, if afterwards there is heaven forever, forever . . . forever!"[40]

But hope is also important when things are going OK. Sometimes the most difficult times are those when everything is humming along well and there are no great problems, but there is no great joy either. This seems the typical mind-set of middle age: Is that all there is? You work

[39] Josemaría Escrivá, *Furrow* (New York: Scepter Publishers, 2002), no. 892.
[40] Josemaría Escrivá, *The Way*, no. 182.

hard; you put in long hours, at work or raising the children; then here you are—you own a house and two cars, you take nice vacations, and life still seems somehow inadequate. Hope is that deep intuition that life is supposed to yield more, something deeper, truer, more extreme than simple, comfortable domestic life. That yearning is for heaven and the beatific vision.

It seems hope is more than just the desire for happiness: it seems almost an enjoyment of a happiness not yet fully possessed. It is like the pleasure of anticipation that engaged couples experience as they contemplate their approaching wedding, or the pleasure of looking forward to a family reunion at the holidays: there is already in the anticipation an element of the happiness and joy that is foreseen.

Advent is an excellent time to foster that understanding of hope. It is as if Christ were going to be born for the first time. We should try to do things to kindle that sense that, at last, the desire of every nation, of every human heart is coming into the world. For that is what we celebrate at Christmas. God created us with a desire for Him. There is no finite good that can satisfy the human heart: we can only attain happiness united to God. And since we do not have the ability to reach God, God reaches down to us, coming in the most accessible, even adorable, way He could devise: as a helpless child.

During Advent, we should encourage this spirit of anticipation with our children. Use Advent candles; use Advent calendars. Do special things, and increase family prayers for special intentions. We should also try to make Christmas as festive and joyous as possible.

The Rosary and May Pilgrimages

Since May is the month devoted to Our Lady, I am going to speak about two very traditional and very popular Marian devotions: the Rosary and May pilgrimages.

The Rosary is a devotion of the Latin rite Church that was developed to allow laypeople to join in the Liturgy of the Hours. (Now, most of you probably know this, but when I first converted, this was not explained to me, so I am going to go over what is obvious and familiar ground.) The Roman Catholic Church has official, liturgical prayers that are recited every day throughout the day. All priests are bound to recite these prayers, though with varying degrees of completeness. The psalms of the Old Testament form the major part of this liturgical prayer. In the course of reciting the entire office, one goes through all 150 psalms. The full fifteen sets of ten Hail Marys correspond to the 150 psalms. In this way, people who simply could not recite the liturgical prayers could, nevertheless, join their prayers to those of the Church.

The practice of reciting the Rosary was promoted after Saint Dominic received a revelation from Our Lady, who told him that the Albigensian heresy would be defeated through promotion of the Rosary. The Albigensians were very puritanical and took a dim view of marriage, childbearing, and human nature in general. The mysteries of the Rosary focus attention on the humanity of Jesus and the dignity of His Mother, thereby asserting the supernatural dignity God has conferred on human nature and relations within the family.

For many centuries after Saint Dominic, the Rosary continued to be one of the most popular devotions of the Latin Church.

In the past century, however, it has become abundantly clear that Mary wants to increase devotion to the Rosary. Her appearance at Fatima should have been enough to settle the question for all time. Those of us who are mothers know that saying something once never suffices for all time, so Mary has taken the trouble to appear numerous times to many different people, reiterating this little piece of maternal advice: "Say the Rosary."

Now, many people today think the Rosary is too old-fashioned. They think that, since the time of Vatican II, we have moved beyond simplistic, repetitious, maybe even superstitious, vocal prayer into the superior realm of "centering" prayer, or praying in tongues, or conversational, spontaneous prayer. I do not mean to disparage any other form of Christian prayer—all have their good points, and we should all be developing our prayer life to include other forms of personal prayer. But people: if the Mother of God, who stands, body and soul, in the presence of God already enjoying the beatific vision; if the Mother of the Church, the creature whom only God Himself is greater than; if this lady from heaven says, "Pray the Rosary", well, I think we should just do what she says, no matter what. Chances are, she has a pretty darn good reason for being so insistent about asking us to say the Rosary.

Think about the way you deal with your children. You tell them to brush their teeth. You tell them to wash their hands before eating. You tell them to change their socks regularly. They usually do not see the efficacy of doing what you say. They complain that it's too hard, or too boring, or too time-consuming to do all of these dumb little things. But we know that if we can bludgeon them into forming these habits, then they won't lose their teeth, they won't die of typhus or dysentery, and their socks won't be reduced to shreds in a matter of days. It takes time, but most children come to realize that their mothers were right about these matters.

Why don't we recognize that the same thing applies to our relationship with Mary? We should just do what she asks and trust that she really does know what is for our own good. She wants people to say the Rosary each day.

Now, of course, the Rosary is closely linked to the practice of making a May pilgrimage. The destination of the pilgrimage is typically a shrine, a church, or a suitable image of Our Lady. You recite all fifteen decades of the Rosary en route to, returning from, and at the site of the shrine, the church, or the image. It is a beautiful way to give outward expression to our devotion to Mary. It is a good way to include children in the recitation of the Rosary: most children find it a little difficult to sit still in one place through the entire fifteen decades, but if they are walking around outside, able to look at trees, flowers, statues, etc., it is a bit easier for them to carry on praying.

God has organized things with a view to our salvation. It is no coincidence that the Resurrection took place at the beginning of spring, when many human cultures experience the return of hope after the desolation of winter. The same applies to Marian devotion in May:

the beauty of the flowering trees, the fresh pale green of the new grass and leaves, the delicacy of the spring flowers—all these things put us in mind of the extraordinary beauty of the Blessed Virgin, the Bride of the Holy Spirit, this youthful Mother of the living.

Mary is our Mother. A May pilgrimage is a little bit like observing Mother's Day. You know you love your mother. You know she knows you love her. And yet it is important to give outward, even somewhat formal, expression to this love. So when Mother's Day rolls around, most of us make a point of doing something extra to let our mothers know that we appreciate what they have done for us, even if it is just a small thing like a phone call or a card.

In dealing with our own children or grandchildren, we recognize that it is important to teach them how to observe a holiday like Mother's Day. It is good for children to learn how to express that they are grateful for all their mothers do for them.

A May pilgrimage is an excellent way for us to show our devotion and gratitude to Mary, our heavenly Mother. Think of how it is when your child gives you some small gift. Don't you love him all the more because you see how much he wants to give you something to show you how much he loves you, and you see how powerless he is to give anything except that fact—that he loves you and wants to give you something to make that love visible?

There is nothing we can give Mary, our heavenly Mother, except that same thing—we give her the fact that we want to show her our love. And she will accept that little token just as we accept the bouquets of limp dandelions and the construction-paper cards dripping with Elmer's Glue.

The Church attaches great significance to the Rosary. In fact, you may gain a plenary indulgence by reciting the full fifteen decades with others or in front of the Blessed Sacrament. The usual conditions apply: sacramental confession, attendance at Mass, reception of communion, and prayer for the Pope's intentions.[41]

[41] [One might also note: "Regarding the plenary indulgence for the recitation of the Marian rosary, the following is prescribed: (1.) The recitation of a third part of the rosary is sufficient, but the five decades must be recited without interruption. (2.) Devout meditation

And of course, we are doing this not because we are confused about whom we are worshipping. The reason we love Mary is because she brought Christ into the world. She is our Mother because she was Jesus' Mother first, and He gave her to us. Mary plays an essential role as the spiritual Mother of each and every individual Christian. It would be obtuse and ungrateful if we were to fail to acknowledge her. And if we consider that Jesus is fully human, it becomes clear that He wants us to recognize Mary.

"Are you not moved to hear some affectionate word addressed to your mother? The same thing happens to Our Lord. We cannot separate Jesus from his Mother."[42] To hear praise of one's own mother: as adults, isn't this a great joy for us? So it is for Jesus, as for the Holy Trinity who made her.

Abortion and the Culture of Human Rights

Transcript of LEAP (Life Education Awareness Project) presentation, Saint Peter-Marian High School, Worcester, Massachusetts, November 12, 1997

The immediate reason for my coming to speak to high school students this time of year is that this January will mark the twenty-fifth anniversary of the Supreme Court decision *Roe v. Wade*, which is the reason why abortion became such a controversial issue in our country. This was the decision that legalized abortion on demand. And the

---

on the mysteries is to be added to the vocal prayer. (3.) In its public recitation the mysteries must be announced in accord with approved local custom, but in its private recitation it is sufficient for the faithful simply to join meditation on the mysteries to the vocal prayer." Apostolic Penitentiary, *Manual of Indulgences: Norms and Grants* (Washington, D.C.: United States Conference of Catholic Bishops, 2006), pp. 58–59, a translation from the 4th ed. (1999) of *Enchiridion Indulgentiarum: Normae et Concessiones*.]

[42] Josemaría Escrivá, *The Forge*, no. 243.

Pro-Life Office is going to be sponsoring three buses for high-school-aged students to go down to Washington for this March. I'm sure that you know some students who have gone to the March—there have been several students each year from this school. But this is the first time that the diocese itself is going to sponsor buses and organize a trip for high-school-aged students to participate in this March, because it's the twenty-fifth anniversary, a significant and sad milestone.

Obviously my job is to get interested young people to go to this March, and how do you sell the idea of getting on a bus at ten in the evening and riding through the night, getting out before daylight in the dead of winter, spending the entire day outside—going to some of the official buildings and museums, but for the most part you're outside, you're going to walk for about an hour in a huge March, with tens of thousands of people—and then getting back on a bus and riding through the night again, and coming home in the middle of the night? It doesn't sound that attractive, and this is not a trip for sightseeing. It's not a pleasure trip.

I think the only way I could realistically inspire anybody to want to go on this trip is to talk about what the purpose of this March is and talk about what unites all of the tens of thousands of people who will be there for this March.

So I'm going to cover *Roe v. Wade*—what that decision represents in our country's history and development. And then I want to talk a little bit about what value systems are competing for your allegiance in this country. I'm not exaggerating. There are two diametrically opposed value systems in competition—in conflict—in the United States today, and they are trying to win over *you*, your hearts and minds. The Holy Father refers to these two world views as the Culture of Life and the Culture of Death. So that's what I want to do today— talk about *Roe v. Wade* and then talk about those two cultures.

You were born after *Roe v. Wade*. So you obviously have no memory at all of what it was like before abortion was a big business and freely available on demand. But prior to 1973, abortion was a crime in almost every state in the United States of America. There were about a half a dozen states that, during the sixties and the very early seventies, changed their laws in response to [followers of] certain ideological movements—people concerned about "overpopulation", people who were in favor of eugenics (eliminati[on of people] with genetic defects), [members of] the feminist movement, and advocates of the sexual revolution. These four ideological strains began agitating to change quite a few of the laws—the divorce laws, laws about marriage, and also, in our country, the laws that prohibited abortion. And by the end of the sixties and very early seventies, they had had some very modest success in a handful of states that had legalized abortion in the first two trimesters, the first six months [of pregnancy]—in Florida, New York, California, Colorado, and one or two others. *That's it.* Everywhere else in the United States, abortion was a kind of crime.

Now, you know that crimes are divided up into different types of crime. What do you call the crime of going on property where you are not allowed? Trespass[ing], right? What is the category of crime that involves taking property that does not belong to you? What are different names for these sorts of crimes? Larceny. Theft. That is taking property. Now, where do you think in the categories of crimes abortion was classified? What kind of a crime? [*Audience member:* Murder?] No, not technically murder. What is the general term for crimes of which murder is one particular form? [*Audience member:* Homicide?] Homicide, exactly. It's not as if people didn't know what an abortion was. Everyone understood what it was. And it was classified as a crime, as a form of homicide. Not murder—murder needs to be a deliberate, freely chosen, intentional act. That's got a technical meaning in the law. And there is also manslaughter, and there is vehicular homicide. There are many different forms of taking human life. And abortion was understood to be one of them.

But the Supreme Court of the United States was composed at that time of seven people, out of nine, who had been very much influenced by those four ideological groups I named before—[people concerned about] overpopulation, [supporters of] eugenics, [supporters of] feminism, and [advocates of] the sexual revolution—and when this case came before them, *Roe v. Wade* ... Of course, this case didn't just come out of the blue; there had been a nationwide campaign by these ideological groups—the American Civil Liberties Union, NOW [National Organization for Women], Planned Parenthood—they were looking for a good test case. They had many going on across the country, but the first one that got to the Supreme Court was this one from Texas known as *Roe v. Wade*. And in one decision, overnight, seven men sitting on the Supreme Court of the United States interpreted our Constitution to say that, embedded in the Constitution—I always bring a copy, just in case anybody wants to look—somehow embedded in this document is an unfettered right to an abortion—though you can look: the word "abortion" does not occur; the word "privacy" does not occur; the word "choice"—it just doesn't occur.

It was a highly criticized decision at the time by constitutional scholars. But the effect of that decision was to just erase every single law in all fifty states that prohibited or restricted abortion in any way. And it's interesting, they even erased the laws in the most permissive states—California, Colorado, New York, Florida—because those states did not permit abortion in as broad a way as *Roe v. Wade* required.

Now what was the immediate impact of *Roe v. Wade*? I think there are three basic categories of information that I want to get across to you that help you picture what happened after *Roe v. Wade*. Something that had been a crime and considered a form of homicide went overnight from that category to being a constitutionally guaranteed right. That's a very radical change. So three [questions] that help you understand what has happened in our country around the practice of abortion as a result of *Roe v. Wade* are: (1) How many abortions are there? How common has it become? (2) At what point in pregnancy are abortions typically performed? and (3) What are the reasons that women have abortions? If you know those three things, then you have a pretty good sense of the actual subject matter of this conflict—how abortion is going on, day in, day out.

So I am going to start with the number of abortions. The first year abortion was legal (and it was legalized in January, so it was almost a full year), there were eight hundred thousand abortions performed. By the second year, 1974, there were a million; by the third year, 1.2 million; and by the fourth year (that would be by the end of 1977), 1.5 million. And it has stayed at that level ever since, hovering between 1.5 and 1.6 million.

Now, this is an interesting observation. What is the ratio between 1.6 million and eight hundred thousand? What fractional part of 1.6 million is eight hundred thousand? It's half. Abortion advocates (and I'm very familiar with what they say because I frequently do debates, and I've debated every abortion advocacy group in this state, so I know what they say)—one of their claims is that there have always been abortions, a million illegal abortions every year. They claim that even if abortion is illegal, there are going to be just as many desperate women resorting to illegal abortions. But it is impossible to believe that, because it is very clear from the numbers that, at the very least, legalizing abortion on demand doubled the number of abortions over the span of four years. That's what happened; the numbers are there. And it's pretty difficult to contend that there were eight hundred thousand illegal abortions in the year prior to abortion becoming an unregulated industry which did advertising and was also tax funded, since immediately Medicaid began picking up the tab for abortions of women who were in low income brackets. So legalizing abortion on demand at the minimum doubled the number of abortions in our country— more likely quadrupled the number, but we can't record the number of illegal abortions.

Another way for you to visualize the impact: the abortion rate in Massachusetts is one out of three pregnancies. So today there will be women who will go to the drugstore [and] get a home pregnancy test, or go to their doctor's office, and for every three women, today, who discover they're pregnant, one is going to have an abortion. That's been going on in this state for almost the full twenty-five years. So the corollary of that is that if I were to put you in pairs, for each pair of you in this room, there was another human life, conceived the same year you were conceived but [that] did not get born. And that's true for every grade—high school and preschool, toddlers at home, and the babies that come into the world today in hospitals in Massachusetts. For every two of them, there was another—that was aborted.

Now, at what point in pregnancy are abortions typically performed? Again, when I do debates—you can take that color brochure [*points to a picture in a brochure on fetal development already handed out to each of the students in the audience*]—abortion advocates love to look at this picture, a zygote, what a human being looks like in the first twenty-four hours; abortion advocates will say, "Who can look at that, a one-celled animal, and say, 'Ah, I recognize there a fellow human being with the same rights and immunities as a grown woman'?" And I agree, it's extremely difficult to identify with a one-celled animal. But that's irrelevant to the abortion debate, because you cannot do an abortion this early—it is impossible, physically impossible, to destroy the developing human life at this point. The earliest any abortion can be performed, even an abortion using the abortion pill, RU-486—turn to the next page of the brochure—is five weeks after conception. That's the absolute earliest abortion. I agree, I would not call that a baby. It's not a baby. It doesn't look adorable and cute. On the other hand, this is what a woman will be told is a "clump of cells", or "pregnancy tissue", or a "product of conception". Those are the typical phrases that are used to describe *that*—even though I think every reasonable person looking at that photograph can say they see a head, an eye, arms, legs, spinal cord. And you can see that red bulb located in the picture above what will be the thumb is the heart—a heart that has already been beating at this point for two weeks. That's true in every abortion. The heart is already beating. And in the vast majority of abortions, all you would have to do is lay an electronic stethoscope on the woman's abdomen, and everybody in the room [*taps on the wooden desk at a fast rate approximating an unborn baby's heart rate*] would hear [*stops speaking for a moment and keeps tapping*] that fetal heartbeat, just a lot faster than an adult's heartbeat. But they don't do that in abortion facilities. I think you can figure that out. Why don't they do that? They don't. They never do.

Now, this would still be an unusually early abortion. The typical abortion in Massachusetts—you've got to turn two pages over in the brochure—is between the eighth and the ninth week. That's the median gestational age for abortions in Massachusetts—which means that half of all the abortions done in our state, which would be about fifteen thousand per year, are done between this point [*points to the picture of the five-week-old fetus*] and this point [*points to the about-nine-week-old fetus*]. But of course that means that the other half are done after this point [nine weeks] in pregnancy. And again, abortion advocates would love for everyone to continue to believe that abortions are only performed—what?—before there are any recognizable human features, just unformed tissue. But that is simply not true. No abortions are performed that early. And in fact, half of the abortions in this state take place after the ninth week of pregnancy.

Now, most Americans remain very unaware [of] and oblivious to how routinely late abortions are performed. And what astonishes me is that it's not as though you've got to go dig this information out of medical archives or anything. All you need to do is look in the Yellow Pages [*holds up a page torn from the Yellow Pages*]. You will see, next to all the tiny, modest ads for other businesses—like dry cleaning, sales and services, deposits, accessories—there are these big, very expensive ads for abortion clinics. And right in the Yellow Pages, it says: "Reasonable fees. Most health insurance accepted. Evening hours. Prompt appointments. MasterCard and Visa accepted. Abortion to twenty-two weeks." In the Yellow Pages.

Now this is what a developing human looks like eighteen weeks after conception [*holds up a plastic model of what appears to be a small baby*]. This is life-size and anatomically correct. And in the Yellow Pages, [abortion clinics] advertise that if you've got your MasterCard or Visa, you can walk in off the street, and if you can pay for it, they will destroy *this*. You don't need a doctor's note. You don't have to prove that your health will be jeopardized, or anything. It's just: you want an abortion; you can pay for an abortion. And a full four weeks—a month—further along in pregnancy than this [*continues to hold up the model*], they will just destroy this. This is what will be described as a "clump of cells", "pregnancy tissue", "product of conception".

I even brought the Informed Consent Form used by the state of Massachusetts, where all that is said about *this* is that "the contents of the uterus will be evacuated." That's what this is [*again holds up the model*]— contents of the uterus. Now, of course, abortion is legal and performed even later than the twenty-two-week point.

You have heard by now of partial-birth abortion? This is the debate that's raging in Congress. Twice our Congress has passed a law to ban a particularly barbaric method of doing a late abortion, and President [William] Clinton, who is very much in favor of abortion on demand, has vetoed this. The paper that began this whole debate was given by the doctor, Dr. Martin Haskell, who developed this technique of doing abortions. And he explained why he developed the technique and at what point in pregnancy this technique can be used. If any of you doubt me, you can come and look at the photocopy [*gestures to the document she is holding in her hand*]. He says right at the opening of the paper that he routinely uses this technique in women twenty to twenty-six weeks pregnant. (Let's see, twenty-six weeks, and four weeks to a month, so that's six and a half months.) But then towards the end, he says he's familiar with another surgeon, using a "conceptually similar technique", who performs these procedures up to "thirty-two weeks or more". It says it right there in black and white. [How long does it take to carry a baby to] term, does anybody know? Any mothers or aunts or cousins who have had babies, when everybody's counting the weeks? The baby comes on the due date, and how many weeks is that? Right, it's forty. So "thirty-two weeks or more" means [it is] the seventh or eighth month of pregnancy when this technique is used.

This is a paper that was given at a convention. You know how insurance salesmen go to conventions, and dentists go to conventions—and abortionists also go to conventions. This was held in Dallas, September 13–14, 1992, and it was hosted by the National Abortion Federation. This was where Dr. Martin Haskell got up and gave his paper about how to do a partial-birth abortion. And right here in public— it's written in this article—it's said that this is used into the seventh or eighth month of pregnancy.

All right. Enough of that. You know how many abortions there are; you know at what point in pregnancy they are typically performed; and the final little piece of the jigsaw puzzle: Why, why do so many women choose abortion?

Again, I have heard abortion advocates, and I know what they use in their rhetoric, in their advertising, and in their PR. They focus on women who are victims of rape and incest. Women for whom pregnancy poses a serious risk to their physical health. And women who are carrying children who are known to be handicapped. But now they've changed a little. They don't even just say "handicapped" because it's not PC to be in favor of killing handicapped people anymore. So they say "children with profound handicaps who are certain to die". And who would not feel sorry for a woman in that circumstance, who is carrying a child, and she is going to go through labor and birth knowing that the child is going to die? And similarly, victims of rape and incest, and women who are really risking their physical health being pregnant. I think everybody in this room would say that we all feel a lot of sympathy for women in those circumstances. But it is a realistic question to ask, "OK, how many of the 1.55 million abortions done every year are actually done for those reasons?"

Now, I know from dealing with the media, dealing with the public, that nobody believes pro-lifers. Why should they? We're supposed to be irrational fanatics. So I don't ever tell you things that come from pro-life sources. I brought with me the photocopy of an article. It appeared in *Family Planning Perspectives*, which is the research journal put out by Planned Parenthood. Planned Parenthood operates the largest chain of abortion facilities in the United States, and they are also the biggest funders of pro-abortion advocacy and lobbying in the United States. So this is not pro-life propaganda. This is a research paper: they handed out questionnaires all across the country; they got a very good, very representative sample of women that were having abortions, who filled out this questionnaire in the abortion facility. The question was: What is the principal reason you are having this abortion? And I am going to read to you the top six reasons, given by the women themselves, why the woman was having an abortion. If you add up all the percentages, it comes to about 90% of all the abortions done in the United States. And these are the reasons: "I can't afford a baby now"; "I'm not ready for the responsibility"; "I'm concerned about how having a baby could change my life"; "I have problems with this relationship and want to avoid single motherhood"; "I'm not mature enough to have a child"; "I already have as many children as I want."

Now, again, without being harsh or judgmental—I'm sure a lot of these women were in extremely difficult circumstances—but I think we can all agree these are a far cry from women who are victims of rape or incest; women who are going to jeopardize their physical health; or women who are carrying a profoundly handicapped child. How many of the women in this questionnaire said, "I was a victim or rape or incest"; "My health is threatened"; "This child is fatally handicapped"? If you add up the women who said that, it comes to less than 3% of the 1.55 million abortions done each year in this country.

Now, that's really significant, because this was a headline, in the *Boston Globe* [*holds up a newspaper*], back in 1989, which was a very startling headline. (One of the members of the board of directors of Massachusetts Citizens for Life, which is the pro-life lobbying group in Massachusetts, had a friend who worked for the *Globe* and heard the editorial staff shouting at them the night they were trying to decide how to print this headline, because the headline did not come out the way they wanted it.) They had commissioned a poll, a public opinion survey, with WBZ-TV, about what Americans think about abortion, and, of course, don't we all know that we are the most pro-choice state in the union, and the vast majority of people are pro-choice and favor a woman's "right to choose"? But the headline says, "Most in U.S. favor ban on majority of abortions." How is that possible? Well, if you look carefully at their pie charts and everything, what you find out is that if you ask people detailed questions like this: "Do you think all abortions should be illegal?" "Do you think all abortions should be illegal except those to save the life of the mother?" "Do you think all abortions should be illegal except those to save the life of the mother and those of women who were victims of rape and incest?"—what you find is that if you keep going until you get to "Do you think you should have our current policy, which is abortion on demand?" about 52 or 53% of Americans believe that abortions should *only* be legal for the "hard cases"—those ones that I just cited. So basically, if we could make laws—which we can't, because once the Supreme Court rules, you can only go against what the Supreme Court says if you pass a constitutional amendment, which is very difficult, or if the Supreme Court itself sees fit to change its mind, which does happen but takes a long time ... So we cannot pass laws that actually reflect what the majority of Americans believe. What the majority of Americans believe is that abortion should only be legal for the 3% of the abortions that are actually going on day in and day out in this country.

Now, I think at this point—I could go on and on—you've got a clear sense how abortion became legal, how many there are, at what point in pregnancy they really are done and are legal, and what are the reasons that are driving women to this. A lot them are just plain old socioeconomic reasons. You could solve a lot of these problems in ways that are a lot less drastic and final than taking the life of the unborn child.

Now, I want to try very vividly to impress upon you what are the two value systems competing for your allegiance. The first is the pro-life position, which I think is pretty obvious—no, it's not obvious, because of the way that the media always portrays people like [me]. I am a pro-life activist; I have been doing this for a decade; a lot of my free time goes to trying to teach people and persuade them to be pro-life. Now, what is it that motivates me? The media portrayal of people like me is that we are religious fanatics, just going around trying to make everyone be whatever religion we are, or that we are against equal rights for women—which I always think is a joke, because if I were against equal rights for women, what would I be doing with a job, and out in the public sphere, getting involved in politics and public policy debates? And I don't know a single pro-lifer who is motivated because [he or she doesn't] think women are equal to men or [doesn't] believe in equal access to education or professional training, political life, and everything.

What motivates us is something that is very simple. We just really do believe that all human beings are equal. *All human beings are equal.* What could that possibly mean? Because, as you well know, all of us are not equally smart, equally athletic, equally good-looking, equally proficient, equally nice. We're not equal in any of those categories. But we are equal in our essential dignity as human beings. And that means everybody, not just the ones you like, or the ones that look like you or talk your language. It means every single member of the human race has this innate human dignity. It doesn't matter how old they are, healthy, sick, poor—we just don't care. If you are human, then you have this basic equality.

Now, what is the thing in the womb of a pregnant woman? It is absurd to deny that it is alive. You've taken ninth-grade biology, right? You know what a living thing is. If I put this zygote down in a petri dish, and it was a biology final, and I said, "Tell me, is this inanimate matter—minerals, rocks, dirt, stuff—or is it organic matter? And if it's organic matter (which you can all clearly see), is it alive, or is it dead? Or is it some 'tissue culture' from a living thing?" OK, if it's in the womb and it's swimming around, and it's got a little heart beating, and it's sucking its thumb—obviously it's not dead. Equally obviously, it's not some kind of tissue culture. It's not like you took some of the woman's brain cells and grew them in a petri dish. They're not cells from her

263

body. It's some kind of little living animal. OK, that's just a scientific fact. It's *alive* in the sense in which a biologist would use that word.

OK, it's alive. What species is it? It's not like we don't know what species it is. It's not some unknown species—if it were, you could get a Nobel Prize naming it, right? No, it belongs to the species *Homo sapiens.* Everyone knows that. It's living and it's human.

You believe that human beings are all fundamentally equal. *There* is a living human for you.

Now, that's a nice, neat philosophical argument, but what is more important to understand is what people who advocate abortion really believe on this. And I'm going to read an example so that you get the point—what differentiates those who take the pro-life position from those who accept abortion.

The one I'm going to read comes from this interesting book, *In Necessity and Sorrow: Life and Death in an Abortion Hospital,* by this woman—this picture was taken thirty years ago; by now she's grey and wrinkled, but—Magda Denes. She's a clinical psychologist. She opens up her book saying, "I am pro-choice. I am in favor of unrestricted abortion through all nine months, tax funded." But unlike a lot of abortion advocates, she's a very honest woman, which I admire. She's very plain-speaking. She felt that, as a clinical psychologist, she ought to go to an abortion facility and witness—how is it done? How does it affect people? She talked to everybody involved with it—the doctors, the nurses, the counselors, the women having abortions, everybody who came with them—and this book is a collection of her observations and her interviews. She wanted people to see the real emotional turmoil around this issue. And as part of her honesty as an abortion advocate, she thought she ought to witness an abortion and describe it. So I'm going to read to you her description of an abortion that took place—if you look at that brochure that describes Mass[achusetts] Citizens for Life, with the picture of the earth and the moon, and you turn to the back panel, there's a picture of a child at fourteen weeks after conception—that's the same gestational age as the abortion she witnessed. And I'm going to read to you how she describes an abortion.

264

"The person doing the abortion is Dr. Holzman. There was a nurse in the room, a man, who was named Mr. Smith, and the woman having the abortion is under general anesthesia." Ask yourself, would they have spoken like this if she were under local anesthesia, if she could hear every word? I don't think so. "Dr. Holzman pulls out something which he slaps on the instrument table. 'There,' he says, 'a leg.' I turn to Mr. Smith. 'What did he say?' 'He pulled a leg off', Mr. Smith says. 'Over here.' He points to the instrument table, where there is a perfectly formed, slightly bent leg, about three inches long. 'I have the rib cage now,' Holzman says, as he slams down another piece on the table. 'There, I've got the head out now.' I look at the instrument table, where next to the leg there lies a head. It is the smallest human head I have ever seen, but it is unmistakably part of a person." [43]

Now, I obviously want to get across the anatomical details. Because the way people talk about abortion, you would think there is nothing there and that it just sort of dissolves and goes away. But that's not true. That slogan, "Get laws off of my body", "My body, my choice"— these slogans are drawing your attention away from the fact that there is another life and that there are body parts in an abortion. That's just a fact that cannot be avoided if you are going to be honest.

But that's not what's really so disturbing. What is really disturbing is her last phrase, "unmistakably part of a person". Because here is a person who has just told you that she supports abortion, but she understands it to be the deliberate dismembering of a helpless and innocent human person.

And I could go on. I make a point of collecting quotes like this. There are dozens and dozens of them. Abortion advocates—people who are like me, only, they are on the other side—they're well informed on this issue. They know perfectly well that abortion is the taking of a human life. There is no doubt. There is no doubt on that question. And that's the big divide, and those are the two cultures competing for you. And you have to choose. It would be lovely if you didn't have to choose, but you do. You have to choose whether you are going to take the stand that, no matter how serious the problems, no

---

[43] [Magda Denes, *In Necessity and Sorrow: Life and Death in an Abortion Hospital* (New York: Publisher, 1977), p. 222.]

matter how burdensome, no matter how problematic, we will not take innocent human life to solve problems. We won't take human life, deliberately, to solve problems—that would be what the death penalty is about.[44] The other side says, "Yeah, we may not like [abortion]. We wish it wouldn't happen. But, under some circumstances, we take human life to solve problems." That's the Culture of Life and the Culture of Death. And you live in a country where four thousand innocent lives are being killed by abortion every day. So merely by doing nothing, you are, in fact, sort of taking a side. You're saying, "Oh, I wish that weren't happening. I don't like it. I wouldn't have an abortion myself. But isn't it too bad—four thousand innocent human lives are snuffed out every day in my country."

A Myth, an Error, and a Lie

Opening statement, debate at MIT, Cambridge, Massachusetts, January 18, 1989

The Supreme Court decision that legalized abortion on demand has made a mess of constitutional law; it has placed ridiculous inconsistencies in tort law; and it has polarized society on this difficult and volatile issue. But what may prove worse than all of these, it has done immeasurable harm to the cause of true equality for women.

The feminist movement has split into several camps, but one crucial point of division arises from the way one understands the relationship between personal identity and physical being. The pro-abortion, establishment feminists view personal identity as something which can be

---

[44] [Ruth held, of course, that the state has the right to use the death penalty and could exercise that right if bloodless means did not suffice. She would sometimes say, however, that it was simpler and rhetorically more effective in debates to deal with the death penalty as she does here. Also, as a diocesan spokesperson, she believed that she should represent the death penalty in presentations in the way that her bishop wished it to be represented.]

detached from physical being. Most of them betray in their writings an actual hostility, or at least a resentment, toward the reproductive biology of women. Fertility is regarded as a curse, and pregnancy is regarded as if it were a disease.

Pro-abortion feminism regards male patterns of sexual behavior as the ideal. Since the dawn of time, it has been possible for men to engage in sexual intercourse and walk away from the consequences, free of any responsibility toward the new human life which may be conceived. Women can imitate men in this behavior if and only if they will submit to abortion. Abortion makes women into pseudo-men, and it allows society to abandon pregnant women, leaving them to fend for themselves because, after all, it's a woman's choice now if she allows a pregnancy to continue.

This view of women and of what makes for equality between the sexes is fundamentally flawed. Tonight I hope to convince you that pro-abortion feminism is based on a myth, an error, and a lie.

The myth is this: pro-choice advocates talk as if women who have abortions fully understand the procedure, know the facts about fetal development, know there are other options available to them, and yet freely "choose" abortion because they believe it is the best option available to them.

This is a myth. While it may be true for a very few ideologically pure leaders of the feminist establishment, it has nothing to do with the reality of the experience of millions of regular women who are exploited by the abortion industry.

Anyone who reflects for a moment on the standard procedures in an abortion clinic will immediately see the truth of what I am saying. A woman who appears at an abortion clinic is already in a stressed state of mind. Why? Because she thinks she's pregnant, and she is distressed at the prospect of having a baby. She thinks she cannot have a baby for a variety of reasons, usually reasons that stem from a lack of support from friends, family, employers, and—most importantly—the father of the child.

Does she want an abortion? In most cases, no. In fact, if you read interviews of women who chose abortion, the recurring theme is this: I didn't want to do this, but I had no choice. I had no choice.

Many of these women actually think that abortion kills a baby and say so in just those words. Others are worried about that question. What do you think abortion clinic counselors [i.e., those who counsel on behalf of abortion clinics] do to "help" these women? Do you think they show them a medical school textbook with a picture of a fetus? Do you think they tell a woman what a fetus is like and let her decide for herself whether or not she thinks it is, in fact, a human being?

Of course not. If abortion clinics showed women pictures of seven-week-old fetuses, many women would decide not to have an abortion. And that would be bad for abortion clinics.

Naturally, the clinic counselors think they are helping women, that they are shielding them from painful experiences and helping them to make what the abortion clinic counselor is convinced is the "right choice". And the counselor "knows" that if the woman sees what that "product of conception" looks like, then that silly woman will think it's a baby, and she won't have the abortion. But, the counselor reasons, she really needs this abortion, so I will withhold this information so she will make what I know is the right decision for her.

Reflect for a moment on how patronizing an attitude that is. For any other medical procedure, feminists would scream bloody murder if health professionals withheld information from women in order to influence their decision in favor of elective surgery. But when it comes to abortion, ignorance is not only tolerated, it is mandated. You may not be aware that abortion advocacy groups fought against informed consent legislation for women seeking abortions. The legislation required an abortionist to inform a woman that a pamphlet was available, if she wanted to see it, which would describe the fetus. The Supreme Court struck down this legislation because it might distress women and might have a "chilling effect" on their freedom of choice.

We have come to a sad pass when the Supreme Court feels obliged to protect women from painful truths and thinks women are more free when they are more ignorant.

So much for the myth of women freely choosing abortion. Now let's turn to the error. Abortion advocates insist that we must respect a woman's right to control her own body, a right which supposedly springs from the constitutional right to privacy.

I don't have time to lay out fully how ridiculous this claim is. But I want to draw your attention to the short circuit in this flawed argument. Abortion comes under the right to privacy if and only if you have already determined that no one else's life is at stake. It is a woman controlling her own body if and only if it is possible for women to have incompatible blood types, for women to have male reproductive organs, or for women to donate their own brains and livers to scientists involved in fetal tissue transplants.

Must I belabor this point? The creature who lives inside a pregnant woman is not a part of her body. Justice [Harry] Blackmun was being blind or disingenuous when he said, "We need not resolve the difficult question of when human life begins", for *Roe v. Wade* is based on the tacit assumption that there is no other human life involved.

Finally, the lies. It has recently come to light that both of the women who were represented anonymously in the Supreme Court decisions that legalized abortion lied to the courts. There is something fitting in this. *Roe v. Wade* is based on the lie that we don't know when human life begins. That is a joke. Professor Fried knows as well as I do that the thing in the womb is alive[45]—it takes in nourishment and grows: that is the elementary-school definition of a living thing—and that it is biologically a member of the species *Homo sapiens*. It is living, and it is human. Where we differ is here: abortion advocates believe it is OK for individuals to kill other living human individuals under certain circumstances. Or they believe that you can be alive, you can be biologically human, but that is not enough to make you a human being with human rights. I hope you all appreciate both the irrationality of that assertion and the historically demonstrated danger of that assertion.

And the final lie—that abortion helps women. No one says that a woman who chooses prostitution, or who chooses an abusive partner, or who chooses to shoot up with heroin is choosing this self-destructive behavior freely or is choosing it because she alone knows

[45] Marilyn Fried, a feminist philosophy professor, then teaching at a Boston area college.

what is in her best interest. Women, like men, are fully capable of choosing something that is actually harmful. So just because women appear to choose abortion does not mean either that they do so freely or that it is in fact in their best interest.

Now, it should be obvious that abortion is not actually good for a woman's health. After all, it is an invasive surgical procedure that forces open her cervix and scrapes the living tissue from her womb. Nobody is seriously going to contend that this procedure improves the woman's health. Pregnancy is not a disease. A woman's body is designed to conceive and nurture new human life. An abortion is a violent thwarting of what physically a woman's body is meant to do.

Often, abortion advocates misunderstand what I just said. I did not say that, because a woman's body is designed to bear children, that means that this is the only significant, or even necessarily the most significant, thing a woman can do. What it *does* mean is that abortion is a violent attack on a woman's physical being, and it represents, at the very least, a profound alienation between a woman's physical and mental being.

We are told that abortion is safer than childbirth, but that is a phony statistic. A pregnant woman is more likely to die in a car accident than of anything related to childbirth. The leading pregnancy-related killer of women is ectopic pregnancy. Now, a leading cause of ectopic pregnancy is pelvic inflammatory disease—which also happens to be the most common post-abortion complication.

Women who die in childbirth usually die because they already have an underlying health problem, like diabetes or heart disease. Even under the Human Life Amendment, these women would be able to choose abortion to save their lives. But some women will always risk their lives in order to have children. It is insulting to use their deaths to argue that abortion is safer than childbirth.

It has been widely documented that previous abortions increase the likelihood of complications in subsequent pregnancies, though this is a highly controversial topic. The surgeon general recently issued a report which basically says—despite the fact that abortion on demand has been legal for sixteen years, that it is the most common form of elective surgery performed in the U.S., and that four thousand women undergo this surgical procedure every day—despite all this, there have been no careful, scientifically reliable studies conducted to determine whether abortion is safe or not.

Several factors account for this lack of information. First, it is almost impossible to find someone who is completely objective regarding abortion. It is not the sort of thing about which an informed person can remain dispassionately neutral. And that goes for both sides.

Second, aside from the immediate physical complications of an abortion (things like death, hemorrhage, puncture of internal organs, etc.— things which, admittedly, are rare), the major physical complications of abortion tend to show up only years later, when the woman wants to have a baby. That is when problems like infertility, miscarriage, premature birth, and rupture of the uterus are likely to show up. It is very difficult to track these kinds of long-term consequences. Third, the Supreme Court has struck down legislation that would require abortion providers to keep records of post-abortion complications. It is hard to see how that benefits anyone but the abortion providers.

As for the mental health problems suffered by many women who have undergone abortions, it is even more difficult to trace the connection in a scientifically reliable manner because typically women who experience psychological trauma following an abortion do not recognize the source of their problems until many years have elapsed, sometimes as many as thirty years.

You should also know that there are very few studies of any mental disorders, even of well-known, commonly accepted classifications like depression or phobia, which meet the strict canons of scientific reliability. The information upon which mental health professionals rely is largely [from a patient's] case history and anecdotal. This is precisely the kind of evidence that is accumulating regarding post-abortion syndrome.

You will hardly ever meet a woman who is happy about her abortion. But you can find thousands of women who don't like to talk about their abortions and who seem to have a lot of conflict surrounding it. You can read the testimonies of hundreds of women who became convinced that abortion scars women emotionally, because that was what happened to them.

Women will enjoy full equality of opportunity in this society when society recognizes and values appropriately the fact that women conceive and nurture new human life. That kind of supportive environment will never come into existence as long as society offers abortion as the answer to unwanted pregnancy.